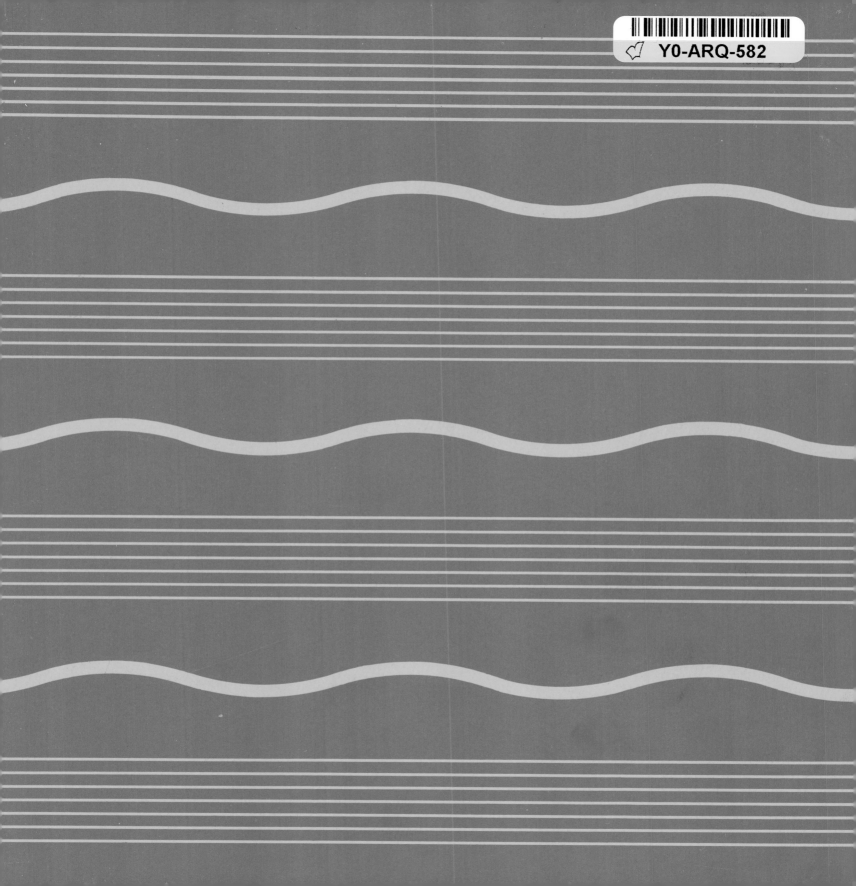

Y0-ARQ-582

Contemporary
American
Painting

The Encyclopædia Britannica Collection of

CONTEMPORARY

AMERICAN

PAINTING

WRITTEN AND EDITED BY

Grace Pagano

WITH A NEW INTRODUCTION BY

Donald Bear

ENCYCLOPÆDIA BRITANNICA, INC., 20 NORTH WACKER DRIVE, CHICAGO 6, ILLINOIS

Copyright in the United
States of America, 1946, by
Encyclopædia Britannica, Inc.

●

Copyright 1946. Copyright under
International Copyright Union
by Encyclopædia Britannica, Inc.
All rights reserved under Inter-
American   Copyright   Union
(1910) by Encyclopædia Britannica, Inc. Printed in the U.S.A.

SECOND EDITION

ABOUT THE *Encyclopædia Britannica Collection*

OF CONTEMPORARY AMERICAN PAINTING

That the painter has no more place in the garret than the symphony orchestra has become evident to more people in recent years than perhaps at any other time since the Renaissance in Italy. He has been beckoned out of his solitude by a suddenly receptive public eager to know and enjoy his work, to defend him, promote him, subsidize him, use him. He has been sent to war to record those subtleties of combat the camera couldn't catch. He has gone into the market place as a novel and startlingly successful salesman of radios and soft drinks, drugs, tobacco, whiskey and jewels. His agents are prodding him for increased production. Museums are clamoring to show his work. Sometimes ineptly and clumsily, to be sure, but firmly and genuinely his contemporaries are making his pictures an accepted, familiar part of their everyday living.

It was a chance and happy set of circumstances that led the Encyclopædia Britannica into the business of collecting and exhibiting contemporary American paintings. When, in September 1943, the company decided to commission the production of a number of pictures to illustrate several articles in Britannica publications, it had no idea that hardly two years later it would have gathered together, as the result of this idea, a representative collection. In 1943 Britannica was 175 years old. From its first edition in 1768, when it boasted 160 full-page copper engravings, to its 1943 printing with 19,000 line drawings, black and white and color plates, Britannica had been probably the most lavishly illustrated reference work.

Consequently, because it wanted to heighten interest in several of its articles, particularly in Britannica Junior, and because it considered American art to be the most virile in the contemporary world, Britannica commissioned several famous United States artists to make these further contributions to its publications. And then, as their paintings began arriving at the Britannica headquarters offices in Chicago, the idea of extending the project to form an adequate collection of contemporary American painting became so obvious as to be inescapable. These pictures, though few in number, were living representations of America, her land and factories, her people, her politics, fashions, her growth and strength. Why not try to complete the survey? Why not try to get the best work of other Americans who express their thought and emotion in paint—then put the entire group on tour of the country to be seen to best advantage in the greatest number of museums by the most people?

The collection was shown publicly for the first time in April and May 1945, at the Art Institute of Chicago. While Britannica considered the group of pictures to be quite an admirable accomplishment, it nevertheless regarded it as a provisional one. It was evident to the company that if the collection were truly to reflect the best among the tremendous number of paintings produced in 20th century America, it would necessarily have to be subjected repeatedly to capable public and professional scrutiny to winnow the inferior from the good and to add more of the good.

In this, the second edition of our book about the Encyclopædia Britannica Collection of Contemporary American Painting, is ample evidence of the change and growth in the collection. We have reproduced twenty-eight new paintings, twenty-one of them by artists who were not represented in the first edition. Seven are substitute paintings by artists formerly included. Each new acquisition has been made with the best critical consideration of competent persons. Each substitution has been made because the artists represented joined us in the belief that the new picture was a better one.

In the many exhibitions of the paintings thus far completed we have had an unrivalled opportunity to learn the reactions and suggestions of critics and laymen and have been able to measure the worth of our pictures against those in the permanent collections of important museums. We have become more critical, more analytical at each new opening. We have wandered through the galleries at each exhibit seeing the paintings again in a different light, surrounded by different neighbors. There are many that we have learned to like better with each new view, an experience twice pleasurable in that it confirms our original judgment. There are some pictures that are still on probation in our estimation, and there are perhaps still a few that, in our later and more considered judgment, may not belong.

Our goal is evident. Obviously, to gather together so fine a collection of contemporary American painting that it will stand up solidly against the judgment of future generations is an ambitious and difficult undertaking. But we have it before us because we believe it is highly worthy. Perhaps as well as any other medium, and in many respects better, it bespeaks the current American temperament. It is a good objective also because we think the American people should be on more intimate terms with painting, particularly the painting of the United States, for these pictures are products of their own creativeness. The great mass of the paintings produced today, as was always the case, will be forgotten. Only the best will remain and it is from that best that we hope our collection will be comprised. For it is with that best which history will choose that our paintings must eventually stand comparison.

It is manifest to us after these many showings of our pictures that Americans have an avid appetite for painting, a boundless desire to learn more about it, and a pride in the achievements of their countrymen. There has been a legend about an unbridged gulf separating the artist and the layman or those who like art and those who are disinterested. A similar legend in the case of music is disappearing. Radio has built a very substantial bridge between the musician and the listener. As we encourage people to see Britannica's paintings we like to feel that we, too, are helping to build a bridge. For we have observed how very substantial and enduring can be the layman's reward in return for a small investment in honest inquiry.

President, Encyclopædia Britannica, Inc.

ON THE TECHNIQUE OF PAINTING

TECHNIQUE—THE PAINTER'S ALPHABET

However hard we may search for a quality in art which is not connected with craftsmanship, we shall not be able to find it, because in art technical and esthetic considerations are inseparable. Of course, there are aspects of art other than those resting on esthetics alone: archaeological, philosophical, social, historical. Whatever sublimation is materialized in a picture, however, will depend solely upon the artist's skill with paints and tools. Whatever thought may flash through his mind will be registered on the canvas in paint quality, light, color, composition.

There are other elements than craftsmanship in the process whereby the mind of the painter objectifies itself, but even these—imagination and originality, usually associated with abstract qualities of the soul—are earthbound, since they are entirely dependent on technique. Imagination and originality must, perforce, be revealed through technical proficiency. I have linked these two qualities together because originality presupposes imagination. However, an imaginative painting need not necessarily be original.

What is it, then, that makes a painting original? Color, light, paint quality, composition. These are the elements upon which original conception rests; they are all concrete matters, ponderable, calculable and subject to classification. It was long ago agreed that subject matter cannot be responsible for originality in a painting, for there could be greater originality in the representation of a potato than in that of an apocalypse. Through the medium of imagination, new and ever-changing aspects of nature are revealed. Originality unfolds for us visions as yet unfelt, unseen, unsensed.

PAINT QUALITY—BRUSH STROKE

Whereas technique or craftsmanship is a term denoting the all-around skill employed in a work of art, paint quality refers to the manner in which paint is applied to a surface. Paint quality is composed of three distinct elements: brush stroke, contour, texture. Utilization of brush stroke in painting has not always appeared desirable to painters. Painters before Titian's time avoided the imprints of brushes on their paintings. Leonardo da Vinci's desire was to effect a soft transition of light and shade, like smoke thinning out imperceptibly in the air until it fades entirely in celestial light. "Sfumato," he called this blending of light and shade; evidence of brush strokes would have greatly interfered with such an effect. Much subtlety is to be found in the delicate merging of tonal transitions, but in the end this will flatten out the individual nervous habit of the painter's hand; only a brush stroke can reveal his personal method and his temperament. However, the reasons why the early painters did not explore the possibilities of brush strokes lay not only in their different esthetic outlook, but also in their dependence on an older manner of painting. The masters of the early Renaissance were still following the dictates of the tempera school of painters, and in tempera painting brush strokes cannot be executed in the manner common in oil painting.

The first manifestation of brush strokes appeared in the later work of Titian and El Greco. Although the emphasis on brush strokes has not continued uninterruptedly, at times the manipulation of the brush has become a purpose in itself. As in music, the Paganinis of the brush have often delighted in the sheer skill of their hands.

CONTOUR—THE OLD MAGIC

Brush stroke, which we have just discussed, and contour and texture as well, are all interdependent, since texture is made up of brush strokes, and the appearance of contours depends on texture and reflects the nature of the brush stroke. Realization of the importance of contours had already manifested itself in antiquity. Said Pliny 1900 years ago: "Contour in painting is the very highest point of skill. To paint substantial bodies and the interior of objects is a great thing, no doubt, but at the same time it is a point in which many have excelled; to give the finishing touches to the painting in rounding off the contour, this is a point of success in art which is but rarely attained. For the extreme outline to be properly executed requires that it be nicely rounded and so illuminated as to prove the existence of something behind it and thereby disclose that which it also seems to hide." Pliny, it appears, had a realistic representation in mind; the contour he praised was one that created an illusion of third dimension. However, technical and artistic ideas of painters have not always been concerned with an object's bulk and roundness. The technical equipment of the early tempera masters was not suited for a fade-out rendition of contours, as Pliny would have liked to see them. The contour in their paintings is always hard and unyielding, but this limitation does not detract from their artistry; linear emphasis has often great beauty unattainable by any other technical device. With the development of oil painting, treatment of contour often became a preoccupation of the virtuosos. El Greco orchestrated his contours with a symphonic sweep; in Rembrandt space and contour merge as rivers merge with the waters of the ocean.

TEXTURE—EVER-PRESENT, REDISCOVERED

Texture in painting refers to the appearance of the paint-surface. The paint may lie on the canvas in a thin film like a transparent veil —it is then called a glaze. It may be put on thickly, with impasto. Not only the physical characteristics of paints but painting tools as well—soft or hard brushes, or palette knives—will create textures different in form and structure.

Considering the tactile values of various objects, let me state that it is not the painter's task to imitate these textures so as to create illusion of an object's verisimilitude. A vaporous sky, for example, may be painted with impasto, and a rough rock surface may be done with a smooth glaze. In fact, the rocks in the magic paintings by Pieter Brueghel or Quentin Massys were all painted in glazes, and they suggest more a stone-like character than the thickly stippled-on rocks of the Impressionists. Textures in painting have, like brush strokes and contour, autonomous life. They are independent of the nature of material as it appears in reality.

In periods following the Renaissance, understanding of textures and their function in painting deteriorated; but with the advent of Impressionism, and later, abstract art, textural emphasis gained enormous importance; indeed, such emphasis became frequently the chief object of the painter's attention.

LIGHT AND COLOR

Intensity and character of colors depend on the general treatment of light and shade. It follows that the type of light used in painting, chiaroscuro or plein air, will be responsible for the artistic effect. Chiaroscuro is a light condition such as is found indoors, with a clear division between light and shade, hence it is referred to as "studio-light." At times chiaroscuro can be found also out of doors. A focal light emanating from an opening in clouds will create such a light effect. The setting sun will also act as a focal light. In both instances, the characteristic of colors will be as when seen indoors. Especially the colors in shade will appear almost monochromatic as compared with the multi-colored shadows caused by direct sunlight, that is, under plein air conditions. In the work of some post-Impressionists there is neither chiaroscuro nor plein air lighting; color is here used for its own sake regardless of light and shade.

The Old Masters, on the other hand, painted even landscapes as though they had viewed them indoors. Nevertheless, the coloristic power of these masters is unsurpassed; in art it is the subtlety of tonal gradations rather than riotous color which gives coloristic beauty to paintings. Almost monochromatic variations of light and shade, as seen in some of Rembrandt's paintings, can convey a powerful sensation of color. Said Goya, "In nature, color does not exist any more than tone. Give me a piece of charcoal, and I shall make you a picture."

COMPOSITION

Design, composition, perspective—in painting they are all linked together. Whereas design refers to the disposition of an abstract pattern, composition relates to the balance of masses and volume. Where there is volume, there is depth, and depth is the soul of distance. The picture's depth need not be suggested by the convergence of parallels on the horizon at eye-level, the axiom in scientific perspective; distance can also be suggested through the use of colors. As a color recedes from the local plane to the middle ground and then to the picture's background, it loses its identity and intensity. Even a strong hue like vermilion will fade out on the horizon in a pale blue haze. This phenomenon is known as aerial perspective. Illusion of space can be created by other means. Cézanne suggested depth through planes, which, while receding into the middle ground, do not diminish in size or weaken in color. This sensation he achieved through a system of overlapping planes.

In composition, not only the masses but also the empty space around them—negative space, as it is known—will account for the picture's balance.

HISTORY AND TECHNOLOGY

Coloring materials have at all times been abundant; painting with colors was already being practiced by prehistoric man, that is, in so far as he was artistically inclined. Plants, insects, berries, produced various coloring matter. Earth pigment and brightly colored minerals (of the heavy metals) were used in earliest recorded history. Even artificial pigments were made, perhaps five thousand years ago, for we have evidence that at this time oil painting was known.

Although easel painting as we understand it was not uncommon in antiquity, the great era in art started with the perfection of oil painting technique some six hundred years ago. In oil painting, the dry pigment, which is a finely divided coloring matter, is mixed with oil, mainly linseed oil. The oil is its binder; upon drying, it forms, with the pigment, a solid film. Under favorable circumstances the color-film may preserve its appearance over centuries and even millenniums.

It is generally assumed that the colors of the Old Masters were superior to ours, but this is not confirmed by facts. It is rather the knowledge of craft which made the work of some of the Old Masters virtually indestructible. However, some of their colors were fugitive, and often an evaporated color has had to be conjured up by the hand of a restorer. The deterioration of so many of the nineteenth century paintings has two principal causes: neglect of sound craftsmanship and the unscientific manner in which the paints and their vehicles were manufactured. Today, a painting executed carefully with native materials—which are, by the way, superior to the foreign products—has a good chance of surviving a cathedral or a railroad terminal.

How much technique and esthetic consideration are interdependent can be realized from the fact that an unstable color or vehicle will in time affect the entire coloristic appearance of a painting. To some extent, all paints change in time. A fresh color, no matter how subtly chosen, is always somewhat raw. It takes time and aging until a paint-surface acquires that precious glow inherent in some of the great works of the Old Masters. This is not to say that time improves all oil paintings. It is noble work which ages nobly for the knowing hand of the master builds his work with nobility of spirit and of craft.

THE BODY AND THE SOUL

In the preceding pages I have endeavored to demonstrate that technique, although it is suggestive of mechanical exercises and manual skill, far from encumbering the volatile soul of a painting, is in fact its very essence. Art is not an ethereal goddess free from physical toil, untouched by consideration of craft. Art relies more on the painter's knowledge of his tools than on the vagaries of inspiration. Lofty ideas about freedom in art took root at a time when art divorced itself from craftsmanship—when it became an individual rather than a social function. The greater freedom it acquired, the more complete became the painter's disdain for craftsmanship.

Today, the notion that all the equipment a painter needs is a burning desire for self-expression is, fortunately, abating. We may as well expect presently the official declaration that the art of painting is a skilled profession after all. Let us face it with equanimity; in art thought and form are one. The painter's thoughts dwell in forms commensurate with their magnitude. Form and content in art are indivisible, for the technique of a painting is its soul as well as its raiment.

Frederic Taubes

X

CONTEMPORARY AMERICAN PAINTING

THE ENCYCLOPÆDIA BRITANNICA COLLECTION

This collection is a lively and interesting reflection of the aspirations and accomplishments of the American artist who has seen and experienced much; who has felt the impact of two world wars and has watched his own art pass through many trying periods under the confusion of diverse influences. These influences have ranged from internationalism to blatant nationalism and coy provincialism. Somehow through it all there has been a basic integrity inherent in the minds of American painters which has prevented a complete loss of native equilibrium. Constantly they have attempted to forge new symbols, to mint new meanings and to find the fresher, more exact, more daring pictorial phrasing for their plastic and graphic message. One cannot help feeling, though, that the search for a new symbolism, and a personal one on the part of the American painter today, is a result of a poignant tension of thought, habit and experience which has been brought about by the impact of the organic aspects of an old culture against the inorganic mechanized facts of a certain kind of new civilization that has grown with terrible speed. This tension has not occurred in America alone, because certainly it has been increasingly evident in Europe, especially from the nineteenth century up to the present. But in the United States the divergencies have been greater, just as the distances are still immense. Through this struggle between the biological elements of a culture and the synthetic forces of a civilization, the artist has sought to find redemption in some form of personal symbolism which will re-establish his equilibrium. This is the problem of the American artist today.

Because America is the melting pot and because World War II has given us such a great influx of talent from all over the world, the American artist has not only the greatest opportunity but the greatest struggle in several centuries to prove the validity of his own art and to maintain his own spiritual integrity. This is our artist's debt to circumstances and to the past, as well as his impetus for the future.

Accompanying the plates which illustrate the work of each artist represented in this collection, is a statement regarding his or her work and intention. These are honest and revealing interpretations of the artist's point of view to the public. When reading these statements by the artist, and the carefully selected critical opinions, one feels that here are words that attempt to define the need, desire and fulfillment of symbols and expressions that modulate the differences between the concepts of painting of the past and of today.

Whenever possible, it is desirable to be able to read and to attempt to understand a picture according to the basic wishes of the artist. Much confusion in general reviewing and criticism can thus be avoided. Fortunately the painter is most articulate with his brush. Fortunately, too, of the fine arts in America, painting shares with music and literature a widespread knowledge and a certain degree of genuine popularity.

The twentieth century inherited much in tradition and mannerism from the brilliant personalities in American art history. These were internationalists, teachers and painters of quality—Whistler, LaFarge, Mary Cassatt, Duveneck, Sargent and Chase. Innes was a leavening influence upon the American scenic school. Today we think of the three outstanding individualists, Homer, Ryder and Eakins, brilliantly epitomized by Daniel Catton Rich "the masters of loneliness," as our immediate "Old Masters." These three masters remain secure, a source of inspiration and renewal of tradition, but they defy imitation.

Following Homer, Ryder and Eakins, were the American impressionists. They freshened the vision of the artist and at first dismayed the public. Soon their theory of color, upon which their painting depended, became familiar. It was the perfect vehicle for the sketch and was used by every student and amateur. Clean color, sparkling light, little or no earth tones, temporarily removed the gloom from the period that is referred to by Lewis Mumford as "The Brown Decades." Through the leading impressionists, Theodore Robinson, John Twachtman, John Alden Weir and Childe Hassam, the American eye became accustomed to sunlight within the confines of the picture gallery as well as recognizing it as an aesthetic medium out-of-doors.

Childe Hassam, founder of the group known as "The Ten," is represented in this collection by a canvas of sparkling color activity entitled "Avenue of the Allies." "The Ten" was made up of the following artists, all of diverse aims, talents and accomplishments: Frank W. Benson, Joseph deCamp, Edmond G. Tarbell, John Alden Weir, John Henry Twachtman, Thomas W. Dewing, Willard L. Metcalf, Robert Reid, Edward F. Simmons and Childe Hassam. Hassam, referred to as the "Dean" of American painters, maintained a spectacular performance throughout his career. Before embracing the broken color of French impressionism, he painted many solid and beautiful canvases with line, tone and texture, recreating the mood of the old metropolitan world. Perhaps because of this, and also that he essayed in the new movement of French

impressionism, he may be considered a direct forerunner of the revolutionary group whose leaders were Robert Henri and John Sloan, known as "The Eight."

For the most part, American art has been devoted to various interpretations and aspects of realism. Sometimes this realism is given the power of superrealism. In the hands of some of our contemporaries it is used with crystalline clarity. Again this superrealism, coupled with a flair for illustration, easily veers toward the superchromo, or at its worst, the old-fashioned calendar.

For better or for worse, realism in American painting is motivated by an intense energy. It dominates the interpretation of nature in landscape and in the life of the city, even nature presumably static in still life, although some of the most dramatic paintings of modern times, including those of the American school, have been achieved within the limitations of still life.

The year 1908 introduced to the art world a new group of painters of great gifts which labeled itself "The Eight." These artists, led by Robert Henri and John Sloan, formed interesting and inspiring company, together with Arthur B. Davies, George Luks, Everett Shinn, Ernest Lawson, Maurice Prendergast and William Glackens.

"The Eight," named in pre-tabloid journalism, the "Newspaper School," the "Ash Can School," and the "Revolutionary Black Gang," collectively and individually set the stage and opened the theater of American painting as we know it today. They were bound together by the need to revolt and, although their talents and accomplishments had seemingly little in common, their contributions were immeasurable. "The Eight" interpreted American life in every-day terms with a gusto and flair for the picturesque. Street scenes, ever-day incidents, the mood of the city, the temperament of obscure and surprising characters, and every kind of vignette were placed on canvas for public exhibition. This was a shock to the professional gallery visitor. Actually these men did for the American audience a service similar to that accomplished by the innovators of impressionism in nineteenth century France. But their use of color and their lacing of pigment had little in common with the French school of that period.

Most of these men had journalistic experience and worked as illustrators for newspapers and magazines. Ernest Lawson was primarily a landscape painter, whose solid decorative impressionism made him appear as a Monticelli with an outdoor vision. Maurice Prendergast gave us broad tapestries of lyrical gaiety teeming with colorful groups of people done in compelling designs and set in a luminous sunstroked landscape. Distinctly personal in style, a great formal designer, Prendergast combined the scintillating color and brilliant light of the impressionists with a knowledge of the great architectural decorative arts of the past. While his pictures of picnic, promenade, park and street scenes have a striking vitality based upon nature, he generalized the individual characteristics of his impressionism by using mosaic-like strokes of paint in his compositional arrangements.

A bulk of bibliography has accumulated concerning the contributions, eccentricities and achievements of "The Eight." Today Robert Henri's book *The Art Spirit* is still read and holds its place as one of the significant documents on the development of the American artist. It was a genuine gift to his host of students and friends.

Of "The Eight" in the present collection, Robert Henri, George Luks, John Sloan, William Glackens, Arthur B. Davies and Everett Shinn are represented.

Robert Henri's painting does not merely summarize his admirations of the past, which were Manet, Velasquez and Hals, but indicates the art of a sensitive and exciting personality whose performance was variable according to pressure and influence. Henri sought, as did George Luks, the picturesque, and placed it on canvas with the enthusiasm and reaction which generally accompanies the first impression. Regardless of color key, blond or dark, Henri's effusive stroke remained very much the same.

Typical of George Luks is the picture "Cabby." In this character vignette, Luks is represented by painting that is authoritative, epigrammatic and straight from the shoulder. This is another example of a fragment or "slice of life" which made this artist a virtuoso in interpretation of the life of the city and its incidental people. George Luks was one of the "little masters" of his time and his sympathy and understanding of his subjects is genuine and profound.

John Sloan has long been a leader and prominent figure, adding to the living history of American artists through his own work and by his activity as an organizer in vigorous, independent groups and as a compelling influence on other painters. Though experienced as an illustrator, the painterly approach equals, if not exceeds, the graphic in Sloan's work at its best. "Chinese Restaurant" is filled with rich brooding quality. Typical of Sloan's painting, it is so fraught with the atmosphere of the time in which it was painted that it seems to be the portrait of an era in American art.

William Glackens also gathered experience as a newspaper illustrator. His series of drawings made while artist-correspondent during the Spanish-American War are interesting visual documents of the period. They are filled with activity and have a suggestion of pageantry. Glackens changed from the intimate low key of tonal poetry used in his early work to the luminous coloration of the impressionists. He made of the art of Renoir a specialized personal tradition.

Arthur B. Davies brought to his fellow artists many important contributions. Although a highly individual person in his art, a lyrical painter with a feeling for mystic beauty which almost amounted to a special symbolism, Davies had, in common with John LaFarge, a lively curiosity about the revival of nearly forgotten techniques. He experimented with various mediums. The most important thing that Davies had in common with "The Eight" was his friendship for his fellow artists and his desire to welcome innovations of any kind. Perhaps the most violent episode in American art history took place in the revolutionary Armory Show in 1913, which was under Davies' direction. He and Walter Pach, Max Weber and Walt Kuhn accomplished a turning point in American painting through their relentless, courageous efforts in assembling this exhibition and making it an artistic success. Walt Kuhn's *The Story of the Armory Show*, published in 1938, is a first-hand document which is of interest as well as importance. Jerome Mellquist also handles this turbulent chapter of our art history both in his provocative book *The Emergence of an American Art* and in the *Magazine of Art*, December 1943.

Everett Shinn's famous canvas "London Hippodrome," in the Art Institute of Chicago, is one of the finest pictures by any American contemporary painter. It is a masterpiece well worth a pilgrimage to see. Based on tradition, the understanding of Degas, Lautrec, and perhaps Menzel, it is filled with sturdy painting and succinct passages of rich pigment.

After the advent of the Armory Show and the growing acceptance of "The Eight" painting in this country was not confined to any one school or set of ideals. From the time of the Armory Show, the development of "The Eight" and the rising spirit of internationalism, we are compelled to think almost altogether in terms of the individual artist. Each one who helped establish a direct exchange of European ideas, such as Davies, Weber, Kuhn and Marin, was highly individual, too, and contributed forcefully to the collective energies of our advancing creative abilities. Through the genius of Alfred Stieglitz, we were given a tradition in photography, and, at the same time, Stieglitz, by grouping around him some of our most advanced painters, helped to force the patterns of our growing "modernism."

The United States has furnished a market for all the schools of French painting from Millet and the Barbizons to the present day. Our private collections and museums are rich in material. French painting of the last hundred years, even though its development was revolutionary, gave our artists and public understanding of the consistent enactment of tradition. It is sensuous and organic, always in taste and therefore calls to mind the much repeated cliché comparing the art of France to its native wines and national cooking. The quality of French painting is not only delectable but satisfying.

In essence, the very cadence, timing and space arrangement, the touch and pressure of pigment and its realization as a plastic medium has largely controlled the reactions and response of the American artist and art lover. This response on the part of the public has formed a métier of appreciation. For example, such diversified artists as Max Weber, Walt Kuhn, Marsden Hartley and Yasuo Kuniyoshi, to mention but a few, have built largely upon the textural qualities, the color modulations and the structural architecture of the French painting of the post-impressionists and the rich but eclectic approach of the modern school of Paris. The twentieth century tradition of France is both archaeological and experimental. Perhaps its dominant criterion is the recognition of the elusive elements of taste and inherent quality. But in the end it returns safely to tradition. American painters have absorbed these French influences, as have the artists of the rest of the world, because after all they form the only truly international tradition of our time. However, American painters have used them primarily to gain a wider and more easily expressed range for their own personal expression. This has been a good and inevitable experience for the American artist and his audience but it has forced us to neglect much that is important in near-contemporary painting throughout the rest of the world. It is only in the greatest of our art centers that the painting of middle Europe and the northern countries seems to be appreciated. The most widely known artist working in America today, who is of the northern or Gothic tradition, is Lyonel Feininger. Feininger's art, even though predominantly northern, springs from a personal mysticism. In many exhibitions held in the large art centers in the United States one may find that some of the younger artists have been specially influenced through the color expression, the willed but characterful distortion of drawing, the violence of composition arrangement and the emotionalism which marked both the middle-European as well as the Russian contemporaries of the school of Paris. The entire conception of form and the meaning of tradition as interpreted by Kandinsky, Beckman or Kokoschka is different in continuity, impact and timing from the ideals that have mainly guided the development of contemporary American painting as a whole. It should also be mentioned that many of the influences from Europe, other than from Italy or directly from France, have been tempered by the school of Paris. However, as one views this collection of American pictures of our own times, one sees much use of color, much characterization of line and design, space interval and timing which is based upon the consideration and appreciation of all the active traditions.

Not being translators alone, American artists have sought new symbols. George Bellows is perhaps the foremost example of the modern American artist who was open to all suggestions but bent to no convention. Bellows invented his own particular kind of form with which to express the great power of his direct and uncompromising realism. Despite his vitality and incredible energy, Bellows often handled his subject matter with romantic insight which is kindly, sometimes nearly tender. Though he is thought of as the print maker and painter of the prize fight and the world of sports, his portraiture and landscape reveal an artist of enormous natural gifts and many varied accomplishments. With Bellows, the tempo of modern American painting was set. Because he achieved his position in American art without European training, critics especially consider him to be authentically the American artist.

After Bellows, we find in American painting a confusing number of divergent influences and traditions. Contemporary French art, the study of post-impressionism, abstract or nonrealistic painting appears and then there are the beginnings of regionalism and the American scene.

American painters developed much in common with many of the leading literary spokesmen of the day. Sherwood Anderson and Theodore Dreiser are mentioned most frequently in this connection. American painting today, with its excitement, variation and unevenness, calls to mind the unpredictable genius of the late Thomas Wolfe, who was so richly laden with talent. Thomas Wolfe especially comes to mind because he was constantly reshaping and reconstructing the portrait of America in his novels and short stories. He understood the enormous distances of the country; he appreciated the quality of places that were remote from the metropolitan areas. As many of our painters are trying to do, he seized upon multiple places and personalities that compose America. Rich, effulgent and extravagant, and at times obviously disorganized, Wolfe interpreted his subject matter with emotional accuracy and the tang of direct observation.

Both regionalism and the American scene have been the cause of much critical conjecture, controversy and widespread publicity. In reading the commentary and the statements by the artists opposite reproductions of the paintings in this book it is interesting to note that a few of the artists more or less disparage each of these movements in our painting. Both regionalism and the American scene are convenient labels for a certain type of painting which is grouped together more because of subject matter or geographic location than for any other reason. However, regionalism is probably not as limited as generally supposed. Nor is regionalism a particularly new approach. Somewhere along the line the painters of the regional areas and the artists of the American scene converge. In the future, the stigma of a militant nationalism, bordering on provincialism, will be removed from these schools of thought and the work of many of the artists will come shining through, regardless of nomenclature.

It has often been said that regionalism and the American scene are broad considerations for painting that is localized in subject matter but gains national prominence. In this case the artist uses his experience along with tradition but hopes to say something that is important to the country as a whole. He hopes to combine his intimate experience along with a tradition that he can make further important, even though his statement may be based upon narrative or limited facts. Certainly at best this type of painting should be far removed from the coincidence of mere pictorial gossip.

Regionalism in the arts became the theme song of the 1930's. But long before this movement gained headway as a "movement," there were men and women seriously and modestly working throughout the country—in California, New Mexico, Texas, Colorado—in the great cities and busy towns of the middle west and along the eastern seaboard. Each of these artists was painting something which might be significant of the American scene or could be representative of a particular region. Among the painters represented in this collection, those who could be considered the aristocrats of the American scene are Charles Burchfield and Edward Hopper. Many others with diversified points of view have added to this tradition which began with "The Eight" and has been carried on steadily since that time.

The work of Charles Burchfield reveals him as a master of poetic mood. Burchfield seeks to express the nostalgic, the haunting, and the miraculous in the commonplace, and he more than often succeeds. Each picture is a pictorial motif or fragment in which a combination of literary and painterly feeling have been merged into a composition of breadth. As did Sherwood Anderson in his short stories, Burchfield, through a particular twist of fancy and lyrical feeling, recreates from the average, the everyday, and the more or less ordinary incident, work of unusual beauty and compelling interest.

The painting of Edward Hopper once seen is quickly memorized. His art is overtly objective. Economical in paint quality, it is also so simplified in concept that it is removed from the category of illustration. Throughout Hopper's work there is an integrity that almost seems to begrudge any overtones of romantic or imaginative nature. Yet Hopper has produced many fine portraits of houses, places and situations that, through their special quality of starkness and what amounts almost to an astringence of handling, create a sensation of dramatic impact to the eye of the beholder.

Ernest Fiene has always sought to reach the American mind by a conscientious effort to understand and study the sources of our art and to identify its background with the contemporary spirit. He has done a series of pictures devoted to the changing aspects of New York City which capture the tempo of the day. He has explored many sides of the American character in his forthright New England landscapes. He is aware of the social sources of American art; he believes in its integrity.

The regional school is by no means limited to Thomas Hart Benton, John Steuart Curry and the late Grant Wood, although they represent its chief exponents in the popular mind. While not known as regionalists, Andrew Dasburg, scholarly painter and a great teacher in New Mexico, B. J. O. Nordfeldt, formerly of New Mexico, and the late Willard Nash, along with Josef Bakos, contributed greatly to the development of the art of their region, as did R. Vernon Hunter. In Colorado there are the late John Edward Thompson, Vance Kirkland and Boardman Robinson, contributing to regional understanding although they are not themselves regionalists in the accepted sense. Henry George Keller of Cleveland and Clarence Hinkle of California, though both widely traveled, have also thoroughly painted their own locale and have brought out younger talent of importance.

Dale Nichols, Millard Sheets, Joe Jones and the late Frank Mechau have painted much that is of regional content but this does not necessarily typify them as regionalists. Frank Mechau, Fletcher Martin and Peter Hurd have revived the rugged history of the west, and produced many interestingly composed pictures of violent action which are done sometimes with a lively spirit of invention. Joe Jones has painted a series of simple and unaffected canvases filled with the rich color and baking light of the Missouri farm country. Millard Sheets often interprets his subjects, either in water color or in oil, with a feeling for design structure, and embellishes forms and spaces with flourishes of ornament. He appears essentially to be a designer.

Actually regional painting may depict the big city just as easily as the open country, places of remote distance or some illustration of the picturesque. It may or may not lay emphasis upon the importance of social content.

Altogether, neither regionalism nor the American scene are matters of fixed ideology. Both movements occurred partly as economic and partly as emotional necessities. The depression of the 1930's brought many artists back to the United States from Europe and also many who were living in New York turned to other parts of the country. The federally supported and organized government art projects of the Treasury Department and Works Progress Administration helped re-establish the American painter in his own city and region. While not every artist was helped directly through the government's art program, he was aided indirectly, so to speak, because this activity increased public awareness of the artist's work and his value to the community. Particularly from 1935 to 1941, the United States government was the greatest patron of the graphic and plastic arts. The record of the amount of work accomplished through murals, easel pictures, prints and sculptures reaches an astonishing total. One of the most valuable experiments made by the government was the creating and establishment of community art centers which brought exhibitions of all types of material, quality and interest to the rural communities, and introduced a teaching program, among other activities. These art centers were not limited to the small towns but had their place in the congested areas of metropolitan centers also. The success of the projects was especially due to the careful planning and valiant services rendered by Holger Cahill, the late Edward Bruce and Forbes Watson. There were also many others who, in the face of severe criticism, gave their best efforts toward the continuation of this work during this period.

Playing an important part in the evolution of American painting during the last few years have been the great exhibitions which have brought together the art of our own time from this country and Europe. There were the "Century of Progress" exhibits, the great show of the independents in New York, and the gigantic exhibits held in 1939 and 1940 at the two World's Fairs—one in New York and the other in San Francisco. Outstanding and brilliant work in the presentation of American art has been accomplished by the Whitney Museum of American Art, the Art Institute of Chicago, and the Museum of Modern Art in New York. Aside from the huge exhibitions conducted annually, the Carnegie Institute in Pittsburgh, city and university museums all over the country have made a special effort in recent years to conduct well publicized showings of American painting. A new development is the organizing of large exhibits, some of them competitive, by commercial enterprises.

Burchfield and Hopper, Benton, Curry and Wood have succeeded in creating certain symbols of meaning to describe particular aspects of American life. Sometimes this symbolism expresses a quality or an overtone of the suggested, the unseen presence—in short, a mystical experience. This is often true of Burchfield and Hopper; Benton, Curry and Wood have described through a highly personalized sense of individual style, types and actions of a limited phase of American life. The latter three painters have created a contemporary Americana.

The late Grant Wood was not an artist's painter in the accepted sense, but the public loved his clarity, his craftsmanship, and simplicity of design. His admirers also understood his psychological portraits and his toy-like landscape panoramas. It seemed as though one could look down into a world that was as precisely laid out as a relief map executed in patterns of polychrome. Grant Wood sometimes succeeded in producing a modern folk art and at other times, as in "Daughters of Revolution" and "American Gothic" he created documents of emotional and historical importance.

Although John Steuart Curry often paints pictures of dramatic episodes, there is no pretension in his well known series of pictures illustrating life on the prairie and the farm genre of Kansas. He has a determined sense of the graphic and a natural love and sympathy with his subject matter. He is close to the earth and his art springs directly from his simple love of the soil and his respect for all men and women and living things that belong to the windtorn, sunbitten plains and farm country. Curry's pictures seem painted with grave and careful consideration and as though they were very slow in gestation. Sometimes carried to the point of dullness, this tends to lead to a monotony of surface quality and texture, and to add to the general uncertainty and awkwardness of his compositional arrangement.

Controversially, at least, Thomas Hart Benton is the most widely discussed of our contemporary painters. Gifted, inordinately articulate, knowledgeable, and greatly experienced, Benton has created a one-man movement in American art. Sometimes his sense of satire imparts an expression of the grimace to the forms and furniture of his pictorial world. At other times he handles landscape with a suggestion of lyrical sensitiveness, but everything he paints bears the stamp of his style. In his murals there is relentless use of his personal brand of political caricature. Much of Benton's work is devoted to a revival of hillbilly and backwoods folklore, which is interpreted in his own deliberately baroque manner. Benton builds the best of his work solidly and with great thoroughness. Although many of his pictures seem to be almost improvised, the procedure from the first sketch-notes to the finished work is one involving great concentration and effort. He abstracts the elements of his picture-making after long analysis of his subject; then he takes these rhythms and forms and places them in relation to the particular pattern of speed, cadence and phrasing that he wishes to use.

The very strength of the scenic artist is his weakness. He becomes identified with the light, the climate and the peculiarities of the terrain, and we are apt to be interested only in this identification process with subject or place. Subject matter, handled in this case as an isolated phenomenon, often forces the painter to sacrifice the deeper aspects of painting as a medium of aesthetic communication— a communication which we recognize today as resulting from tensions between the formal and abstract elements of art, from the exigencies of the medium itself and from the dominant interpretive meaning of the motif taken from nature. There is little or no scenic pioneering left to be done. In the nineteenth century the painter could still thrill his audience with facts. Today color photography has replaced the need for this type of recording or reportage.

The marine compositions by the late Frederick J. Waugh were for many years the most popular pictures in current exhibitions of American painting. Waugh's painting represented a direct connection with the past of the immediate yesterday before American artists became adjusted to the new influences from France or "The Eight" had gained recognition and acceptance. Waugh recorded his observations of the sea with assurance and certitude.

Rockwell Kent, Dale Nichols and Luigi Lucioni each are accorded great acclaim by the public. Much of their painting, done in clear, vivid color, has the precision of a print-maker's process or the direct message of the poster and the illustration. Each artist magnifies the picturesque in landscape through a crisp technique and a tendency for laying emphasis upon local color. Rockwell Kent has created a romantic, individual tradition for himself that has greatly influenced the graphic artist as well as the public.

Throughout the country there are a number of accomplished and seasoned artists painting specialized subject matter, particularly landscape, yet they have developed no essential mannerism or peculiarity of style which identifies them in any limited sense with their own locale. Clarence Hinkle, of California, has repeatedly painted pictures of the sea and the mountains. He works broadly and structurally with a fine understanding of scale and space. Paul Sample paints landscape with a marvelously adjusted eye, timed to the inspiration of a flawless technique. He understands how to interpret effects with candor and sparkle. Francis Speight also paints with the speed of a fresh impression taken directly from nature. His brush is guided by vigorous suggestion and the certainty of good taste. Then there is Francis Chapin, a sound painter who seeks freedom in directness and ease of handling and whose love of color is best expressed through his spontaneous use of fresh, flowing pigment.

Alexander Brook, Adolf Dehn, Doris Lee, Georges Schreiber and Arnold Blanch are among the travelers and interregionalists. They have painted various landscapes with figures in relation to special locale, such as the deep south or the west. Sometimes their painting conveys social meaning, although this is not often apparent. Adolf Dehn has a fine sense of landscape which he expresses in careful purity in water color. Doris Lee always appears to sparkle with wit and takes great pleasure in her observations whether her picture has to do with expressing modern Americana, a single figure, or a study of the south. Her work is generally informed with a quiet whimsical gaiety that has no need to turn to severe satire. Alexander Brook and Arnold Blanch often steep their landscapes in quiet, gentle melancholy.

Portraiture in contemporary American painting, like all other forms, is treated as a means of individual expression. It is no longer distinctly a standardly recognized art of social communication with a regular economic foundation. Therefore there are two types of portraits which are recognizable at first glance; the international academic manner, which does not belong to any one country, and, on the other hand, the serious interpretive portrait which is first of all a picture, with due attention given to the formal elements of painting, and secondly a study of individual character. In spite of modern photography, there still seems to be a need for a straight middle course to be followed in portrait painting today. It is not possible to suggest a return to the past, but a re-interpretation of the integrity and values established by the American portraits of John Singleton Copley and those by Gilbert Stuart might be of great value. Both artists at their best maintained an equilibrium between character, likeness and formal values.

Eugene Speicher, Leon Kroll, Bernard Karfiol, Alexander Brook and George Biddle, have more or less formed the Museum school of portrait and figure painting. Also Reginald Marsh, Robert Brackman, Robert Philipp, Gladys Rockmore Davis and Jerry Farnsworth, have produced a long line of figure studies, compositions, vignettes and arrangements which are seen in most of the museum exhibitions and are in many collections. Both Eugene Speicher and Leon Kroll have developed a recognizable type in their interpretations. Alexander Brook, along with Eugene Speicher, has accomplished a series of mood portraits of personages. Brook appears to stay well within the confines of his particular style of mood and interpretative values, and even his landscapes of the south are predominantly brooding essays into portraiture. Bernard Karfiol is primarily concerned with abstract painterly problems in his approach to his subjects. The values of individuality and the essential personality of the subject are secondary matters to him because he concentrates upon painting a good picture for its recognizable worth. Grigory Gluckmann presents a series of figure compositions which may be considered 19th century French in feeling and conception. However, they are strictly contemporary in the manner in which they seize upon the varying moods of modern woman and her relation to her environment and fashions of the day.

George Biddle makes a concentrated effort to analyze the special attributes of his characters, including their foibles and the properties which seem to surround or be essential to them. When Biddle is at his best, he conscientiously probes with line. In paint quality he is economical to the point of being astringent. To a certain extent George Biddle is a social painter. He is interested in revealing the purpose and reason that create character and motivate action. He is inspired by "humanity" and he controls this approach through rationalization and analysis.

Henry Varnum Poor, exceptionally versatile, handles all of his subjects in the various mediums in which he works with a profound respect for the fundamentals and exigencies of structure. Regardless of varying quality in performance, his faith remains uncompromising. Robert Brackman often works his figure compositions with a feeling for the formally set "dramatic" incident. He uses the figure with stayed or delayed action. It is almost as though he sought the quiet architecture of still life even though painting figures presumably capable of movement. The painting of Gladys Rockmore Davis lingers in the "Glackens-Renoir" tradition, but it is authentically a fresh and direct statement. Fluency, gusto and physical vitality mark the painting of Waldo Peirce. Peirce paints with an easy flow of line and many simplifications of the figure. He is of the earth but the earth always seems freshly washed. In landscape, figure painting and still life, Russell Cowles has an admirable sense of space and a feeling for the adjustment of space relationship and volume to his natural compositional motifs. He recognizes the essential continuity of tradition without obstructing his own work with mannerisms. At times Paul Cadmus restates something of the Mantegna-Signorelli tradition in the hard brilliance of his busy figure pieces, while Jon Corbino's vignettes are devoted to a restatement in miniature of the Rubens-Delacroix heroic or "grand" composition. Rico Lebrun must be mentioned whenever figure composition is discussed. Still best known for his masterly drawings, his painting consistently gains in scope and intensity. As a draughtsman he may be counted among the foremost in the United States.

Guy Pène du Bois, Louis Bouché and Randall Davey, each in his individual way, are painters of manners. Not literary painters in any sense of the word, they have consistently documented certain situations, characters and types. All three of these artists are cosmopolitan in their point of view and quality of sophistication.

Guy du Bois has created a number of portraits and compositions of solid, thoughtful analysis. Randall Davey, often painter of the elite at play, understands the temperament of his subject matter and places the appropriate accent upon its importance. Sometimes his brush is so glib that his painting seems a matter of reflex. Louis Bouché has feeling for the quality of paint itself and an accurate sense of punctuation and contrast, through which he describes the world with bright humor and pleasant, inquiring curiosity, inevitably smart and to the point. Zoltan Sepeshy is strictly disciplined, has a fine sense of observation and a thorough understanding of the place and value of individual details. He controls his forms partly through the clarity of his draughtsmanship, as well as the careful direction of his modeling. Frederic Taubes is essentially a painter of studio composition. Abstractly interested in the Old Masters, the Venetians, and perhaps the Spanish, he imposes both mood and manner. His subjects may or may not be important but he reduces and controls his contrasts of color, texture, shadow, space and light according to his sense of fundamental pictorial structure. Taste, quality, the background of an intelligent continental eclecticism have leavened the style and approach of Eric Isenburger. He brings to a wide variety of subjects grace of handling, directness of color, and his figures reside in surroundings and colors of decorative ease.

Max Weber is known as the "Dean" or "father" of the American moderns and experimental artists. He brought to this country a sympathetic understanding of the modern French school before the advent of the Armory Show in 1913. Weber also had a larger sense of art history than most of the other artists of his time and he therefore became, both directly and indirectly, a teacher as well as an influence. The depth of integrity in Weber's painting is backed by a lifetime of striving to express something so deeply personal that it is of nearly religious meaning. In his many figure compositions of racial types there is the devotional quality of the icon. Whether in still life, landscape, figure or portrait, Weber expresses himself with thoughtful, brooding fervor. He exhibits his knowledge and background modestly and abstracts the emotional meaning of his subject matter with infinite care. One feels that Weber has such a passionate regard for art that he often paints with a feeling of reticence, as though he were revealing some truth or secret too profound and too spiritual for direct statement.

John Marin, Georgia O'Keeffe and the late Marsden Hartley, also have contributed greatly to shaping the definitions of American painting today. They are so secure in their maturity that they seem not to have any close relation to immediate European influences. This seems especially true of Marin and O'Keeffe, because it was only in the latter part of his career that Hartley produced his most compact statements.

Marin is not merely "the painter for other painters." However, his pictures do require concentration on the part of the spectator and an extremely careful reading. He expresses the depth and volume of landscape, the dynamic direction which seems to be taken by the elemental, invisible forces of nature in a language that is personal yet universal in final meaning. This is amply shown in his water colors, in which the power of the sea swells from the paper.

With lines and zigzags, Marin expresses simultaneous action with a few terse phrases. He is one of the few painters who places the spectator in the midst of the controlled chaos of natural forces and makes him a part of the violence of action rather than permitting him to peer through the window of the picture frame. Other examples of this strange genius of Marin's are to be found in many of his New York street scenes, cityscapes and bridge compositions. He feeds into the eye with this simultaneous action of phrase more than the eye can possibly hold when looking directly at the subject. He makes one a part of it. He places the spectator on the avenue and makes him feel, with one powerful gesture, the entire vertical façade of a skyscraper.

There are times when Marin uses a pattern which results in either a geometric or a designed symbol. This may be the suggestion of labeling of a force, such as the direction of the wind or the power of the shaft of light, or again, the heavy construction of the earth. These patterns are never on the surface, but are prone to lie inwardly toward the boundary of the picture's space. No artist says more with so little detail. It is as though one had the construction of an entire page in three or four key words.

While it is true that one has to learn almost a special language to understand Marin's painting, there is nothing precious about it. Marin is an artist who is still several generations ahead, and he looks from afar and muses. He cannot be contradicted; he can only be accepted or evaded.

Toward the end of his career, Marsden Hartley became more and more powerful as a painter. He translated his reactions to nature with rugged, almost brutal impact. His very simplicity of handling and reduction of nature's forms and forces to plastically designed contrasts brought a new source of inspiration and vision to American painting. Only since his death has his true stature begun to be apparent.

Georgia O'Keeffe, along with Charles Sheeler, has a feeling for austere objectivity and an immaculate eye. While she is not a surrealist, her juxtaposition of objects, her combination of subjects, coupled with the precision of her painting, sometimes induces the element of shock. By her very economy of subject matter and means she, too, recreates with symbols. Not only in her magnified flower compositions has she originated a new approach and sought out new forms, but her landscapes of New Mexico bring an entirely fresh interpretation to the themes of the southwest. O'Keeffe and Marin, particularly the latter, have strongly influenced some of the later painting from this section of the country.

Warmed by fantasy and possessed of tremendous imagination, Lyonel Feininger has escaped the brittle and the inorganic quality of so-called abstract or geometric picture-making, although his lyrical art is partly based on cubism. It is well known that Feininger is profoundly interested in music and that this interest is coupled with that of mathematics. These interests are an important factor in forging his highly sensitive and delicate art. Through the architectural details of his subjects—the springing curve of an arch, the cube of a tower, the proud lift of the bow of a ship, the concentrated power of a locomotive—he imparts the essence of the touch of the human hand, whether in architecture or the building and control of the machine. The devices and furniture of the world of commerce and machinery move through his compositions leaving, seemingly, but the memory of a dream mingled with a moment of nature.

For years Walt Kuhn has worked independently and has remained aloof from controversy. He has produced picture after picture, portraits of circus people and troupers of burlesque, which are psychological documents. He has also painted landscape and still life. He tries to retain an archaic, rugged structural finality in his costume studies and compositions of the actor and the clown. Striving to adjust the exact amount of finish to the character of his subject, Kuhn creates in each canvas a feeling of tension and measured evaluation.

Yasuo Kuniyoshi is one of our most cosmopolitan and sophisticated painters, whose work is consistently shown in every major exhibition. His pictures are always distinguished by a personal sense of color, a feeling for its close interval and a highly original, often witty, arrangement of subject material. His draughtsmanship is lucid and sensitive, with a superb energy of line which is never weary in delineation of character. This delineation, however, stops this side of caricature or the grotesque.

These seven artists, all of whom are represented in the collection, have so consistently merited special attention in critical discussion that at this time they would seem not to fall in any general grouping, but must be considered among the leading individuals and independent creators. At best any grouping is an arbitrary matter and one of convenience. Its chief value, possibly, is to stimulate controversy. However, from this point we shall proceed to make deliberate and limited groupings as some of the outstanding trends in contemporary painting obviously seem to suggest.

During the rise of regionalism and the impact of the Mexican renaissance, many critical voices were heard denouncing exhibition pictures of the figure and studio pictures of still life, because it seemed as though these subjects reflected an unawareness on the part of the artist of "current events" as well as defining his apathy and general shameless social irresponsibility. For the most part this pseudo-critical attitude was unrefreshingly journalistic and op-

portunist in origin. No doubt it had some justification and meaning, considering the number of amateur painters who devote their energies to traditional and even limited problems of subject material. But still life and figure painting as composition continue to occupy an honored place in our museum collections and exhibitions of contemporary art.

Both subjects demand imagination and an understanding of abstract values on the part of the painter, and require an unbiased approach from the spectator or art lover. One could hardly fail to find elements of nobility, grandeur and dramatic meaning in a great still life by Chardin or Cézanne, and the history of painting is filled with posed figures and nudes which have been of sufficient beauty to provide both study and enjoyment for their abstract as well as vital worth.

Among the masters of still life in American art is Henry Lee McFee. Maurice Sterne was counted as part of the vanguard of the modern movement. Both artists have also painted the figure with scholarly care and understanding. They deserve a special place in the annals of contemporary American painting.

Both Luigi Lucioni and Florence Julia Bach are poets of the meticulous in the art of still life. Their personal aesthetic arises from a tender and passionate regard for each nuance of texture. Clarence Hinkle, on the other hand, paints still life with the same breadth and feeling for form that he imparts to landscape. With Hinkle every picture is more-or-less the conclusion of a semiabstract problem.

Actually all art expresses social criticism in some degree, even if it does no more than reflect the state of mind of the individual, or his reaction to a limited segment of society or a particular social condition. But painting practiced as an easel form and deliberately designed to fulfil a social purpose is more widespread today than ever before. In contemporary American painting social criticism may be impressionistic or analytical, kindly or severe in understanding, gay or grim. It takes many directions, from passing observation and comment to militant protest. Certainly social criticism is not limited to any single pictorial device. It runs the gamut from illustration to abstraction, surrealism and fantasy. Protest may ring through any of these approaches, but whatever the weight, burden or portent of the message may be in expression, it is by no means limited to caricature.

It is logical that mural painting should have become the vehicle of a social message or protest, or, in some instances, of propaganda. Its very form suggests and permits a greater extension of time element in pictorial narration. The influence of Diego Rivera, José Clemente Orozco, and other leaders of painting in Mexico not only gave rise to the beginnings of a serious school of mural painting in this country which attempted to interpret subject matter through a critical point of view, but it left a strong mark on easel painting as well. More than social conviction alone, it was also the graphic intensity of these artists of Mexico, coupled with narrative power, that stirred the energies of the American painter. Many of the younger painters, like their colleagues in the other arts, were compelled by the social unrest and upheaval of the day. They were also museum-minded, and were studying Goya, as well as Daumier and other masters of the revolutionary instinct in the not far distant past. The time was ripe for reform; there was indirectly the influence of George Grosz and others at hand, and more directly that of Boardman Robinson and Henry Varnum Poor.

A change from a self contained art form to one of social critical impact and literary overtones is not always due to economic forces alone. Artists can be and often are inspired by innovation and change solely for their own sake. Even the use of a new or revived technical medium may serve as an impetus to accomplishment. This is a

matter of will, arising out of the artist's necessity. The causes of a reformation are not to be lightly dismissed on the social and economic side, but such causes are by no means complete in themselves. Sometimes, however, the artist's message burns with such belligerent flamboyance as to destroy the art form in which it is cast. This weakness is too easily recognizable to demand further comment, except to remark that it appears most obviously when painting loses the directness of the black and white cartoon and fails also in the more expansive qualities of color and pictorial organization.

Internationally known as the most brilliant satirist of modern times, George Grosz has run a full scale of experience from his scathing caricature of the German military and the profiteers of the first World War to his Marin-influenced glimpses of New York. He now paints still life, figure and landscape. Like a veteran he recalls images of the past. Often the path of the "Four Horsemen of the Apocalypse" marks the way of his reminiscence. William Gropper sometimes succeeds in translating the absolute statement of black and white into simplified color compositions wherein he describes, satirizes or sympathizes with his subjects and their place in the class system. Georges Schreiber has been constructively influenced both by George Grosz and William Gropper, and has sought to understand and interpret the varying aspects and habits of the American people. Social significance is undoubtedly present in most of the work of the gifted Robert Gwathmey. However, this is of minor importance in comparison with his original and distinguished use of the elements of line, color and design. Philip Evergood is a draughtsman whose searching honesty of temperament demands that he constantly explore and seek to define new situations of character, with the result that he has given us a set of human documents of highly specialized meaning. Jack Levine, considered both a satirist and an expressionist, relieves the terse abbreviations of his images and the extravagance of his distortions by his opulent use of rich color. Here is a young artist to whom the term "talented" may be aptly applied. One always feels the strength of intention in the work of Mervin Jules. He documents his figure compositions in terms of uncompromising faith, and at times an almost smoldering bitterness. Intensity of social conviction likewise marks the work of Anton Refregier, Mitchell Siporin, Louis Gugliemi, Paul Burlin, Joseph Hirsch and Fletcher Martin, although they have little else in common. Siporin has his individual form of expression. Gugliemi is always interesting in his approach to social problems through realism and fantasy. Burlin, an inveterate eclectic, constantly experiments with new mannerisms and fresh social points of view.

Reginald Marsh, William S. Schwartz and Raphael Soyer as, well as a number of other painters, have developed an expression of the life and drama of the large city. They might almost be named "city regionalists." Marsh can be considered a painter of manners as well as an acute observer of city life. He is a painter of crowds in all their dispositions and vagaries of mood. His is not a socially critical point of view. He seems to mingle with his subjects and setting, and relays his experiences with brilliant action and swift line. Many of his paintings and prints are complex, enthusiastic and energetic, and extraordinarily American in their exuberance. Raphael Soyer is concerned primarily with the individual in relation to environment. He seems to brood over his characters and to register sensitive protest concerning their destiny. Schwartz is interested in the character of background and setting. He does not limit himself to one aspect of the city but has painted a number of solid, carefully analyzed statements in glowing, burning color, which describe its personality and very physiognomy with a feeling almost of pathos. Aaron Bohrod has painted a number of accomplished and sensitive translations of the mood and general façade of the city and village streetscape. With town, city or industrial setting, Bohrod paints richly with an amazing ability to express character through the varying layers of texture in pigment. He has made of solid textures and granulations of paint a medium of true emotional force. William Thoeny has made an original contribution in his vibrant and highly ornamental compositions of the grander aspects of New York City, the harbor and waterfront. There is a spontaneity, but at the same time a wise and telling use of colorful, explosive phrasing, which ricochets throughout his canvases and describes each familiar aspect of his subject with great tension and certainly fresh enthusiasm. He is a modified expressionist.

*   *   *

There are always a certain number of artists whose painting defies classification except for one thing which they appear to have in common, and that is a feeling for romantic personal vision. They remain more or less aloof from any of the "isms" and do not belong to the conservatives. Their work may have mystic evocative power, like that of Henry Mattson, or a wistful nostalgic quality such as is felt in some canvases by Franklin Watkins. The work of each of these artists, and of others associated with them in feeling and approach, seems to depend upon immediate emotional tension or the long forgotten word "inspiration." This does not imply that their painting is not carefully pondered. For the most part their pictures are thoroughly planned and often slowly constructed. If, on occasion, their performance is uneven, this, too, is all the more to be expected because of their approach through feeling and sentiment. Painters of mood are apt to be the least consistent of all artists, and also to suffer the most from repetition. But the few finest pictures of the best of them, and most of Franklin Watkins', are far above those of the recognizedly good painter who is able to maintain a higher average level of production.

XXV

Franklin C. Watkins molds character and style through the gesture, and sometimes almost frenetic pantomime, of his figures which are expressed with wealth of mood. Within the range of his work is style and stylization, manner and mannerism, qualities of richness and surprise that are deeply provocative. Peppino Mangravite is more interested in organic synthesis than clinical analysis or factual description of life. His work attempts to convey the warmth and vitality of people engaged in play, in conversation or communing with nature. Often his figures seem to move with the cadence and rhythm of the dance. Sometimes he seizes upon the intimate moment, the half obscured human situation, seemingly the unuttered thought, and reveals the emotional tension of his subject with startling effect. John Carroll works in a world of personal fantasy, far removed from everyday experience. He often plays a color-scale of pearl-like tones with a few rare chromatic flashes of light. His dream-world is no accident of the subconscious but of the will, constructed of adroitly aroused phantasma and fragile mannerism. Jack Gage Stark is an artist devoted to recalling the intimate quality of the fleeting moment. In his painting, line, plane and tone merge, meander and coruscate to create a sensitively modeled figure, often reduced almost to the simplicity of a silhouette.

Henry Mattson, Hobson Pittman and Julian Levi each has identified himself with a particular kind of picture or subject, which he repeats and revises with interesting variations. They are painters of poetic sensibility. Mattson, considered a mystic painter, interprets the turbulence of the sea in his own powerfully romantic idiom. Pittman makes his whole world into a gently lighted interior, and repeats his haunted theme and variations of wistful vagary with the practiced hand of a minor master. Julian Levi's many quiet pictures of deserted nature along the beach are filled with an imposed sense of isolation, loneliness and escape. Herman Maril is a romantic painter of modest introspection whose sparsely furnished landscapes have a classic sense of order in the handling of space and silhouette.

*   *   *

Any collection of contemporary American painting naturally includes examples of the various experimental and advanced schools: surrealism, nonobjective, geometric or abstract art, and neo-romanticism.

Surrealism is devoted to a hypothetical realism or truth based upon the combination or juxtaposition of ideas, objects and events not objectively or noticeably related. These images or concepts are placed in such violence of contrast as to produce an effect of imaginative fact. Dream, shock and paranoia are part of its paraphernalia. Even though the craftsmanship of this school of painting is accomplished with exquisite finality and perfection of finish, the total effect is often so disarming as to appear quite academic and almost pleasantly conventional.

"The Madonna" by Salvador Dali quietly introduces this international figure to American art. Dali's painting impulses have resulted also in an exhaustive personal literature. This particular picture from the brush of an acknowledged modern "Old Master" appears to be innocent even though typically "Dalinian" in certain details. George L. K. Morris has expanded the devices of abstraction as it is commonly understood, combined with a suggestion of surrealism, in his picture in the collection. Julio de Diego is not strictly a surrealist. His pictures are filled with plastic and literary symbols which are being used to create a new symbolism to express the chaos of our time. He has invented his own special and interesting vocabulary for painting war, in which the terror of the machine monster is described with anthropomorphic attributes.

As a whole, the abstract or geometric painters revitalize and restate their subject matter in simple concentrated terms of design, pattern and color. They seek to establish a new kind of pictorial and plastic energy through the terse statement. French abstract painting has a patois or vernacular all its own which came through the innovators of this movement. American nonrepresentational art does not have this, at least in the same degree as European painting.

Charles Sheeler and Stuart Davis have both expressed many interesting aspects of American life through a highly stylized personal idiom. Sheeler may be interpreted in various ways. His work is always beautifully clean, and his subjects are recreated with the care of the engineer-architect. Because of his close association with photography, which he practices as an art along with painting, his work is widely accepted. Since he disciplines his vision, his subject matter and his medium, his art seems abstract and impersonal. He might be considered at once an abstract painter, an objective painter and a "painter's painter." He handles the tools and craft of painting with surgical precision; at the same time, his work reveals the painter's interest in the quality of light, and he states the textural design of familiar objects with exquisite but formal simplicity.

Stuart Davis may be considered both an abstract artist and a realist. His punctuated passages of vivid color describing activity along the water front, harbor scenes and street scenes, are symbolically simplified, yet they are highly realistic. Through his adroit simplifications, Stuart Davis creates something that is nearly classic yet related to folk art. In some of his pictures, Davis, by various changes of cadence and accent, and by exchange of color-weight, by size of pattern and intensity of color and ornament, has translated into pictorial effects the relentless and mad speed of modern "hot" music. Yet if one looks at Stuart Davis's pictures without taking their titles too seriously, one will find something of the gaiety of the "friendship" quilt of early times. Davis's pictures are often as American and colloquial as a barber pole.

Francis Criss and Ralston Crawford, different as they are, could be considered along with Stuart Davis and Charles Sheeler as objective abstractionists or simplified realists. Criss has more the quality of a modern miniaturist when placed alongside Davis. Crawford dramatizes the silent, sometimes the nearly terrifying vistas of space as an organic foil to his world of structural engineering. He makes imagined blueprints spring to exhilarant life with abrupt shock. His world is one of steel and concrete, speed and wonder. Joseph Stella has also aided greatly in building up the living tradition of American painting, especially in the great series of industrial landscape studies, and the imposing group of pictures devoted to the Brooklyn Bridge.

At various times Morris Kantor's work has been associated with surrealism. Whether in landscape, still life or figure composition, the painting of this gifted and unpredictable artist has an element of surprise. An eclectic painter, Abraham Rattner composes with semi-abstract forms and improvises in light and color. Expressionist in feeling, his use of singing, glowing color for its own sake seems to be his main contribution in his otherwise genuinely experimental art. Following in something of the same pattern, Samuel Rosenberg has a more measured and objective approach than Rattner.

The neo-romantic school is nostalgic, manneristic and sophisticated. It has in common with surrealism an archæological excursion into the past. It seeks to revive the emotions and properties of the late Baroque era, and to reform our contemporary materialism. Eugene Berman and Pavel Tchelitchew are the most widely known of the neo-romantic painters in this country. Francesco di Cocco is probably the most poetic.

It is obvious that American contemporary painting seeks to join or infuse new forms with older, perhaps quite localized realities and familiar facts. Long has the Negro spiritual been a source of stimulation in the various arts. Its handling has varied from a folk approach to fantasy, and it has engaged the attention of some of the most accomplished artists, musicians and writers of our day. A form that seizes upon the imagination, it is capable of infinite interpretation. Dan Lutz, a painter of growing stature and great emotional power, has created his own individual plastic symbolism, through which he depicts the inherent richness of this material with smoldering fervor. Raymond Breinin has painted a number of highly arresting pictures which convey a strange and eerie sense of fantasy. He combines his color and draughtsmanship with an unusual and magical use of silhouette, through which foreboding shadows acquire volume and are disciplined into release. Darrel Austin, possessed of a strange, self-evoked vision, has been aptly summed up by that able critic Alfred Frankenstein as "the past master of the lyrical chimera." A colorist of distinction, Karl Zerbe has developed a type of lyrical subjective painting wherein each pictorial situation he deals with is analyzed, magnified and reconstructed with the touch of the storyteller who knows where to place the precise accent that touches just this side of fantasy. Gifted with a strong graphic sense, further enhanced by an exuberant use of color, Iver Rose paints his subjects with a smashing sense of action whenever action is required. He has a fine sense of character, which stays fittingly with his talent as a painter and does not encroach on the more static field of illustration.

* * *

The pictures of the so-called "modern primitive" and popular artist bring a fresh point of view to an old set of forms, and yet are acceptable to the public and much publicised as being of value to the student of art as well. In this collection, for example, is a painting by Horace Pippin entitled "The Holy Mountain." Here is the art of the "modern primitive" at its spiritual best. Pippin reminds one of Edward Hicks, the American sermon painter of the nineteenth century. His painting conveys its meaning quite clearly by virtue of its great sincerity.

Many of the artists represented in this collection laid the foundations for the general understanding of the experimental movements that play such an important part in our art today. Among these painters not represented or already discussed, mention must be made of S. MacDonald Wright and Morgan Russell, who evolved a movement in painting that had to do with an abstract and dynamic use of color. This movement was known as "Synchronism." Also the work and influence of three artists no longer living were of vast importance: Jules Pascin, Alfred Maurer and Charles Demuth.

Man Ray has never ceased to experiment with all forms and mediums, including his inventive approach to photography. Among the many artists whose work is colored both by surrealism and fantasy, we specially list Loren MacIver, Morris Graves, Gina Knee, Leon Kelly and Arshile Gorky.

Karl Knaths, L. Moholy-Nagy, Jean Helion, Carl Robert Holty, Hans Hofmann, Vaclav Vytlacil and Hilaire Hiler, each have contributed to a recognized form of abstract painting. Of all the American artists working in the field of abstraction, Arthur G. Dove seems the most individual, the least predictable and, in a personal sense, the most highly inspired. Charles Howard adds a new note of clarity and brilliance of both color and invention to nonobjective painting today. There are many other names which could be included and especially those of the European artists who are now in America more or less in exile. The Museum of Modern Art, the Museum of Living Art, and the collections of nonobjective painting of the Solomon R. Guggenheim Foundation have repeatedly presented, with due documentation, the work of the international experimental groups of our time. It is significant that the newer schools are not confined to the direct line of modern French painting but have taken into consideration new forms and ideas appearing throughout the rest of Europe.

*   *   *

There are a number of young artists throughout the country who have developed personal styles of recognizable authority, some of whom are represented in the collection—David Fredenthal, John Edward Heliker, Louis Bosa, Frank Kleinholz and Andrée Ruellan. "No More Mowing" by John S. de Martelly was one of the most strikingly original pictures in the painting section of the huge exhibition "American Art Today" in the New York World's Fair of 1939. It has a quality that seems essentially American, that is super-real, and at the same time romantic. Copeland C. Burg has a refreshing approach to his subject material. His art is directed by genuine taste and understanding of the eclectic forms of modern painting. Marion Greenwood is consistently evolving a style of genuine individuality; likewise Lily Harmon, who also paints with sensitive feeling.

An artist who cannot be included in any grouping, because of her personal devotion to highly specialized subject matter, is Doris Rosenthal, who brings us some of the most convincing pictures of Mexico by any American. She has developed her own honest sense of humor. Her paintings are vigorously fresh, as personal as a letter, and she never goes tourist or leans heavily against the pillars of the Mexican renaissance.

*   *   *

Certainly it appears that the American artist today is seeking to express the forces and energies of his own country. He is not content with being eclectic, but wishes to seize upon all forms in order to bring greater clarity and intensity to his own talents, background and equipment.

Donald Bear

Director, Santa Barbara Museum of Art

XXIX

ADVISORY BOARD *of the Encyclopædia Britannica Collection*

• Encyclopædia Britannica wishes to say thanks and to express its sincere appreciation for the assistance it has received from members of the Advisory Board, from museum and gallery directors and from the artists themselves in helping to solve many of the problems pertaining to the selection of the paintings for this collection. Without their kindly help and consideration it would have been a far more difficult task.

PHILIP R. ADAMS, *Director, Cincinnati Art Museum* — Cincinnati, O.
DONALD BEAR, *Director, Santa Barbara Museum of Art* — Santa Barbara, Calif.
THOMAS HART BENTON, *Artist* — Kansas City, Mo.
GEORGE BIDDLE, *Artist* — Croton on Hudson, N.Y.
ADELYN D. BREESKIN, *Acting Director, Baltimore Museum of Art* — Baltimore, Md.
ALEXANDER BROOK, *Artist* — New York, N.Y.
CHARLES BURCHFIELD, *Artist* — Gardenville, N.Y.
PAUL BURLIN, *Artist* — New York, N.Y.
CLYDE H. BURROUGHS, *Secretary, Detroit Institute of Arts* — Detroit, Mich.
JERRY BYWATERS, *Director, Dallas Museum of Fine Arts* — Dallas, Texas
JAMES CHAPIN, *Artist* — Andover, N.J.
JAMES CHILLMAN, JR., *Director, Museum of Fine Arts* — Houston, Texas
STEPHEN C. CLARK, *Vice-President, Metropolitan Museum of Art* — New York, N.Y.
RUSSELL COWLES, *Artist* — New Milford, Conn.
STUART DAVIS, *Artist* — New York, N.Y.
JULIO DE DIEGO, *Artist* — New York, N.Y.
ADOLF DEHN, *Artist* — New York, N.Y.
GEORGE H. EDGELL, *Director, Museum of Fine Arts* — Boston, Mass.
PHILIP EVERGOOD, *Artist* — Woodside, L.I., N.Y.
DAVID E. FINLEY, *Director, National Gallery of Art* — Washington, D.C.
JULIANA R. FORCE, *Director, Whitney Museum of American Art* — New York, N.Y.
PAUL GARDNER, *Director, William Rockhill Nelson Gallery of Art* — Kansas City, Mo.
BLAKE-MORE GODWIN, *Director, Toledo Museum of Art* — Toledo, O.

MARION GREENWOOD, *Artist*	Woodstock, N.Y.
WILLIAM GROPPER, *Artist*	Croton on Hudson, N.Y.
PAUL H. GRUMMANN, *Director, Society of Liberal Arts*	Omaha, Neb.
ALEXANDRE HOGUE, *Artist*	Dallas, Texas
PETER HURD, *Artist*	San Patricio, N.M.
FISKE KIMBALL, *Director, Philadelphia Museum of Art*	Philadelphia, Pa.
FRANK KLEINHOLZ, *Artist*	New York, N.Y.
LEON KROLL, *Artist*	Gloucester, Mass.
REEVES LEWENTHAL, *Director, Associated American Artists, Inc.*	New York, N.Y.
SAM A. LEWISOHN, *Vice-Chairman, Museum of Modern Art*	New York, N.Y.
ESTELLE MANDEL, *Vice-President, Associated American Artists, Inc.*	New York, N.Y.
REGINALD MARSH, *Artist*	New York, N.Y.
DOROTHY C. MILLER, *Curator, Museum of Modern Art*	New York, N.Y.
WILLIAM M. MILLIKEN, *Director, Cleveland Museum of Art*	Cleveland, O.
GRACE L. McCANN MORLEY, *Director, San Francisco Museum of Art*	San Francisco, Calif.
DALE NICHOLS, *Artist*	Tucson, Ariz.
ANNA WETHERILL OLMSTED, *Director, Syracuse Museum of Fine Arts*	Syracuse, N.Y.
WILBUR D. PEAT, *Director, The John Herron Art Institute*	Indianapolis, Ind.
WALDO PEIRCE, *Artist*	Pomona, N.Y.
DUNCAN PHILLIPS, *Director, Phillips Memorial Gallery*	Washington, D.C.
RUSSELL A. PLIMPTON, *Director, Minneapolis Institute of Arts*	Minneapolis, Minn.
PERRY T. RATHBONE, *Director, City Art Museum*	St. Louis, Mo.
DANIEL CATTON RICH, *Director of Fine Arts, Art Institute of Chicago*	Chicago, Ill.
FREDERICK B. ROBINSON, *Director, Museum of Fine Arts*	Springfield, Mass.
NATHANIEL SALTONSTALL, *Institute of Modern Art*	Boston, Mass.
PAUL SAMPLE, *Artist*	Hanover, N.H.
GEORGES SCHREIBER, *Artist*	New York, N.Y.
MILLARD SHEETS, *Artist*	Claremont, Calif.
LEWIS P. SKIDMORE, *Director of Art, High Museum of Art*	Atlanta, Ga.
LAWRENCE BEALL SMITH, *Artist*	Cambridge, Mass.
EUGENE SPEICHER, *Artist*	Woodstock, N.Y.
FREDERIC TAUBES, *Artist*	New York, N.Y.
HUDSON D. WALKER, *President, American Federation of Arts*	Washington, D.C.
SIEGFRIED R. WENG, *Director, Dayton Art Institute*	Dayton, O.

Contemporary
American
Painting

DARREL AUSTIN

Darrel Austin weaves for us exotic legends of bewitched creatures in a muted moonlit world. For anyone who has within him a love of fantasy, who seeks escape from a factual world, Austin's painting is enchanting stuff.

The artist, who admits quite calmly that he has little interest either in the art of the past or the techniques of his contemporaries, came upon the palette knife and for a time believed that he alone had discovered its possibilities. He uses no brushes and starts with no preconceived story—but out of tiny hillocks of pigment, applied with the knife, his opalescent tones obediently take the shapes of enigmatic nymphs and charmed beasts who perform mysterious rites in an aquatic lunar world. Almost as imperturbable and remote as the creatures who people his canvas world is the man Austin who proffers neither explanation nor defense against any criticisms of his work. He paints them—that is enough.

Despite his art, he stems from a down-to-earth western background. Born in Raymond, Washington, in 1907, he moved, at two years of age, with his family to Portland, Oregon. His school career was an average one. Instead of high school he attended Polytechnic in order to study printing and typography. During his teens he earned his way at lettering. As a sparring partner, he taught young boxers the tricks of that profession. Finally came the burning desire to paint, and he began to study at the University of Portland with Emile Jacques. Later he followed Jacques, who was then teaching at Notre Dame. It was there that he met Margot Helser, whom he married in 1933, and who has since acquired a reputation as a writer and illustrator of children's books. The next four years were an arduous struggle for both of them. He had his first one-man show at the Putzel Gallery, in Hollywood, Calif., early in 1938, and every picture was sold. The year 1939 marked the beginning of Austin's purely imaginative and creative style, of which Sheldon Cheney wrote, "When so much of painting is statement and copy, it is something like homecoming for the soul to encounter these distillations of feeling imaged forth in paint."

That same year he went to New York. He was rebuffed by practically every gallery, but finally found an understanding dealer in the person of Klaus Perls, who previously had specialized in modern French painting. His success was immediate and overwhelming. As a result of his first one-man show in New York six important museums acquired his works. Museum directors and trustees bought them for their personal collections. In 1943, at the age of 35, he already had earned a retrospective show and today his star is still rising. He is represented in the permanent collections of many museums, including the Metropolitan, and the Museum of Modern Art in New York, Boston's Museum of Fine Arts, Albright Art Galleries in Buffalo, and Detroit Institute of Art.

● *Darrel Austin makes no statement. He prefers to have the painting speak for him*

CUB AND INSECT

by Darrel Austin

painted in 1945

Oil, 24 x 30 inches

1

FLORENCE JULIA BACH

Something akin to religion seems to be the very essence of F. Julia Bach's painting. One can visualize this woman lost in wonderment over the miracle of God's creating—desiring only to record it with reverence and exactitude. She says: "Nothing is left to chance. Long hours and many are spent on the paintings. I admire and am fascinated by the casual and free painting of today, but for several years my studies have been defined realism—it is what I choose to do and I uphold it—endeavoring to subordinate all means to an idea, and technique only interests me in giving facility for expression."

To Erwin S. Barrie, Director of the Grand Central Art Galleries, Miss Bach expresses profound gratitude. In 1940, at a Syracuse exhibit, Mr. Barrie saw a small flower painting. He sought out Miss Bach and it was his encouragement and understanding that gave her the incentive to paint rather than to teach. In December 1944, Barrie gave her a one-man show, and in the *Art Digest* Margaret Breuning wrote: "It is remarkable that a painter of sound accomplishment should have waited so long to present her work to the public. . . . It is to be hoped that Miss Bach . . . will continue to paint flowers not merely as gay decorations, but as portraits of ephemeral beauty at its moment of fullest realization."

Miss Bach was born in Buffalo. Her art studies began there at a very early age and her teachers included such names as Mary Bowman, Wheeler Coxe, Frank Vincent DuMond, William Merritt Chase and, in Paris, Louis Lejeune, the famed sculptor. Her devotion to art seemed to have been without ego, and she contented herself for many years as instructor of creative drawing, painting, and modelling from life at the Buffalo School of Fine Arts. In 1932 she was awarded the Buffalo Centenary Medal for distinguished service in the field of art. In 1940 she won the Purchase Prize of the Syracuse Museum of Art and it was shortly thereafter that Erwin Barrie persuaded her that painting, not teaching, should be her goal in life. Today she is represented in many private collections, as well as in the permanent collection of the Buffalo Fine Arts Academy of the Albright Art Gallery.

It may seem highly presumptuous to attempt the painting of flowers—but they are so appealing that to resist is impossible. There is constant wonderment at their perfectness, at their fragile, exquisite beauty, and that anything so lovely can spring from the earth, also at the infinite variety presented in line and mass. Petals, leaves and stems similar in the kind of plant but endless in individual character and detail. Such creations have power to humble and make one reverent.

F. Julia Bach

MARSH MALLOWS
by Florence Julia Bach
painted in 1943
Oil, 36 x 28 inches

2

LOREN BARTON

Too often artists are suspicious of beauty, afraid of sentimentalism, and thereby lean over backwards against such betraying will-o-the-wisps. But from California comes a woman who believes in beauty and courage and high ideals, and fearlessly she presents a world tempered of its dross. The people who come into being on her canvases are strong, healthy lovers of life, who face a world courageously and defiantly. Her messages are the heartening ones of gallantry and challenge and triumph.

There is no sense of laboring in Loren Barton's painting, but there is a clear conception brought to completion through the smooth and telling use of her brush. It is beautiful, effortless painting, in young, clean, sparkling color.

She can turn to oil, water color, pencil or etching needle with equal efficiency and enthusiasm. Whether her subjects are steel mills, portrait sketches, or the tenderest of Madonnas, she approaches them with a directness and decision that results in a brilliantly executed work of art.

Loren Barton was born in Oxford, Massachusetts, in 1893, in the home of her great-aunt Clara Barton, the beloved founder of the American Red Cross. However, California claims her for its own, since she moved as a child to the West Coast, where she attended the University of Southern California and began her painting there at an early age.

She has distinguished herself in three fields of art—painting, illustrating and etching. In the latter field her "George Arliss as Disraeli" and "Manuel" are considered to be among the most outstanding prints by living artists. She has illustrated numerous books, among them *Spanish Alta California* (Minton Balch), *Beppy Marlowe* (Viking Press) and *The Little House* (Harcourt, Brace). She also devotes a great part of her time to teaching and lecturing on art in various universities and organizations.

Her honors and awards are noteworthy, among them the George A. Zabriskie prize in 1941 presented by the American Watercolor Society. Her paintings and etchings are represented in the permanent collections of the Metropolitan Museum, the Art Institute of Chicago, National Gallery in Washington, D.C., the Brooklyn Museum, the New York Public Library, the California State Library, the National Library of France and many others.

● *The vast magnificence of the Pacific Ocean, with its rugged coast and windswept skies, gives to the artist a fascinating subject upon which to build with line and color, and there could be no more inspiring models than the seafaring people who share the seeming strength and patience of the rocky cliffs that form a background for their daily lives. I find increasing interest in the problems offered by the beauty and drama of the sea.*

Loren Barton

PACIFIC

by Loren Barton

painted in 1943

Oil, 29 x 37 inches

3

GIFFORD BEAL

There is no typical "Beal." Which makes him a bit confusing to critics, for the job of evaluating him is not a simple one. The mood of the sea, the carnival atmosphere of the circus, the carefree gaiety of park equestrians, the deep serenity of a river—each has its own spirit and essence and Gifford Beal goes toward each with a different approach.

One critic writes: "There are the circus pictures, perhaps no more than six or seven all told, and yet so fine of their kind that they have established a reputation for the artist in this particular field. The lover of skies and clouds and extravagant sunsets will always find his canvases breath-catching, without the critic's endorsement that 'his bright color is based on form.' "

Gifford Beal was born in New York City in 1879 and at the age of twelve began his formal studies under Chase. All through his college years at Princeton he continued under Chase's guidance, where George Bellows was included among his fellow students. Later, when he entered the Art Students League, he paid careful attention to Du Mond and Bridgman but it was Chase who always exerted the more important influence.

His first canvas appeared in an Academy exhibition before he was twenty-one years old, and although success came early it had no unhappy crystallizing effect upon his art. Beal has never worked on any one subject until he has exhausted it. His creative impulse shines on too many facets of life, and in turning from one subject to another he keeps a freshness of viewpoint. He believes that the first fine flash of inspiration cannot be long sustained—but he will never bore you with his theories. Homer Saint-Gaudens once wrote "For while he knows his rules and regulations, he never preaches what he practices."

His student days were spent in America, his subjects are the American scene and in spirit his art is American.

Beal won prizes in the Academy as far back as 1910, 1913 and 1919, and became an Academician in 1914. He has won medals at the Carnegie Institute and the Corcoran Gallery in Washington, D.C. He is represented in the Metropolitan Museum, the Chicago Art Institute, the Syracuse Museum, the San Francisco Art Institute, the Detroit Museum of Art, the Harrison Gallery in the Los Angeles County Museum, the Phillips Memorial Gallery, among many others, and is also a member of the Academy of Arts and Letters.

● *This picture was painted from sketches made at a circus in Gloucester, Massachusetts. As I remember I spent the whole day and evening making drawings in the different parts of the circus. It was an unusual day for me because from the drawings I made I painted five pictures, four of which have been sold. It was one of those rare days in the life of an artist when everything seems to go just right. The picture is painted in the oil tempera method which is so popular these days.*

Gifford Beal

CIRCUS TENT

by Gifford Beal

painted in 1937

Oil, 20 x 30 inches

4

GEORGE BELLOWS

The mauve decade was over. A boisterous new century was kicking over the traces, taking the bit in its teeth and setting a new pace. And by some very neat arrangement of fate this was the moment for the dramatic entrance of George Wesley Bellows on a jaded art horizon.

In speaking of him, Saint-Gaudens says: "Changes were coming in all forms of art and an American master was saying his say. Bellows understood us, appreciated us and expressed us and our social structure, with an imagination that constantly gained in strength and inherent dignity. One man like George Bellows is a sufficient output for seven years' worth of any nation's art."

Seldom is there the acknowledged master without a few voices raised in dissension, but in his case there seems to have been complete accord. Bellows was a creative artist, neither academic nor impressionistic, who depicted the every-day scene from the romantic to the brutal. His prize-ring series are among the most reproduced, and certainly no one else has ever painted them with such physical vitality.

Columbus, Ohio, in 1882 was his birthplace. He was a descendant of Benjamin Bellows who migrated from England in 1632 and founded Bellows Falls in Vermont. Bellows' rare talent began to assert itself from the time he went to kindergarten. At Ohio State University he was star shortstop on the baseball team, but the love of art proved stronger than the aptitude for athletics. His wealthy father was decidedly in favor of a business career, but eventually relented when the young man began working during summer vacations as a cartoonist with a Columbus newspaper.

Later he went to New York to study with Henri who was already rebelling and preaching against the static sentimentality of current exhibits, and such principles found instant response in the Americanism of Bellows. He never set foot on foreign shores. From 1913 to his untimely death in 1925, was the short span of time in which he fulfilled a great artistic destiny. He instructed at the Art Students League and gave liberally of his time in teaching underprivileged youngsters. He was a devoted husband and father and found in his wife and children constantly recurring pictorial inspiration. Equally distinguished in lithography and drawing, his book illustrations are considered among his most outstanding work.

Twenty-five museums own his paintings and he is represented in every important American collection.

(1882-1925)

SUMMER CITY

by George Bellows

painted in 1908

Oil, 38 x 48 inches

5

THOMAS HART BENTON

"The gusty realism of his boyhood colliding with the artificially stimulated life of the Left Bank"—and out of his chaotic struggle came the direct and unblushing representation of American life, the embodiment of its strength and even its crudeness, with honest defiance that lifts Benton's art to its high estate—an art of swinging rhythms and plastic color that does no borrowing from other techniques.

Born in Neosho, Missouri, in 1889, Benton's childhood environment was that of Huck Finn, Tom Sawyer and the rushing energy of a maturing mid-west. His father was a criminal lawyer and his great-uncle was the famous Missouri senator for whom he was named. Parental plans notwithstanding, Benton had to paint. At college his interests went no further than football, and his next step was to Chicago's Art Institute. Inevitably, he found himself in Paris, wallowing with all the intensity of his nature in all the cultural isms of the Latin Quarter, studying the old masters and experimenting with new techniques and changing theories.

Back in America, he still floundered—these were the years of disheartening struggle—he worked as a stevedore, tried book illustrating, taught art and served as architectural draftsman in the Navy.

But a visit to his native Missouri gave him the earthy inspiration that finally "jelled" in the four murals that provided him worldwide attention. These were the New School, Whitney Museum, Indiana State and Missouri murals.

When Benton painted the murals for the Missouri State capitol he pulled no punches. His choices of representative subject matter were not the legendary heroes; they were instead, the lusty figures of Jesse James, Boss Pendergast and Frankie and Johnnie. He painted with the doors open so that all who liked might come to criticize.

Benton is more than a great artist—he is a great American with a pioneering mind ready to fight for his beliefs—his headstrong qualities tempered with a humorous slant on life. His picture "Boom Town" was painted in 1927 and shown in 1928, and was the largest he had painted up to that time.

Other work of his may be found in the Metropolitan Museum of Art, the Wanamaker Gallery Collection, the Museum of Modern Art, the Brooklyn Museum and others. He was awarded the gold medal for decorative painting by the Architectural League of New York in 1933.

● *This painting, "Boom Town," is an interpretation of Borger, Texas, as it was in 1926 in the middle of its rise from a road crossing to an oil city. Out in the limitless stretches of the Panhandle as the rigs went up and the drills went down, Borger was born and raised in the traditional fashion of the western boom town—speculators, gamblers, sporting ladies, rich men, poor men, beggar-men, thieves— and eventually the Texas Rangers to straighten them all out.*

Thomas H. Benton

BOOM TOWN

by Thomas Hart Benton

painted in 1928

Oil, 45 x 54 inches

6

GEORGE BIDDLE

Altruism is the opposite of individualism or egoism and embraces those moral motives which induce a man to regard the interests of others. If an example were necessary, the man who fits the statement is George Biddle. In the world of American art few men have earned such honest approbation, not only for his own work but for his unselfish crusading in behalf of all artists, for his belief in art for the people and for the development of mural art as a cultural national expression. His friendship with Franklin D. Roosevelt, which dated back to his school years at Groton, made it possible for him to sponsor the Federal Arts Project of the WPA through which hundreds of artists, working at mechanics' wages, were given freedom to express the social ideas of America, its government and its people, in public buildings throughout the country.

His most recent book, *Artists at War*, published in 1944, is eloquent proof that Biddle can take up a pen with equal facility.

Born in Philadelphia in 1885, of a socially prominent family, George Biddle bowed to family tradition and via Groton and Harvard emerged with an LL.D. Before he passed his bar examinations, however, he took off for Paris and a happy year at the Julian Academy.

After World War I he went to Tahiti, where he experimented in stone and wood; he modeled in clay, cut block prints, made designs for marquetry, embroidery and pottery. Again he tried Paris, pitting his talents against the best French talent, holding one-man shows, making comparisons. America won the decision, and, having made the full test, home he came to be a vital part of American art. Later he settled at Croton on Hudson with his sculptress wife, Hélène Sardeau.

Biddle's murals in the Department of Justice Building in Washington, D.C., portray his passionate belief that "the sweatshop and tenement of yesterday can be the life planned with justice of tomorrow." He was commissioned in 1942 by the Republic of Brazil to paint two large frescoes for the lobby of the Biblioteca National in Rio de Janeiro, and in 1944 was working on two murals for the Supreme Court Building in Mexico City. His easel paintings and lithographs are owned by the Metropolitan Museum, Museum of Modern Art, Whitney Museum, Chicago Art Institute, Pennsylvania Academy of Fine Arts, the Boston, San Diego, Los Angeles and San Francisco Museums, and many more.

● *Al Lounsberry is an old friend and neighbor. He hasn't done any serious work, or taken a bath or repaired his house this past 40 or 50 years; and he is drunk whenever he can get the price. He believes in God, and has a salty sense of humor and a grand feeling for earthy words. He comes of good stock, was born in a neat farmhouse off Mt. Airy Road and once mowed the cleanest swathe of grass in the neighborhood. Once a fortnight I give him a little "tobaccy" money and he buys "scratch-gut" gin with it. Someone said that "Civilization is measured by the percentage of its individualists." Al helps support civilization.*

MY NEIGHBOR, AL
by George Biddle
painted in 1940
Oil, 60 x 40 inches

7

ARNOLD BLANCH

So perhaps the critics will continue to disagree and he won't fit accommodatingly into any neatly designated pigeonhole. In his pictures there will always be those who will seize upon the acid realism, the irony or the gloomy sentiment, but there will always be others, fortunately, who will see them as art in its finest sense. He can't be summed up, his artistic credos may vary, but Blanch will always find an audience. He says of the public's indifference to art, that the artist in his frantic endeavor for self-expression has lost the art of being understood. He rejects art for art's sake, and the philosophic statements on many of his paintings give evidence of his interest in the world he lives in.

Mantorville, Minnesota, in 1896, was his birthplace; his mother painted on china and his aunt copied "famous paintings" and gave drawing lessons, so his own artistic tendencies sprouted at a tender age. He attended the Minneapolis School of Fine Arts for four years; the winning of a fellowship enabled him to continue at the Art Students League in New York where Henri, Bellows, Robinson, Sloan and Miller were teaching. It was this group which opened his eyes to the adequacy of the American environment without garnishing.

After serving in World War I he managed a year's educational tour through the chateau country in France, then came home to establish his residence in Woodstock, N.Y. Fortunately, at this time, Blanch's love of the pioneer life stood him in good stead and his aptitude for hunting and fishing helped to tide him over some fairly lean years.

Then, between 1926 and 1929, came two one-man shows and an offer to teach at the California School of Fine Arts, which guaranteed substantial recognition as an artist, and Blanch took off promptly, crossing the country in his trusty old Ford.

In 1933 Blanch was awarded a fellowship for further European study. He has done murals for the post offices in Fredonia, New York, and in Norwalk, Connecticut. His paintings are included in the museums in San Francisco, Denver, Colorado Springs, Cleveland, Brooklyn, the Metropolitan, the Whitney and in the Library of Congress in Washington, D.C.

Though he has never worked in his own state (which in turn has never bought one of his paintings) Blanch still confesses a chronic nostalgia for Minnesota. He does not believe, however, in regional painting—feeling too intensely the wealth of material all over the country.

● *In the winter of 1939 I spent some months in the swamp country of eastern Georgia and South Carolina. I made my headquarters first on St. Simon Island, then later at Beaufort, I did many drawings and paintings of this slow-moving country and its people and I think "Carolina Low Country" is one of the best.*

Arnold Blanch

CAROLINA LOW COUNTRY

by Arnold Blanch

painted in 1939

Oil, 18 x 30 inches

8

AARON BOHROD

Chicago's most nationally known gift to art is in the person of Aaron Bohrod, who returns the compliment nicely by finding all the inspiration he needs within her environs. Completely disinterested in her more elegant sections, he finds his material in the shabbier parts of the city—Division Street, Maxwell Street, markets and ramshackle houses. Yet, despite satiric intent, they turn out to be pictorially beautiful, probably because beneath the irony Bohrod loves his Chicago and because he uses color lusciously and with a profligate hand. Bohrod, if asked, would prefer to call himself a general practitioner in art—landscapes, architectural structures, figures and still lifes, all offer pictorial temptations "because he is too interested in too many subjects to be tied to one kind of painting."

This shy, blond young man, who is not overly talkative, but quick-witted and observant to a rare degree, was born on Chicago's west side in 1907, the son of a Russian émigré grocer. He attended Crane High School and spent one year at Crane Junior College. He was in turn a printer's devil, broker's messenger, mechanical draftsman and commercial illustrator in order to pay his way at the Chicago Art Institute and later under John Sloan and the Art Students League in New York. He says he learned a great deal from Sloan, who criticized his work freely and openly.

He has had a number of one-man shows, has twice won a Guggenheim Fellowship and has done government murals for the Vandalia post office in Illinois. As an instructor he accepted the post of artist-in-residence at the Illinois State Normal College in Carbondale. He is represented in the permanent collections of the Whitney, Boston and Brooklyn museums, Pennsylvania Academy of Fine Arts, Sheldon Swope Art Gallery, Butler Art Institute, the Art Institute of Chicago and the University of Illinois. He has had color pages in *Life* and *Esquire*. Critics consider him as one of the best artists in America in the mediums of water color and gouache.

His home, with his wife and young son, is in Chicago and one of his best still lifes is an arrangement of toys that the youngster, then six, demanded his father to paint. In 1943, as artist-war-correspondent for *Life*, Bohrod brought back pictorial records of the jungle fighting on Rendova Island in New Georgia. In 1944 Bohrod went overseas on his second assignment, this time to London and the Cherbourg Peninsula.

● *The sketch for this painting was done outside the railroad station of the town of Clinton, Ill., a typical mid-western city, while waiting for my train (actually the 3:30) to take me back to Chicago. I dashed down roughly the outlines of the setting—March snowdrifts, the play of color in light and dark, and the waiting fellow-traveler combined to offer a subject worth recording, I felt. And, besides, I had to wait for the 3:30.*

Aaron Bohrod

WAITING FOR THE 3:30

by Aaron Bohrod

painted in 1941

Oil, 27 x 36 inches

9

L O U I S   B O S A

In Louis Bosa's America one enjoys a welcome respite from argument and discussion. Here is no picture-maker rebuking us for our sins, no pedant struggling to prove or disprove another fellow's theories. Tenderly, humorously or dramatically he sees a world of realities, of tears or laughter, happiness or tragedy. He says, "It is true that I have a sense of humor, but I do not always find life humorous—on the contrary I often find it very tragic, and this I try to express. I paint people as I see them—sometimes gay, but often wistful and even pathetic. They are so funny at times, they are *sad*."

Bosa's one-man show at Kleemann's in March 1944 brought forth from the critics their handsomest tributes. Critics say that he has in him the makings of a landscape painter analogous to Rubens, that his talent is comparable to Forain, even Brueghel; that his compositions are living things; and that he is a master of the gentlest kind of satire. But that same March of 1944 brought one bitter disappointment to Bosa. He won the Altman Prize of the National Academy of Design only to have the decision regretfully withdrawn because, although a citizen, he is not American-born. So the committee awarded him an Honorable Mention, as a partial compensation.

Louis Bosa was born in Codroipo, Italy, in 1905. As an infant he was so tiny that his father, certain that he would die, proceeded to fashion a tiny coffin for him. Bosa often wonders what happened to that little coffin! He started to draw at the age of ten—mostly pictures of his family—and since there were ten in the family there was no shortage of models. He was fascinated by the murals and frescoes on public buildings. At 18 he went to Canada, and a year later he entered the United States and began formal studies at the Art Students League. His paintings are in the permanent collections of the Pennsylvania Academy of Fine Arts, Springfield (Mass.) Museum and in many private collections. In 1944 he received the $1,500 Third Prize in the Portraits of America competition.

Bosa lives in Bucks County, Pennsylvania, in a house 200 years old, which had been unoccupied for 40 years. All of his artistry went into the restoration and it became such a showplace that eventually he was compelled to build a studio with trapdoor entrances where he could work undisturbed by admiring sightseers.

● *Regarding "War Bride"—I was sketching in a small town in Pennsylvania when an old Model T Ford drove by, horn blowing, strings flying out behind with tin cans and other objects attached. In it was a pretty farmer's daughter and a sailor, just married and as happy as could be. Two minutes later, along the same road, appeared an old farmer with a lady in a wagon drawn by an old horse, nothing but bones. So I took the bride and her husband out of the Ford and put them in the wagon. The people behind the trees are the kind that don't get along with their neighbors.*

Louis Bosa

WAR BRIDE

by Louis Bosa

painted in 1943

Oil, 27 x 39 inches

10

LOUIS BOUCHÉ

A *bon vivant* in the most acceptable sense is Louis Bouché. He likes good food and good conversation, and fun and people and dogs. In art, he preaches no sermons and offers no advice; his paintings are faithful living recordings of scenes that he has enjoyed.

His approach may be modern but he paints literally, omitting no small truths. He will make any number of accurate and detailed sketches on the spot but, later, the final canvas is painted in his studio. Aside from landscapes, for which he is best known, interiors intrigue him. Barber shops, bowling alleys, cheap flats and theatrical dressing rooms—these he paints with a rare blend of French tradition and true American spirit.

Bouché was born in New York City in 1896. He can trace his artistic inheritance back to a grandfather who was a Barbizon painter and a friend of Millet and Daubigny. When he was twelve his father died, and a distraught mother took him to France. Recognizing the artistic bent of her young son, she wisely engaged a tutor and turned them both loose to wander in Brittany and talk art to their heart's content. Bouché has never forgotten that sojourn in Brittany.

Later, he studied in Paris at the Academie de la Grand Chaumiere and the École des Beaux Arts, where Albert Besnard became his youthful idol. Returning to New York in 1915, he studied at the Art Students League where he teaches art today. During World War I he served in the Camouflage Unit of the U. S. Navy.

His first show in New York was in 1922 at the Daniel Gallery, and the critics took kindly to his advanced ideas in painting. In 1933, through the winning of a Guggenheim Fellowship, he went to Scandinavia and England and it was at this time that his style changed from the more abstract to the type of painting Bouché is known for today.

His paintings are in the Phillips Memorial Gallery, the Metropolitan and Whitney Museums and the Columbus Gallery of Fine Arts. He has proven himself equally versatile as an easel painter and muralist. In the latter field he has done murals for the Department of Justice and the Department of the Interior buildings in Washington, D.C., and also in the Radio City Music Hall in Rockefeller Center, New York City.

● *I painted the "Lafayette Barber Shop" largely for sentimental reasons. I have been one of its customers for more than 22 years. In painting the picture I wanted to faithfully show the shop as it is in even the smallest detail. Of the small staff of two barbers I made actual portraits. The bootblack in the background is also a true likeness. I made accurate drawings of the plumbing, chairs, floor, lighting fixtures, ceiling, even to the whisk broom hanging from the bootblack's chair. In painting an interior that I like, I feel much as I do in painting a portrait—if the subject is good to start with, I don't see any reason to alter anything.*

Louis Bouché

BARBER SHOP
by Louis Bouché
painted in 1941
Oil, 48 x 38 inches

11

ROBERT BRACKMAN

There is a timelessness, a completely impersonal disregard of current trends, in the work of Robert Brackman. His paintings belong to no one life span. They remain undated. In expressing his artistic philosophies he says: "My greatest aim is to bring my art to such a simple and understandable form that the common man can enjoy it regardless of subject matter and without the need for interpretation. Even ignorant people worshipped the old masters."

Brackman, too, admits indebtedness to the old masters. From Ribera came conception of form, realism and composition. Hals and Manet furnished inspiration in their use of color. Cézanne taught him the unimportance of subject matter and Picasso brought him back to classicism.

Figures and still lifes in beautifully balanced composition are the special subjects that flow from his serenely poised and subtle brush. In many of his paintings the theme is recurrent but it is done in varying moods and tempos—each one a distinct harmony though part of the same symphony in form and color.

Odessa, Russia, was his birthplace in 1898. When he was twelve the Brackman family migrated to America. His initial studies took place in the Francisco Ferrer School, and later he continued at the National Academy of Design. He had the good fortune to have as his instructors two of America's greatest painters and teachers, George Bellows and Robert Henri. In 1932 he was elected to the Academy.

In portraiture, he has been commissioned by such people as John D. Rockefeller Jr., Henry L. Stimson, President Charles Seymour of Yale and Mrs. Ellen C. Du Pont Meeds and her children. It created quite a stir when it was learned that he painted Colonel and Mrs. Lindbergh, but the portraits have been withheld from public scrutiny.

In his visored cap and striped sweatshirt Brackman looks more like a stocky sea captain than an artist. He lives in the old fishing village of Noank, Connecticut, in as snug an anchorage as any man could desire—three white buildings against the blue of the bay. Besides his house and his personal studio he built his school, a studio large enough to accommodate fifty students. Brackman is one of America's most sought-after teachers of the painting craft. His paintings are owned by the Metropolitan Museum, Brooklyn Museum, High Museum of Art in Atlanta, Addison Gallery, Newark Museum and many other public and private collections.

● *What I seek to achieve through color and line is to convey to others my feelings and emotions of the life about me, and to give that message through the simple objects and the people I see, without sacrificing the best craftsmanship that is in me or the appearance of the subject matter. Such was the impulse behind "After the Masque" which was conceived in a dressing room backstage in the atmosphere of the world of make believe. It was later created in my studio.*

Robert Brackman

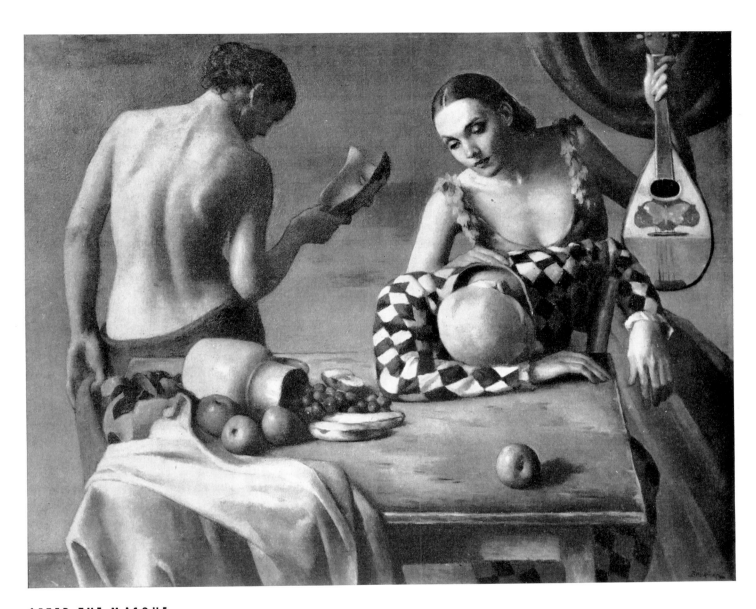

AFTER THE MASQUE

by Robert Brackman

painted in 1938

Oil, 40 x 50 inches

12

R A Y M O N D   B R E I N I N

Late at night, when steel and brick and concrete are shrouded in mystery, when the lake and its great expanse of beach are understated by a subtle moon, when realism is held in abeyance awaiting the first shy stirring of dawn—that is the time when Raymond Breinin wanders the city of Chicago in lone serenity, collecting dreams to be put later into the media of pigment and canvas. Certainly not in the factual daytime could he evoke in a modern American city the pointed spires, the crooked balconies and gargoyles that as a small boy he had absorbed from an ancient city in Russia.

Breinin is completely conscious of the worth of a present-day world with all its erudite scientific explanations attached, but rebelliously and deliberately, he stands as a champion for all the beautiful lost legends. Angels and devils and winged creatures that served so long as builders of dreams and molders of destiny. Besides, Breinin believes that despite his magnificent accomplishments, man's very existence is a legendary thing. He has neither knowledge nor control of the things of the spirit. He knows not whence he comes nor whither he goes—reason enough for a Breinin in his art to prefer a kind of timelessness; not for him the inscribed small date span on a slab of marble.

Quietly, with a small, ingratiating smile, he will, if pressed, tell you his intent. He admits he is not superman enough to divorce himself from the present, but his desire is to set down, not the scene, but its essence; not the transcription, but the dream, and never to repeat a story that has already been told. Critics claim him to be one of the greatest mystic painters since the time of Albert P. Ryder.

Breinin was born in Vitebsk, Russia, in 1910. As a youngster he studied with Uri Penn and at the academy organized by Chaquall. At the age of 13 he went to Chicago and attended the Chicago Academy of Fine Arts. The WPA gave him his first chance to make of painting a full-time job. He completed a 70-foot mural for the high school in Winnetka, Illinois. His first one-man show was held in 1939.

It was then that Chicago stepped in authoritatively to claim her own. He won the Clausmann Prize at the Chicago Art Institute, and his painting "The Night" won the $1,000 purchase prize at the Artists for Victory show.

In 1943 he was appointed artist in residence at Southern Illinois Normal University. He works in oil, water color and gouache. His paintings are represented in many private collections and in the permanent collections of Museum of Modern Art, Metropolitan Museum, Chicago Art Institute, Phillips Memorial Gallery and others.

● *Not as a recorder of times, events, places; not as an interpreter of the future, of which I know nothing; but as an agent free to draw on timeless, limitless material—I paint "Harlequin Horsemen."*

Raymond Breinin

HARLEQUIN HORSEMEN

by Raymond Breinin

painted in 1942

Oil, 26 x 48 inches

13

ALEXANDER BROOK

Another stay-at-home who carried the torch for America, and helped vanquish the French influence, is Alexander Brook. He himself has said:"I haven't jumped any freight cars. I haven't had any desire to go roaming about. I find that my life, like my painting, can be realized on the back porch." And of American art he says,"We are becoming interested in ourselves and our surroundings, in our own particular brand of civilization."

He is classified in the art world as an intellectual romanticist and texturist who handles paint with a personal and lyrical zest and prefers to draw a veil of idealism over cold fact. Only his proven diversity of ability has kept him from being labelled professional portraitist—that and his own statement to clients, "If I don't like it, I'll destroy it; if you don't like it, I'll keep it and sell it as a painting." One glance at his portrait of Katharine Hepburn, painted in 1940, is sufficient proof of his exquisite talent. Thoroughly modern, it also suggests figure portraiture and it was widely hailed as another triumph in his career. His landscapes vary from the lush country near Woodstock to the mute human poverty of a Georgia jungle. In either case he is quick to feel the mood of a scene.

Born in 1898 in Brooklyn, New York, of Russian parents, fate struck out at him cruelly when he was a mere 12-year-old, in the form of infantile paralysis, and it was during this dark period that a kindly neighbor who "did" portraits in oils from photographs interested a sick little boy in painting.

The Pratt Institute was his next step—only a short one—for one day he brought to class a container of beer and the artist-in-residence doubted that it was only the amber color of the liquid that he wished to immortalize on canvas! He studied at the Art Students League under Kenneth Hayes Miller, became assistant director of the Whitney Studio Club and began meeting with one artistic success after another, both at the Art Institute in Chicago and at the Carnegie Institute.

Although Brook recently completed murals for the Washington, D.C., post office and has done some graphic work, he is best known as an easel painter. He is represented in 21 major museums throughout the country, including the Metropolitan Museum, the Museum of Modern Art, Brooklyn Museum, Chicago Art Institute and Corcoran Gallery.

● *I had paused near this particular, small Negro dwelling in Savannah many times. There was a fence around the house and it all impressed me with its love, neatness and care. One day as I sat in my car wondering how I would approach my subject, I saw the father returning from work, affectionately greeted by his wife and child. Immediately, my mental picture took form and composition: the family moving fearlessly toward the spectator, the house their background, the fence their dubious safety from the world. It was a "Family Unit."*

Alexander Brook

FAMILY UNIT
by Alexander Brook
painted in 1941
Oil, 22 x 44 inches

14

CHARLES BURCHFIELD

At a time when the French School was still the traditional "must" for all artists, Burchfield stayed at home and proved the beautiful possibilities of the native scene. American art, therefore, must be grateful for his part in deflecting the attention of her painters from the Paris influence to the home environment.

His is the kind of painting that needs no complicated translation— perhaps a touch satirically, but also nostalgically, he paints the faded grandeur of yesterday's mansions—the drab rows of cheap suburban houses—the relics of what he terms "our tag-end pioneer days." But even these sad and homely subjects he invests with a haunting atmospheric truth—a muted beauty that does not repel—albeit painting with a 20th century feeling for structural organization.

Of Scotch-Irish origin, he was born in Ashtabula Harbor, Ohio, in 1893. His mother, sensing his ability and despite a scant purse, encouraged him to study at the Cleveland School of Art. After his graduation from art school, wherewithal still lacking, he was compelled to work for a company that manufactured automobile parts, so his sketching, mostly water colors at the time, was confined to spare moments.

In World War I he served in the Camouflage Corps but by 1920 had amassed enough material to hold his first one-man show in New York City. Of his maturing art in this show Burchfield said, "I turned square about. I decided I could no longer pretend I was a child and tried to look at life with the eyes of an adult American of the present. This time, instead of my mood determining the manner and style of my painting, it was the subject matter itself." He began winning prizes and awards but art did not offer an adequate living, and for some years he applied his talents to the designing of wallpapers. By 1929, with success smiling more or less shyly, he plunged in full time at his art.

Burchfield, in his latest development (beginning about 1935), is returning more and more to his early romantic and imaginative outlook, to which he has added the knowledge of form and organization gained from his middle or realistic period.

Burchfield's pictures are in the collections of the Metropolitan Museum, Newark Museum, Rhode Island School of Design, Boston Museum, Fogg Art Museum, Albright Art Gallery, Cleveland Museum, Phillips Memorial Gallery, and many private collections.

● *The idea of the advent of Spring being a miracle is the thought behind the picture. The brilliant afternoon sunlight on the fresh half-opened poplar and lilac leaves, gleaming against the clear blue sky, is indeed miraculous but it is made all the more poignant by being juxtaposed to the dirty gray banality of the side of the house and the old fence. By thus balancing conventional ugliness with conventional prettiness both cease to exist, and are translated to complete beauty in one harmonious whole.*

Charles E. Burchfield

HOUSE CORNER IN SPRING
by Charles Burchfield
painted in 1942
Water color, 34 x 26 inches

15

COPELAND C. BURG

He is a big man who looks quite serious, but almost immediately a delightful sense of humor makes itself evident. He works in a pleasant, immaculate studio and there, in one corner, is his bed, draped in black—of all things! There, surrounded by paintings, he lives the life of a recluse, a willing and cheerful one, however, for he feels that such a life is necessary to his profession.

When he shows his paintings to a visitor there is a refreshing absence of showmanship. There is no fussing over whether or not the light is right, no explanations, except perhaps a heartwarming one as in the case of "A Day in the Country." His favorite painters are Primitives and he likes to think of himself as one, too. He is especially fond of Rousseau.

Burg frequently paints in Mexico, where the people and landscape are much to his liking. He paints Mexico just as he does Chicago or New York, without distortion or any mimicry of Mexican style. When he paints a still life he does not make a "set up" or arrangement, but tosses his subject matter about the studio and puts what he likes in the painting. He prefers to work in his studio, away from the scene, to allow imagination and creation full sway.

Briggs Dyer said of Burg that he is a "natural" in the same sense that Utrillo is a "natural." With practically no formal training (except for a few short periods under bad instructors) he has evolved an art of his own, painting with a sympathetic, unpatronizing air which induces the spectator to feel very pleased with it all, in the same way that the painter was. Each picture has its own unity and movement and exquisite relation of colors; he knows how to use a palette knife without getting lost in a maze of gummy smearings; in short, he is a personality to be reckoned with in art.

Copeland C. Burg was born in 1895 in Livingston, Montana, and for many years was a newspaper man—at one time being art critic on a Chicago paper. As a child he had sketched and handled water colors and crayon, but in 1929, at a show at the Museum of Modern Art in New York, he became intrigued with oil as a medium, and by 1935 he was really painting in oil. He has won awards for both oils and water colors in Chicago, Philadelphia, San Francisco, Milwaukee, Grand Rapids and Portland, Oregon; and is represented in the private collections of Harpo Marx, Charles W. Worcester, Frederick Sweet and Mr. and Mrs. Earle Ludgin. His paintings also hang in the permanent collections of the Pennsylvania Academy of Fine Arts and the Art Institute of Chicago.

● I had spent a happy day with delightful friends at Hubbard Woods, Illinois, and I brought home a huge bouquet of wild and garden flowers and shrubs and berries and some tomatoes. The next day I painted them and in the background put some of the things I had seen on the way into the country. I hope the painting shows how happy I was that day in the country with the sky and clouds, the trees and the flowers.

Copeland C Burg

A DAY IN THE COUNTRY

by Copeland C. Burg

painted in 1944

Oil, 30 x 24 inches

16

PAUL BURLIN

Just as one must get acquainted with a different kind of music, so, perhaps, should the uninitiate go toward the art of Paul Burlin. For his is a great talent, a personality to be reckoned with, fortunately cloaked beneath a friendly, disarming exterior that invites further profitable acquaintance. Here is a man who says "When I start to paint, I go out on a limb for sheer imaginative design—I could break my neck." But one suspects that the Burlin neck will remain intact; for he knows art—every structural angle of it—and just as a great composer may deliberately break form for a new creative theme, so does Burlin, giving way to his subconscious, to join, perhaps, the vanguard of tomorrow's art.

Born in New York City in 1886 of a Russian mother and English father, much of his schooling occurred in England. He studied art in New York at the National Academy of Design—and in London and Paris. His leanings were always toward a modern expression—applying conscious distortion for the sake of creative pattern and color—a denial of the rationality of realism.

He left home at seventeen and supported himself via commercial art. In 1916 in Pueblo, Colorado, he was painting abstractions of ma-chinery. He lived for eight years in Santa Fe, New Mexico, and married Natalie Curtis who wrote *The Indian Book*, a study of Indian music and folklore published by Harpers, and who later was killed in a tragic motor accident in Paris.

Always a prodigious worker, he has received notable recognition, and has held two one-man shows in 1942 and 1943. Besides painting in his lighter moments, Burlin relaxes with jive music and has a great enthusiasm for all manner of sports.

In his art he starts with no definite theme. He departs from the visual world to a subconscious automatism, giving free rein to the insistent innate inspiration.

Burlin was among those who exhibited in the historic Armory Show. He worked for *Delineator* when Theodore Dreiser was the editor. His paintings are included in the permanent collections of a number of museums, including the Whitney, the Museum of Modern Art, the Denver Art Museum and numerous private collections.

He is a member of the American Society of Painters, Sculptors and Gravers, the Salon des Independents and the Salon d'Automne in Paris.

● *"Tiger, Tiger" ignores the anonymity of the artist. The tiger and the artist are one. It struggles through life with teeth and hide armored against bourgeois taste; for only a bull or cow goes head-on. But the tiger is canny. It disgorges what it cannot accept, blazing a path for its needs. Its will is but the reflection of its constancy.*

Paul Burlin

TIGER, TIGER, BURNING BRIGHT

by Paul Burlin

painted in 1942

Oil, 33 x 45 inches

17

P A U L   C A D M U S

In 1934 an unknown artist painted a picture called "The Fleet's In!" a very graphic picture of sailors in their relaxed moments holding rowdy revelry with shady ladies on Riverside Drive. By an ironical twist of fate the howling disapproval of the naval authorities booted him not into oblivion but into fame.

Paul Cadmus comes in for more than his share of criticism—as a personality he is a tall, blond, mild-mannered bachelor, retiring, introspective and contemplative. As an artist he prefers the *genus homo* in its unrestrained physical exuberance. He doesn't believe that sailors are Little Lord Fauntleroys and he explains "if there's vice and sordidness in life I don't see why it shouldn't be painted." So he continues to paint "Coney Island," "Greenwich Village Cafeteria" and "Seeing the New Year In"—shocking scenes but done in a noble manner, according to the more broad-minded critics.

Cadmus was born in New York City in 1904, of an artistic family who encouraged and trained him in art at an early age. After high school he studied at the National Academy of Design for four years, and at nineteen became a member of the Society of American Etchers. Another two years at the Art Students League and Cadmus

began to earn his living as an artist. He worked for three years with an advertising agency and, having saved sufficient money, went abroad for a two-year tour of the museums of Europe and a year-and-a-half in Majorca to paint the native scene.

Back in this country and working for the government under the Public Works of Art project, he painted the above-mentioned "The Fleet's In!" which was to be hung at the Corcoran Gallery but due to the "storm" was removed.

Meanwhile, in 1937, having completed murals for the Treasury's Department of Art and the United States legation buildings in Ottawa, he decided to hold a one-man show, remarking facetiously "Thanks to the Navy, I have not previously found it necessary to have a one-man show!" In 1942 his work began to show less of a satiric slant and the critics rave over his subtle and potent draftsmanship.

He lives alone in a spacious New York studio quietly painting, reading and frequently playing the piano. His works have found their way into many public and private collections and in 1937 had already been bought by five important museums.

● *It was painted in a medium new to me at the time, a mixture of tempera and oil . . . Circuses had just come into my life then—I had never been as a child—and I seem to remember that I was greatly fascinated by the acrobats, trapeze artists and especially by the gilded people. I thought it would be particularly interesting to see them contrasted with real flesh and with the dark flesh of the little Negro boy . . . I was also at the time very enthusiastic about the principles of baroque three-dimensional composition.*

Paul Cadmus

GILDING THE ACROBATS

by Paul Cadmus

painted in 1935

Oil, 37 x 18 inches

18

J O H N   C A R R O L L

If, as we have been led to believe, exceptions *do* prove rules, the gossamer veil of illusion that Carroll weaves so delicately has little to do with his rough and tumble Kansas birth. Whereas Benton, Curry and Wood stemmed from the same circumstance and found their idioms in and of the earth, Carroll, no less distinguished as an artist, clings to his dreams.

Unrealistic, unafraid to use distortion when it is expressive, his fragile young girls have a dream-like quality, half ethereal, half sensuous. His tones are silvery and subtle, and superb draftsmanship shows in every line.

A railroad train at Wichita, Kansas, in 1892, when his parents were migrating from Virginia to California, was his unique place of entry into the world. Raised on a California farm, he studied engineering at the University of California, and later, in favor of art, studied under Frank Duveneck in Cincinnati. "After six months," says Carroll, "I was sure I knew more about painting than Duveneck and he threw me out of his class." World War I intervened, but in the navy his portrait heads of his shipmates became so popular they went up in price from twenty-five cents to five dollars per capita.

New York City and Woodstock came next and an amazing assortment of artistic activities. He helped Bellows build a house—made picture frames for Speicher and copied pictures in the Metropolitan Museum. In 1922 he held his first one-man show. In 1924 the winning of a Purchase Prize at the Pennsylvania Academy of Fine Arts granted him a year abroad. Two years later he won a Guggenheim Fellowship. He developed a habit of winning awards and fellowships. In 1930 he was appointed head of the Department of Painting of the Society of Arts and Crafts in Detroit.

"So now," to quote a charming writer, "his bright flamboyant star permits him to create his figures in baroque style, be petted by his tiny wife, to own horses and lead the local hunt as master. Festooned by sport and romance a man can want no more."

Carroll is represented in the Los Angeles Art Museum, the Pennsylvania Academy of Fine Arts, the Toledo Museum, the Detroit Museum, Newark Museum, Indianapolis Museum, Andover Academy, Honolulu Museum, and Whitney Museum among others.

● *The picture "Wendy" was painted about 1938, and is a portrait of Wendy Igelhart of New York City. The work was done in a medium of oil on canvas, and I found the subject particularly interesting because of the adaptability of the model. I was especially interested in catching the highlights in the girl's hair and also in the somewhat quizzical expression in her eyes.*

John Carroll

WENDY

by John Carroll

painted in 1937

Oil, 16 x 14 inches

19

FRANCIS CHAPIN

The funny ramshackle houses, the streets and alleys of Chicago, the moods and manners of his own charming little girls—Chapin paints these subjects with the full mastery of the artist and with all the warmth and humor of a man who finds fulfillment in living.

He has steered a course midway between the real and the abstract. He may juggle shapes—he will do daring things with color—but all of it adds only to the joy of the onlooker. Rather than a factual report he gives you his impression, and it is both personal and profound.

Briggs Dyer says of him, "His work is ample proof of the fact, so beautifully understood by the great Frenchmen, that art is in the mind of the artist, not in what the eye beholds in nature."

Just around the corner from a more modern and elegant Chicago, Chapin has made his home in a street of crazy wooden buildings. Here he dwells amid the whimsicalities of yesterday's architecture, which furnish him with unending painting material.

Here people may gather around him when he paints out-of-doors—his youngsters play happily in and out of his studio—but the extravagantly tall and slender Chapin works on, serene and unruffled. His pupils find him the most patient and painstaking of instructors.

Chapin was born in Bristolville, Ohio, on Feb. 14, 1899, finished high school there and in 1921 was graduated from Washington and Jefferson College. The next six years were spent in study at the school of the Art Institute of Chicago where the winning of a Bryan Lathrop Fellowship enabled him to go to Europe for a year's painting. He exhibited at the Paris Salon d'Automne in 1929. On his return to Chicago he held a one-man show at the Art Institute and another in the galleries of Carson, Pirie, Scott and Company. Later he had three one-man shows in New York.

Since 1930 Chapin has been teaching lithography and painting at the school of the Art Institute in Chicago. He is represented in the permanent collections of the Addison Gallery of American Art, the Brooklyn Museum of Art, the Pennsylvania Academy of Fine Arts, the Art Institute of Chicago, the Metropolitan Museum and numerous other collections.

● *Every afternoon I taught landscape classes, but in the mornings I painted—usually a landscape—during the season at Saugatuck in which "Breakfast on the Porch" was done. I worked on it every gray or rainy morning—painting directly and thinly on the smooth canvas, a root-two rectangle which had been brightly stained with yellow and a few dynamic lines indicated, a method I used that summer. Some of the trees and areas follow these lines. I did no serious rearranging until the very last when, as the composition seemed to get too crowded with three at the table, I washed out Hildur who had posed in the chair at the right.*

Francis Chapin

BREAKFAST ON THE PORCH

by Francis Chapin

painted in 1938

Oil, 28 x 40 inches

20

JAMES CHAPIN

As fluid as his art—as quietly determined as the deep currents of a river—are the mental processes that underlie the painting of James Chapin. Gently, modestly he explains his purpose—to keep his art without labels, to adhere to no one cult, to be able to meet any new painting experience without set technique. He believes that there is room in the world for all kinds of art, but for him—and he states it as a strictly personal need—there must be communion with "living," with human values. He holds no brief for the "Ivory Tower" and "art feeding on art" theories.

Born in West Orange, New Jersey, in 1887, he became art conscious at a very tender age. He worked as a bank runner and studied art in the evenings at Cooper Union. A sympathetic relative sent him to Antwerp for two years of study. Paris followed, where the work of Paul Cézanne made such a profound impression that he began—that was thirty years ago—to paint in so-called "Modernist" directions.

Back in New York and dissatisfied with certain aspects of the intellectual influences on art, he turned from post-impressionism to the painting of the American scene. He rented a log cabin from a country family named Marvin, and "the Marvins" now hang in several important museums as symbols of Americana.

He has a sincere admiration for the structural painters who developed from post-impressionism. He believes in a thorough foundation of schooling as a preventative of "painting tricks" which, given time, will wear themselves out.

A famous portraitist himself, he teaches advanced portraiture at the Pennsylvania Academy of Fine Arts and believes that portraiture, which has fallen into a decadent period, will be brought back to its former high estate.

The critic of the *New York Times* in commenting upon a Chapin exhibit said that "this show establishes his position as second to none in our contemporary roster." His work is represented in the permanent collections of the Duncan Phillips Memorial Gallery in Washington, D.C., the John Herron Art Museum in Indianapolis, the Pennsylvania Academy of Fine Arts, the Art Institute of Chicago and in many important private collections.

● *Because sports provide one of the great channels of folk communication in the United States, they have afforded subject matter for many American artists. "Batter Up" portrays the umpire-catcher-batter group in a small-town baseball game. The three figures silhouetted against the little sun-lit grandstand await with intentness the delivery of the ball from the unseen pitcher. This community of intentness is expressed both in the characteristic individual poses and in the continuity of line developed through the umpire and batter, who are inwardly inclined toward the balanced figure of the catcher.*

James Chapin

BATTER UP

by James Chapin

painted in 1940

Oil, 40 x 59 inches

21

NICOLAI CIKOVSKY

Nicolai Cikovsky has lived two lives. His earlier one in Russia was a rigorous education in art and adversity, the later one in America was a bewildering orientation to strange language and custom.

Originally influenced by the Russian and French schools, his painting has mirrored the alteration in the life and spirit of the man during his years of growth in America. Today he emerges as Cikovsky, without trace of alien influence.

Cikovsky was born in Russia in 1894. He was one of a family of eleven children whose father earned a living by means of a fishing net, cabinet-making and cultivation of a small piece of land.

In spite of the chaotic state of Russia, which was successively living through revolution, civil war and famine, young Nicolai, aged fifteen, took himself off to the city of Vilna to study art. From then on he worked his way, enduring hunger and hardships, along with the other students. Later he went to Penza and Moscow to continue his art studies.

In 1923, upon the death of an older brother who was living in America, Cikovsky came to the new world.

In Russia he had taught and carried out government commissions but had never sold a painting—there was no market—yet he sold the first picture he ever exhibited in America. While struggling to get a firmer foothold, he painted theatrical sets and commercial murals. In 1930 he held his first one-man show.

Everything seems to come readily to his hand—portraiture, the figure, still life and landscape. Making his home in the nation's capital, the Washington scene has intrigued him into the portrayal of many of its vistas. Subject matter aside, he seems enamored of the possibility of pigment, which in his hands has a lush richness of substance that is in itself a sensuous delight, yet he maintains a fine balance between the modern and the traditional.

He has been instructor in the Corcoran Gallery in Washington, and earlier taught at the St. Paul School of Art, the Chicago Art Institute and the Cincinnati Art Academy.

He has done murals for the Department of the Interior Building in Washington, D.C., and for the post offices in Towson and Silver Springs, Maryland. His paintings have been acquired by many museums including the Modern Art, those of Brooklyn and Kansas City, Chicago Art Institute, and the Pennsylvania Academy of Fine Arts.

● *The painting "The Brick Carrier" was executed in the environs of the national capital at Washington, D.C. The subject was found in the suburbs, along the Potomac River, to be specific the actual location was around Alexandria, Virginia, which is considered to be a part of Washington, as it was there that I found the red cliffs I have always admired so much. In this particular picture I have endeavored to consolidate all my knowledge of painting. The picture was on exhibition at the Toledo Museum of Art in the summer of 1944.*

Nicolai Cikovsky

BRICK CARRIER

by Nicolai Cikovsky

painted in 1941

Oil, 26 x 32 inches

22

JON CORBINO

Fiestas, where color and excitement rule, catastrophes where man and beast resort to blind instinctive violence, are the exciting themes of the canvases that flow from the brush of Jon Corbino. Since in Corbino's world the actors so often meet on a physical plane, their creator rightly elects to obscure their countenances and to concentrate on bringing out the intimacy of bodies united in the passionate sharing of physical life. The greatness of Corbino is that he divorces this bodily intimacy from anything banal, topical or coincidental. If life is motion, Corbino certainly comprehends it. He is an avowed disciple of the old masters, but he became acquainted with them only in this country. He has been a modernized admirer, he has done better than copy the old masters, he has absorbed them.

Corbino was born in 1905 in Vittoria, Italy. In 1913 his family migrated to America and he grew up on New York's East Side in the midst of gang wars and rowdy activities. He learned a surprising number of vocations and was in turn, truck driver's assistant and horse handler. Meanwhile he studied at the Art Students League and later at the Pennsylvania Academy of Fine Arts. In 1936 and 1937 the successive winning of two Guggenheim Fellowships enabled him to work as a painter and to learn more about the painting of figure. With the winning of the first fellowship he was intrigued with the idea of going abroad but finally decided he could make as good use of his time here.

He leaves the question of his future development wide open in the belief that the artist who finds a formula is tagged with it and can never shake himself free. He does not feel the need to witness catastrophe in order to paint it. The world he creates is his own and its dramatic intensity a personal symbol rather than a record of experience.

Corbino held his first one-man show in Ohio when he was only 18 years old. His pictures are owned by more than 23 museums, including the Pennsylvania Academy of Fine Arts, the Toledo Museum of Art, Addison Gallery of American Art, Sweet Briar College and Whitney Museum, and in many private collections. He has been a persistent winner of awards and fellowships.

● *A moonlit night can be potent fabric for the imagination. Clouds scudding across the sky can take on mystical shapes. I tried to emphasize the floating rhythm of the sky and moon by means of the faster rhythm of the galloping horses. Here the abstract principles are used, but only to intensify the theme.*

Jon Corbino

MOONLIGHT

by Jon Corbino

painted in 1940

Oil, 30 x 40 inches

23

RUSSELL COWLES

Cowles' art asserts the aesthetic beauty of the frankly sensuous world —a world without fake dramatics, a livable world presented in an exquisitely and richly civilized way. Were Cowles not so thoroughly American, one would say that the urbane qualities of his art were European. Whether painting landscapes, the figure, portrait or essaying into abstraction, his painting shows a clarity and lucidity of thinking. It is joyous painting wherein subtlety masks the underlying mechanics of sound craftsmanship, and color rises at times to full crescendo.

Russell Cowles was born at Algona, Iowa, in 1887. He graduated from Dartmouth College and studied art at the Art Students League and the art school of the National Academy of Design in New York. In 1915 he found himself the delighted winner of the Prix de Rome and the Fellowship of the American Academy of Rome, which permitted him five wonderful years in Italy, of which he said: "I forgot that I was a citizen of the modern world. The intervening centuries were wiped out and I was the intimate contemporary of Tiziano, Veronese, Piero della Francesca and Giotto."

The return to America jolted him rudely back to the 20th century.

His effort at reorientation was the cause of much mental distress. He destroyed a large canvas which had won the Harris Medal at the Art Institute of Chicago because he was dissatisfied with the so-called classical traditions which it embodied. Concerning this he remarked, "I have destroyed every canvas from that period and earlier—a ruthless but necessary gesture of liberation. I had been infected by the germs of the old Armory Show, though the germs had lain dormant so long."

Still seeking, he spent a year in China and Japan, Egypt and Greece. Once again in America, he found himself still closer to the modern trend. He settled in Santa Fe with such associates as Ward Lockwood, Kenneth Adams and Emil Bisttram. The stimulus of these men, the high altitude and clear air of New Mexico, eventually swept away many of the cobwebs and he began to have an increasingly clear idea of what he wanted his painting to be.

Since 1936 he has exhibited in many major American museums, and has had one-man shows in forty museums from coast to coast. Cowles is that rare exception to the rule—an artist who waited for his art to reach maturity before permitting it to be widely shown.

● *"Autumn Wind" is one of my favorite paintings. I think I succeeded in expressing the true character of the place, even while taking some liberties with the facts. And while showing the physical world of our senses to be a glorious thing, as indeed it is, I tried to suggest something more that cannot be stated directly, of which the wind may perhaps be a symbol. But it is useless to try to justify such things in words. If my picture satisfies some people and seems significant to them, that is enough.*

Russell Cowles

AUTUMN WIND
by Russell Cowles
painted in 1940
Oil, 32 x 40 inches

24

RALSTON CRAWFORD

Artists are no misfits in time of war. Some, as morale builders, have brightened the drab walls of army camps with heartwarming murals. As correspondents, they have pictorially recorded history in the making. Others are turning the knowledge of their craft to technical war work. One of the latter is Ralston Crawford, who, before the war, was a painter of the modern school generally termed abstract. The Weather Division, Headquarters, U.S. Army Air Forces, assigned Crawford to duty as Chief of its Visual Presentation Unit which prepared pictorial presentations of weather, air flow and terrain beneath air lines and storm structures. These were for the use of fliers and other military personnel not having technical meteorological background, and require that the picture say something which words alone cannot convey.

These weather paintings of Crawford's, aside from their practical value, are just as pleasurable texturally and for their abstract design as the paintings he executed in peacetime, and in a recent show at the Downtown Gallery in New York they created quite a sensation.

His penchant has always been for painting man-made landscapes such as long causeways, loading derricks, grain elevators and bridges —to abstract from such scenes only the basic pictorial elements in patterns of simplified color, inventive line and beautiful balance.

Born in Ontario, Canada, in 1906, Crawford came to the United States when he was four years old. He graduated from high school at Buffalo, New York. Later he became a sailor, and after a year at sea landed in Los Angeles where he studied at the Otis Art School for a short time and received some valuable experience in Walt Disney's studio. After studying at the Pennsylvania Academy, the Barnes Foundation in Merion, and the Breckenridge School in Gloucester, he spent a year abroad, studying in Paris, Rome, Madrid, Florence and Naples. Returning, he spent much of his time in New York.

Later he settled in Chadds Ford, Pennsylvania, where he lived and worked until 1939. During 1940 and 1941 he taught at the Cincinnati Art Academy, and in 1942 at the Buffalo School of Fine Arts. He has done book illustrating, book jackets, architectural drafting and mural painting. He has had numerous one-man shows, and won many awards. His pictures are represented in the permanent collections of many museums, including the Metropolitan, Whitney, Albright Art Gallery and the Museum of Fine Arts in Houston, Texas.

● *The production of the painting "Whitestone Bridge" was preceded by a series of direct visual stimuli related to this bridge and similar forms. In this painting I have tried to express the sensations and thoughts about the sensations that I have had while driving over such bridges. The simplifications and distortions aim at a distillation of these experiences. Some of the people who have gotten satisfaction from the painting tell me that it clarifies and enlarges their reaction to similar experiences.*

Ralston Crawford

WHITESTONE BRIDGE

by Ralston Crawford

painted in 1939

Oil, 40 x 32 inches

25

FRANCIS CRISS

His is an art of re-creation rather than representation. Perhaps one might say he disciplines the eye-recording of a given scene, preferring to permit the mind and emotions full sway. The meticulously polished pictorial results, though predicated upon factual basis are stark decorative abstractions clarified and uncluttered with surplus accessories. Criss puts down mundane reality austerely in geometric terms and then with delightful perversity proceeds to rival the rainbow in his use of color. But even the inexperienced eye need not shy off, for his particular brand of fantasy is never obscure in meaning.

If you were to walk up the ramshackle stairs of an old building on East 9th Street, New York City, you would find further evidence of the Criss philosophy. Both his "home" floor and the upstairs studio are eloquent of his love of order, color and immaculacy. Most of the equipment is of his own contriving—even to giant-sized projectors and mechanical devices necessary to his profession. But there, over in one corner, is a play-pen complete with sand and toys for his two youngsters (no mercurial temperament here, despite the awesome evidences of efficiency).

He calls himself a contemporary student of life, interested in the problems of contemporary life. He has a special interest in the younger artists whom he teaches today, knowing that the young artist has definite problems of adjustment in a present-day world. Criss is also refreshingly indifferent to those legends of "commercial taint." He likes to eat too—and is never lacking in commissions.

Criss was born in London in 1901. When he was three the family moved to Philadelphia and at 12 he was already enrolled in the Graphic Sketch Club there. At 16, he entered the Pennsylvania Academy of Fine Arts on a four-year scholarship and when he was 19, a Cresson travelling scholarship from the Academy paved the way for European study. Later he studied at the Art Students League and in 1934 he won a Guggenheim Fellowship. He organized the Art Students' Guild and is a member of the American Group and the Society of Painters, Sculptors and Gravers. He is represented in many private collections and in the permanent ones of the Whitney Museum, Brooklyn Museum, Kansas City Museum, Graphic Sketch Club in Philadelphia, La France Institute in Philadelphia, and in the museums of Europe.

● *A painting cannot be posed in advance any more than a news item is a novel. The more I look into Nature, the more I discover and recognize new meanings, ideas, emotions. To represent facts as I know them rather than as I see them, I let my imagined objects dress themselves with real appearances. A good work will stop you. When the above becomes general, the artist will be able to speak in a purely artistic language. Put yourself opposite the picture and let it speak its own message.*

Francis Criss

MELANCHOLY INTERLUDE

by Francis Criss

painted in 1939

Oil, 25 x 30 inches

26

S T E P H E N   C S O K A

A lover of life, a warmhearted participant—this man Csoka voices his artistic reactions with an imaginative kind of expressionism. It is the fine, healthy picture-making of an artist who sees beauty at every turn—who sets it down spontaneously in sweeping strokes of melodic color. If he paints the sorrowful, it is done with profound feeling. His humor is never barbed. He is not afraid to be tender.

That he has kept his talent undimmed is testimonial enough to the character of the man. In 1934, finding the European situation unbearable, he turned to America. He came with high hopes. After all, he was a recognized artist and etcher in Europe, with works represented in important museums. Surely he could make a place for himself in America! But for six years America remained coldly indifferent and Csoka was compelled to turn housepainter in order to support his little family. Csoka, however, continued to paint his pictures, too, and in 1938 entered one of them in the Washington Square Outdoors Show, in New York City. This painting, which he called "Refugees," won the grand prize! Emily Francis of Contemporary Arts Incorporated saw "Refugees" and it was she who en-couraged Csoka and two years later gave him his first one-man show at Contemporary Art Gallery in New York.

Csoka, who is now an American citizen, was born in Gardony, Hungary, in 1897. He studied at the Royal Academy of Art in Budapest from 1922 to 1928, and between 1930 and 1933 he was awarded three prizes by that city. He was also awarded a bronze medal at the Barcelona International Exhibition in 1929.

Since his first one-man show in 1940 Csoka has had four additional shows and critics speak highly "of the lift and feeling of spirit in his spontaneous works." In one show he included a delightful series of the Csoka family's "private life." Each year, as an anniversary gift, he presented his wife with a painting which highlighted that particular year. All of his humor, tenderness, and joy of living are revealed in this intimate group. His etchings and fine prints win prizes consistently. He works in oil, gouache, pastel and water color. His works are represented in the permanent collections of the British Museum, Budapest Museum of Art, the Library of Congress in Washington, D.C., and in many important private collections.

● *Although my main interest lies in figure compositions, I was fascinated by the joyful appearance of horses released from their daily toil. I also like to paint wide horizons. Combining the two—I painted "Released."*

Stephen Csoka

RELEASED

by Stephen Csoka

painted in 1944

Oil, 32 x 38 inches

27

JOHN STEUART CURRY

Curry gives us the earthy and sometimes somber poetry of the Kansas plains and the beauty of Wisconsin hills—factual but moving themes painted with tenderness and supreme artistry, and free from symbolism, romanticism or irony. Born on a farm in Dunavant, Kansas, in 1897, the youngest member of the Wood-Benton-Curry triumvirate also went all the way back through the years to recall a small boy's fascinated awe of nature's elemental conflicts.

Curry's childhood consisted of farm chores first and studies later. His father has said, "With his powerful shoulders and firm build, John was an outstanding athlete, a mediocre student and a devoted artist." He began to draw when he wore "skirts and curls" and an understanding mother encouraged him.

He studied at the Art Institute, first in Kansas City and later in Chicago, supporting himself as bus boy in his spare hours. Art patron Seward Prosser staked him to a year abroad, where laborious study and the endless damp chill of a Paris winter yielded no apparent triumphs.

Back in America, completely discouraged, he vowed to try one more picture before giving up. "Baptism in Kansas," painted from the honest reverence of his childhood memories, was the successful result. Mrs. Gertrude Vanderbilt Whitney purchased it for her museum and subsidized him for the next two years at $50 a week. Again from memory, he painted "Tornado over Kansas" which won him a Carnegie award.

Followed a period when he taught at Cooper Union and the Art Students League and finally went on the spring tour through New England with Ringling Brothers circus. His brilliant circus studies— action captured with split-second precision—are among his most effective canvases.

Westport commissioned him to paint murals for the local high school. Then came murals for government buildings in Washington and an appointment as Artist in Residence at the University of Wisconsin. He has recently completed murals in the Kansas State capitol and in the Biochemistry building and the Law building of the University of Wisconsin, as well as in the First National Bank of Madison.

His easel pictures are owned by the Metropolitan Museum, the Whitney Museum, the Hackley Art Gallery at Muskegon, the University of Nebraska, St. Louis Museum, Addison Gallery and numerous private collections.

● *The painting "John Brown" was a study I made before beginning my mural in the State capitol of Kansas at Topeka. In this study of John Brown I tried to portray the fanatical and vehement characteristics of the man who was so largely responsible for beginning the bloody and fratricidal war of 1861–65.*

John Steuart Curry

JOHN BROWN

by John Steuart Curry

painted in 1939

Oil, 69 x 45 inches

28

SALVADOR DALI

Whether he paints, tongue in cheek, to a gullible audience or takes himself with utter seriousness is a debatable issue. Certainly he exercises the artist's right to create as he pleases without compromise. Obviously, Salvador Dali is good copy and a good showman and though at first his work was viewed with apprehension, amusement or bewilderment, his vogue has had remarkable persistence. He may not have invented surrealism, but it might have met an obscure fate without him.

Known as the Master of the Limp Watches, his exhibition at the Museum of Modern Art in 1936 had the American people scratching their collective heads in astonishment. In 1939 his surrealistic display in Bonwit Teller's elegant windows created another sensation. Dali resented some changes that had been made, and in his rage attempted to destroy a fur-lined bathtub, but unfortunately lost his balance and crashed through the plate-glass window into the street.

Born near Barcelona in 1904, Dali refused to follow his father's career as a notary. At 14 he attended the Academy of Fine Arts in Madrid, puzzling his teachers by his facility for copying the old masters with a touch of personal satire, and for "doodling"—an un-conscious art that has since been publicized. When he arrived in Paris in 1927, surrealism was the talk of the town and Dali took to it with no effort. In 1934, art dealer Julian Levy decided that the people of the United States should get acquainted with the art of Salvador Dali.

He describes painting as "photography, by hand and in colors, of concrete irrationality." Some critics say he wastes a very real talent on nonsense, some find him an amusing opportunist and most will admit that his miniaturist style shows extraordinary facility as a draftsman and a remarkable feeling for color. Although he claims he paints for the "masses" he finds it natural that people do not understand his pictures. "I do not understand them at first myself—there are often some symbols which I can never explain," he says.

Apart from his other activities, Dali has also been the author of two volumes. In 1943 he wrote *Secret Life of Salvador Dali*, and in 1944 appeared his first novel, *Hidden Faces*.

He has held one-man shows at the Julian Levy Gallery, the Museum of Modern Art, and exhibited at the New York World's Fair in 1939.

● *Painting is a combination of eye, brain and hand. Oil is the medium between the three—for oil painting alone is worthy of the name. In truth, the advent of oil in the history of painting gave to the mind of man the same great stimulus as did the first putting of oil in a lamp. On the ideological plane I am against the mediocrity of the modern mechanical world and in favor of the aesthetic splendors of the architecture of the Renaissance, of Palladio and Bramante. On this subject my opinions are exactly like those of Ingres.*

Salvador Dali
1944

THE MADONNA

by Salvador Dali

painted in 1943

Oil, 20 x 11 inches

29

RANDALL DAVEY

In viewing the paintings of Randall Davey one realizes that here is no ascetic, struggling to interpret subtle meanings in cosmic themes —but rather a man of the world who partakes of its material joys with honest satisfaction and finds no quarrel with them!

Horse racing, with all its magnificent and exciting pageantry; lush nudes which have been termed "boldly painted and rather sinfully alluring," are among his most noted canvases. These, according to Henry McBride, "are painted in a clean, direct way, and there is a certain openness in the style of the work that suggests there has been no cheating in the way the effects have been arrived at." He puts them down with spirit, and with the comprehension of a well disciplined brush. He handles a variety of mediums—oils, murals, pastels, water colors and etchings—and in each case has evolved a style highly individual and characteristic of the medium employed.

Davey was born in East Orange, New Jersey, in 1887. After graduation from Cornell University in 1909 he began his studies with Robert Henri, first in New York and later in the capitals of Europe. Henri was a strong influence—Davey particularly admired his use of intense, pure color—and together they made intensive study of the old masters, and out of that study grew Davey's need to find a way of

his own amongst the complexities afforded by tradition. Consistently, through the years, he continued to win distinguished awards. In 1915 he captured the 2nd Hallgarten Prize of the National Academy of Design, and in the same year won honorable mention at the Panama-Pacific Exposition. In 1938 he won the Walter Clarke Prize of the National Academy and in 1941 the Altman Prize. In 1920 he taught portraiture at the Chicago Art Institute, and later he taught at the Kansas City Art Institute and the Broadmoor Art Academy in Colorado Springs.

The West finally won him over, and today he has settled in the beautiful outskirts of Santa Fe, New Mexico, where riding and hunting provide happy hours of relaxation. He is a member of the National Association of Portrait Painters, the Painter-Gravers Society, the National Academy of Design and the National Association of Mural Painters. He has executed murals in the Will Rogers Memorial Shrine at Colorado Springs, and the U.S. post offices at Claremore and Vinita, Oklahoma.

Davey's work is represented in the permanent collections of the Chicago Art Institute, Corcoran Art Gallery, Whitney Museum, Cleveland Museum, Detroit Institute of Arts, Kansas City Art Institute and the Museum of Art and Archaeology in Santa Fe.

● *In painting racing pictures my interest is in the nervous excitement and intensity of the occasion and through the balance of static and moving shapes to develop sensations of suspense, anxiety and moods I experience at the race track. I am keenly interested in thoroughbred horses, but it is the incidental use of them in the composition, their sensitive and vigorous movements, their jockeys, the crowd, the brilliance or dullness of the day, that assist me in arriving at some color and form significance.*

Randall Davey

RAINY DAY AT THE TRACK

by Randall Davey

painted in 1944

Oil, 26 x 32 inches

30

ARTHUR B. DAVIES

Arthur Bowen Davies was another member of the famous "Eight" who turned the spitefully bestowed title of "Ash-Can School" into an honored legend in American art. In his case the term was startlingly incongruous. Though in his open-mindedness he may have experimented for a bit with cubistic patternings, he never went the whole way toward modern expression. He was a dreamer, a romanticist enamored of Arcadian symphonies. The best of Davies was in his cool, harmonious, sylvan scenes peopled with slender young women, legendary animals—a world of primal innocence, wherein facts might be gently altered to suit his own aesthetic fancies; wherein a fine line balanced beauty but overthrew sentimentality; wherein all the external physical aspects were utilized only as a springboard to a spiritual plane of his own.

By nature Davies was a recluse, an ascetic; but he was hostile, too, to the sugary academic art that held sway, and for two momentous years in the history of American Modernism he directed the affairs of the Armory Show group. At a critical time he stepped forth from his ivory tower and boldly allied himself on the side of the open-minded.

Arthur B. Davies was born in Utica, New York, in 1862. He had a youthful fondness for baseball as well as art, but his parents encouraged the latter aptitude. At 15, Dwight Williams was his first tutor and found him an apt pupil and astonishingly productive. The family moved to Chicago, and there he continued his studies at the Chicago Academy of Design.

The need of a practical profession, and his ability as a draftsman, led him to Mexico in 1880 as a drafting civil engineer. The two years there gave him a taste of gaucho life and a knowledge of Spanish ecclesiastical painting. Back in Chicago, he returned to the Chicago Art Institute and then went on to further his career in New York. William Macbeth and Benjamin Altman took over. The latter sent him to Italy to browse among the old masters. The result of this interlude, when he exhibited later in a group show at Macbeth Gallery, aroused lively interest and laid the foundation for his rise to fame.

His was a life of grinding work. He was a lithographer, a muralist, an easel painter—and in all media productive to a staggering degree. While working alone in Florence in 1928, the angina pectoris from which he had suffered for five years finally brought an end to his career. At the time of his death he ranked among the highest of his contemporaries. He painted more than 600 pictures, and is represented in every important museum in America including the Metropolitan, Corcoran Gallery, Phillips Memorial Gallery and Chicago Art Institute.

(1862–1928)

TARTESSIANS
by Arthur B. Davies
painted in 1911
Oil, 18 x 30 inches

31

GLADYS ROCKMORE DAVIS

In one short decade, between 1932 and 1942, Gladys Rockmore Davis abandoned a highly remunerative career as a commercial artist to achieve in American art the title of leading woman artist of women and children in the United States.

Recently she has defied the ghost of Degas, who has frightened most artists away from the ballet, and delighted the world with her exquisite exhibition of "Ballet Backstage" that appeared in *Life* in March 1944. Twenty small gem-like canvases, glimpses from the wings, preparations in the dressing rooms, tableaus on stage, the living spirit of the ballet painted vitally in all the dramatic patternings of dazzling spotlight and shadowy backdrop.

Before that, in 1943, *Life* published a three-page portfolio in color of her charming studies of women, children and nudes. An accompanying article stated that "she has broken all records in her rapid rise to fame until today, at forty, she is considered one of America's best painters."

Gladys Rockmore Davis was born in New York City in 1901, and at sixteen went to Chicago for three years' study at the Art Institute. In 1925 she married the well known illustrator Floyd Davis, moved to New York and began to carve out a career in commercial illustrating, meanwhile accepting joyously the responsibility of two new members to the family.

In 1932, the Davises packed up, bag and baggage and babies, and sailed for Europe. After a few months' tour they settled in Cannes, in the vicinity of the house where Renoir had once lived. The visits to the Renoir home and studio made a vital impression and Mrs. Davis began a sabbatical year of painting seriously. Returning later to America, she found she had lost interest in illustrating, and enrolled for further study at the Art Students League, and for a time with George Grosz.

Mrs. Davis sometimes paints without a model for the sake of greater spontaneity. Of her nudes, it is said that she is the only woman who can paint a nude that does not resemble a department store mannequin. She is equally facile in her handling of pastel and her pictures hang in leading museums, including New York's Metropolitan, Pennsylvania Academy of Fine Arts, Sheldon Swope Museum, Toledo Museum of Art, Nebraska University and University of Arizona.

● *"Emma" was painted in 1940. In this painting I wanted to capture something of the smiling innocence of youth. It was painted directly from the model, which was the method I used at that time. There were many problems which presented themselves in the making of this picture—designing the large shapes of the figure and chair, the brilliant blue of the dress, and the difficult problem of painting the white apron.*

Gladys Rockmore Davis

EMMA
by Gladys Rockmore Davis
painted in 1940
Oil, 40 x 30 inches

STUART DAVIS

Perhaps the Stuart Davis idiom relates to the world of art much as the Einstein theory relates to the world of science. It doesn't invite easy acquaintance. It doesn't even pretend to. To him, the purpose of "naturalism" to ape Nature is historically outmoded. The camera is a better instrument where factual or descriptive statement is the aim. "What is called 'abstract' painting, on the other hand, allows the artist freedom to develop his faculties of invention and synthesis in relation to his subject. Latent potentials of spiritual and emotional experience are realized in abstract art, and evoke their like in the spectator. The innate sense of universal meaning takes objective form in abstract art, as it integrates and reshapes the particularity of the subject."

There is nothing facetious in the point of view of Stuart Davis. He is in dead earnest. He will take material as startling as egg beaters and gas pumps, dissociate them from their actual environments, and remould them to interpretative forms that meet some inner insistence of his own intellectual expressing.

This most daring and powerful of American moderns was born in Philadelphia in 1894. His father was the art director of the *Phila-delphia Press*, and workers in his department included such men as John Sloan, George Luks, Everett Shinn and William Glackens—all of which made it quite natural for the young Davis to develop a precocious interest in art. The major part of his art education took place at the Henri School of Art in New York between 1910 and 1913. During World War I he devoted his talents to map-making for the Army Intelligence Department, and shortly thereafter began to develop the kind of abstractionist painting to which he has remained steadfast through the years.

He has done murals for the Radio City Music Hall, for the New York municipal broadcasting station, and for the Communications Building at the New York World's Fair. His theme for the latter was the development of communication. In it he put a big spiral indicative of the universe, then a succession of symbols to suggest sound, sign language, writing, the printing press, telephone, human ear, radio, light signals, the U.S. mail and many other things!

He is represented in the permanent collections of many museums, among them the Museum of Modern Art, Whitney Museum, Phillips Memorial Gallery, Milwaukee Art Institute, and many others.

● *In my painting "Garage Lights," as in all of my work, there was no intention to make a replica of the optical appearance of the place. Instead, its elements of form, color and space are changed to meet the requirements of a sense of dimensional unity, which develops and becomes complete as I study them. The result is a permanent record of an emotional experience expressed in terms of coherent color-space dimensions.*

Stuart Davis

GARAGE LIGHTS

by Stuart Davis

painted in 1931

Oil, 32 x 42 inches

33

JULIO DE DIEGO

With the true Latin's complete disinterest in reform, with no thought of social context message, purely objectively and because of their sheer fascination for him, Julio de Diego paints kaleidoscopic fantasies of great cities, "the machinery that man has made human thereby dehumanizing himself," the mad chaos of war, the religions of the ancient Aztecs and Mayans.

When he paints, he unleashes an imagination as many-faceted as a rose-cut stone that breaks up form and reflects it again in myriad patternings of utter fantasy. He may solve plastic problems by the invention of symbols, is not averse to abstract areas, but instinctively feels that always the theme must begin with Nature. A prodigious worker, he admits that when he is excited over a canvas he paints himself into a state of complete exhaustion.

De Diego was born in Madrid, Spain, in 1900 and started out in life as an apprentice painter of theatrical scenery. He served in the Spanish army and afterwards spent five years in Paris, mostly struggling and trying to absorb art.

After the death of his father there was enough money for travel, first in Europe and then to America in 1924. His reasons for coming to America were to learn something of this land of Buffalo Bill, Fenimore Cooper and especially to see Indians. The only Indians he saw were wooden ones clutching cigars—it was a bitter disappointment—but he liked the American people and says that America really begins outside of Manhattan.

Despite the dark intensity of his looks, de Diego has the long viewpoint of the true philosopher. He takes life in his stride; has accepted the hardships enroute with a careless shrug and has permitted no irony to insinuate itself either into his work, or into his own soul.

Since 1929, he has been holding one-man exhibits yearly, ranging from the Atlantic to the Pacific, and including New York, Chicago, Wisconsin, San Francisco, Washington, St. Louis, Santa Barbara, Los Angeles and elsewhere.

His work is represented in the Art Institute of Chicago, the San Francisco Museum of Art and the Phillips Memorial Gallery in Washington, D.C., among others.

● *In this picture I have portrayed my reaction when I visit a shipyard and see the men working feverishly on the assembly of strange-appearing shapes—looking like monsters—things for the future. Gradually, a ship takes form. I have tried to combine the raw colors of the shapes—the reds, blues, greens, which lack all dignity—with the somber businesslike gray dress which the boat will assume when the Navy takes over and she is ready to "Sail the Seven Seas."*

de Diego

THEY SHALL SAIL THE SEVEN SEAS

by Julio de Diego

painted in 1943

Oil, 30 x 48 inches

34

ADOLF DEHN

Lyrically beautiful on the one side, wickedly ironic on the other, is the commentary of America that finds expression in the art of Adolf Dehn, who chose but two mediums, lithography and water color, to achieve mastery in both. Despite the twinkling eye, the disarming round face and turbulent silvery locks, one suspects that here one must cope with beauty lover and satirist as well. In him there is a little of the Friar out of Rabelais, of the sharp sophisticate, and of the serious artist intent upon the American scene. As an artist, as well as a person, he shows no deprecatory reticence but expresses himself honestly, and if need be without soft beguilement. Lithography was his first medium and water color came later. The richness of his tones, their precision and infinite range, are the result of his synthesis of skill and creative imagination.

Dehn was born in 1895 in Waterville, Minnesota, his great-grandparents being among the first land-hungry pioneers to settle there. At 19, in Minneapolis, he entered the Art Institute. By way of a scholarship he continued at New York's Art Students League, where Boardman Robinson influenced him strongly. Later he settled in Vienna—about 1921—and the art of George Grosz and Pascin came under his eager perusal. He remained abroad for seven years, but admits that he never could subscribe wholeheartedly to the art of postwar Europe.

Dehn is no ivory tower resident. "Half straight, half salty," said a reviewer, "his squirming lithographs were prized by art connoisseurs as well as magazine readers, and made the grade in leading American and European museums." Edward Alden Jewell, writing in the *New York Times*, said, "These water colors—some so beautiful, and not one that lacks in expertness—do take the breath and shape the response to exclamation, first because they are unexpected and then because at their best they attain so high a pitch of lyric freshness and power. His work exemplifies the happiest of marriages, in which design and color achieve a union that is all give-and-take, all reciprocity."

An exhibit of 52 pictures at Associated American Artists gallery in New York was the pictorial recording of two years' travel in the United States. Among the numerous museums which house his work are the Metropolitan Museum, the Whitney Museum, the Brooklyn Museum and the Minneapolis Museum.

● *"Threshing in Minnesota," which I made especially for* Encyclopædia Britannica, *was done near my home town of Waterville. The old-fashioned threshing rig, with its steam engine burning wood and sending out billows of dark smoke, is a rare sight these days—it has given way to the less picturesque but more efficient combine, just as the horse has been swept aside by the tractor. Threshing day was the most dramatic of all the days of the year on the farm. This picture attempts to be a sentimental document of this passing activity.*

Adolf Dehn

THRESHING IN MINNESOTA

by Adolf Dehn

painted in 1943

Water color, 20 x 28 inches

35

JOHN S. DE MARTELLY

Like Benton, Wood and Curry, John de Martelly allies himself on the side of the Middle West—its life and times, the human and humorous behavior of its people—and very real people they are.

There is nothing of the surface-skimmer in him. He subjected himself to the best of what England and Italy had to say on the subject of art before making any statements of his own. What he has to say is never trivial. It bears all the hallmarks of authority and sympathy, beautifully integrated with the skill of the true artist. As a child he was regarded by his elders as a prodigy in water color. His earliest student years were spent at the Pennsylvania Academy of Fine Arts, under the guidance of Daniel Garber, Albert Spencer and Hugh Breckenridge. Then he went abroad to Florence, where etching on wood and copper and lithography were fascinating pursuits. After Italy came a long stay in England, where he studied at the Royal College of Arts.

Though he was born in Philadelphia in 1903, it was Kansas City and the Middle West that he came home to. It was there, in the things that Thomas Benton was expressing, that he found substance for what he too was seeking. Though he never studied with Benton, he, too, like the masters of the Renaissance, adopted the practice of modeling his subject in clay or wax and then painting it in natural colors to serve as a three-dimensional model for the canvas. Of the procedure he says, "The picture logic that the model contains is of no end of help and establishes itself as a most certain technical aid to the development of the painting." De Martelly records solely from Nature and, as though it were a tapestry, he weaves opaque and transparent color onto canvas, in beautiful unity.

He has been an inveterate student, a hard worker who has proven his skill in many media—as a painter, cartoonist, lithographer, illustrator and teacher. Benton was instrumental in his appointment as instructor in graphic arts and illustration in the Kansas City Art Institute. In 1944 de Martelly was artist in residence at Michigan State College in East Lansing. He has won the Lighton Prize and his lithographs have been selected for the "Fifty American Prints of the Year." He has been written up in *Coronet* and other publications, and has himself written instructive essays for art magazines. He is represented by etchings and aquatints in the Victoria and Albert Museum in London, England.

● *"No More Mowing" is a symbolic picture for the most part, attempting to suggest the abandonment of the once beautiful hillside and mountain farmland. It is ever the same story with the breaking of new land. Often the effort is so great that both land and people become depleted. The girl in the picture is symbolic of this and the scythe represents man's hold of the elements. The turbulent sky and the dramatic symbolic sun rays are the vastness of Nature—bewildering man in appeal and far horizons of reward.*

John S. de Martelly

NO MORE MOWING

by **John** S. de Martelly

painted in 1938

Oil, 30 x 36 inches

36

ARTHUR G. DOVE

There are no neatly coined definitions to fit the fantasies-in-pigment which Arthur Dove puts before you. Before the onlooker may enter his realm the eye must signal, not to recognized realities, but to some free and uninhibited emotion which is willing to walk an untrodden path. Dove knows all about the conventional shapes and substances of things—but they hold no interest for him. Instead he transmutes them into a sphere of his own. In doing so, his vision is clear, unastigmatic in its focus. You may be able to adjust to that focus—and again, you may not. Dove cannot help it. He will neither coerce nor strive to charm.

Dove resents the tempo of our age, yet his consciousness of it is apparent in the swirling movements of his forms. Strangely enough he paints the thing he resents—and the sensitive observer may recognize its almost hypnotic power over him.

Born in Canandaigua, N.Y., on Aug. 2, 1880, of English-American stock, Dove, too, had an antagonistic family to contend with. His father was a successful man of commercial enterprise and had little sympathy with artistic leanings in his son. Private schools and Cornell University were part of his youthful background. Then he tried farming.

He tried magazine illustrating. None of it mattered much after he had the good fortune to meet Alfred Stieglitz. That energetic prophet was already crusading for art in a hostile, non-comprehending world.

Stieglitz took him in hand. He fostered, encouraged, compelled—and Dove responded. Despite financial and domestic worries he held his art inviolate, away from any worldly persuasions. Duncan Phillips, whose artistic opinions are highly valid, was another of Dove's valiant champions. Through the years, Phillips has continued to add to his sizable collection of Dove's canvases.

The work of Arthur Dove is represented in the permanent collections of the Museum of Modern Art in New York City, the Smith College Museum, the Phillips Memorial Gallery in Washington, D.C., and in the Museum of the University of Minnesota among others. He is a member of the American Society of Painters, Sculptors and Gravers.

❧ *The means for painting is very simple. It was developed direct from Nature as in flowers, butterflies and trees. Usually a choice of two or three colors and two or three forms or lines. That gave me a motive upon which the painting was based, i.e., the condition of light in the object or person. The quality of the yellow signified to me the quality of the intelligence. "By their lights ye shall know them."*

Arthur G. Dove

CARS IN SLEET STORM

by Arthur G. Dove

painted in 1925

Oil, 15 x 21 inches

37

GUY PÈNE DU BOIS

Native-born American though he undoubtedly is, there is more than a casual smacking of the Parisian *boulevardier* in the sophisticated and sensuous delineations of Guy Pène du Bois. The flavor of worldly cynicism that creeps into many of his themes, abetted by the subtle polish and exquisite palette he employs, places him in a most enviable spot in American art.

Born in Brooklyn in 1884, his father was a New Orleans writer and critic, and very likely the young du Bois became conditioned to cultural fact and fancy at a precocious age. In pursuit of a career, he first studied at the Chase School in New York City where he was "properly impressed with his mentor's beribboned pince-nez and pointed beard."

Paris followed, and, back in America, he ran the gauntlet of progress from police reporting to the art and music desks of various New York newspapers. Another trip to Europe was included before he finally found his pace and began in his urbane fashion to paint the humorous, chic and sometimes satiric "patter" of the metropolitan scene.

His is the art of a clear vision, a suavely adroit fashion that delights the eye and permits the onlooker to accept or not, according to his concepts. In 1944 he held a one-man show which brought forth the following comment: "Again the Kraushaar Galleries have made way for the paintings of Guy Pène du Bois, 60-year old American artist whose canvases grow more gracious, more gala, more good-humored as the years go by. The point of view here is youthful forever."

He has taught at the Art Students League, and is still teaching in his own schools in New York City and Stonington, Connecticut. For seven years he was editor of *Arts and Decoration*, and as a writer he handles words as fluently as he does his pigments.

Du Bois did murals for the post office at Saratoga Springs of which Saint-Gaudens writes "Any man who has ever been fond of a horse or caught the flavor of the Main Street of that racing center will realize with what charm of execution du Bois forwarded his subject in restricted space."

His paintings are owned by the Metropolitan Museum, Whitney Museum, Phillips Memorial Gallery, Los Angeles County Museum, Addison Gallery and a score of others.

● *I called this canvas "The Beaux Arts Ball." It might be any costume ball. It was painted at Garnes par Dampierre, Seine-et-Oise, France, in a little farmhouse we occupied for about six years. The grange had been converted into a quite magnificent studio. Not much attention was paid to any locale. I never made a sketch at a costume ball in my life. But it seems to me that the costumes at once reveal character better than the regimented clothes of everyday life.*

Guy Pène du Bois

BAL DES QUATRE ARTS

by Guy Pène du Bois

painted in 1929

Oil, 29 x 36 inches

38

PHILIP EVERGOOD

What is happening to the world is the very personal concern of Philip Evergood. The heartbreak of destruction, the braveries and tears of the people, the senseless horrors of war—these he paints with his very soul, and the impression on the beholder is indelible. Even his satiric approach is never trivial; it is dead serious, frequently carrying a portent of tragedy. Not that he is always serious. With his own inexhaustible joy and zest for life he is equally quick to capture the gay and foolish antics of humanity. Evergood can make you laugh. He paints the happenings of today, but in them there is a timeless quality that may be equally poignant to generations far in the future. Evergood has never felt the constraining harness of exact representation. He will use expressive foreshortening or exaggeration of form for the sake of dramatic emphasis. He is one of the most plastic painters among today's moderns.

He explains his type of painting thus: "A painting can have all the abstract forces at work within it, all the precious qualities of pigment and surface, all the electric aliveness of a personal calligraphic line of sensitiveness and strength—and at the same time tell a story or make a statement." What Charles Peguy said of authors is equally applicable here: "One tears it from his guts. The other pulls it out of his overcoat pocket." Evergood belongs to the former category!

The son of an Australian landscape painter, Evergood was born in New York City in 1901. At ten he was sent to England to be educated at Eton and Cambridge, but at 18 renounced the further pursuit of academic study to follow his inborn love of drawing. He stormed the London studios of Harvard Thomas the sculptor, and Henry Tonks of the Slade School and spent three arduous though fruitful years of drawing in apprenticeship under them.

When he was 22 he returned to America and for a time worked with George Luks at the Art Students League. In 1927 he held his first one-man show, at the Dudensing Galleries. Since then he has had more than ten one-man shows here and abroad. In 1931 he married "Juju" Cross, a student of the ballet, who inspired his large picture "Juju as a Wave." His paintings hang in the Metropolitan Museum of Art, Museum of Modern Art, Whitney Museum, Arizona University, the museums of Boston, Brooklyn and Denver and the National Gallery, Melbourne, Australia.

● *My object in painting "Orderly Retreat" was to show the futility of selfish aggression and the ultimate extermination which has always been meted out to forces defying the laws of human justice. Although my picture symbolizes the obliteration of the cruel and vile Nazi military machine by the courageous Russian people, it is intended to carry a universal and timeless connotation. The symbols employed are purposefully simple, because I believe that in visual communication the greatest impact is effected by the most direct means.*

Philip Evergood

ORDERLY RETREAT

by Philip Evergood

painted in 1943

Oil, 40 x 25 inches

39

JERRY FARNSWORTH

Hung alongside of spectacular and flamboyant neighbors, Farnsworth's paintings might not force a first, quick glance, but the glance when it happens will be a lingering and delighted one. Instead of showmanship or bravado, he deals in subtle, quiet charm, and even the layman can appreciate every studied stroke of his honest brush. Never wrathful, never violent, he manages his quiet chords with a sublimated Puritan kind of sensuousness. His brush takes delight in the chaste adventures of a little fold in a blouse as it circles a slim arm or veils a rosy undergarment.

Jerry Farnsworth has kept clear of European trends. As a product of postwar American schools he has developed in the oldest American tradition of all—conscientious realism. He believes that painting is a stern craft to be learned through diligent application on the part of the practitioner. His own work, with its fine sense of composition, integral draftsmanship and delicacy of color, proves his adherence to the creed.

Farnsworth was born in Dalton, Georgia, in 1895. His father died when he was three years old and his mother, a trained nurse, assumed support of the family. His boyhood years were spent in Georgia and New Orleans, and when he was 16 the family moved to New York. By chance he visited a class of Sunday painters conducted by Clinton Peters and immediately knew that art meant something very special to him. At the outbreak of World War I, Farnsworth joined the navy and was stationed in Washington for two years, managing meanwhile to attend night classes at the Corcoran School. After the war he studied with Charles W. Hawthorne in Provincetown, and worked on the staff of *The Nation's Business* magazine.

He married Helen Sawyer, herself a well-known artist, and travelled a year in France and Spain. He taught at the Art Students League and Grand Central Art School and in 1933 established the Farnsworth Art School in Cape Cod. In 1942 and 1943 he was visiting professor of art at Carnegie and artist in residence at the University of Illinois. His paintings are in many private collections and museums, including the Metropolitan Museum, Whitney Museum, Delgado Museum, Pennsylvania Academy of Fine Arts, Museum of Fine Arts in Houston, Texas, the Vanderpoel Art Association and many others.

● *There is no particular significance of the painting "The Spring Hat" from the point of view of storytelling, or any special inner meaning. It holds simply the painter's approach. It is a reserved and quiet canvas in which the painter portrays a young woman in an unobvious and undated costume, and he has the greatest interest in the color, textures and arrangement. The range of color is rich and subtle, and the handling of the flowered burnt straw hat above the girl's ruddy and brooding face made an interesting problem in contrast with the white blouse which is full of pattern and modelling but has conscious simplification of color.*

Jerry Farnsworth

THE SPRING HAT

by Jerry Farnsworth

painted in 1940

Oil, 20 x 16 inches

40

L Y O N E L   F E I N I N G E R

A little old woman of humble birth had been taken one day for her first visit to a famous museum. After having looked at a great many paintings she stopped before a Feininger abstraction of a church. Very simply she said, "That one . . . I like!" "But why?" protested her friends, "it doesn't even look like a church." "No," said the old lady slowly, "but it *feels* like a church."

Many fine things have been said about the work of Lyonel Feininger, but one wonders if such a simple anecdote doesn't sum up his rare ability more deftly than all the rest. For Feininger's painting is not for the light and thoughtless. His pictures are delicately wrought translations to the abstract—spatial compositions of precise line, angular, light and shade, that yet hold intact the essence of the scene as he envisaged it.

Feininger spent a great deal of his life in Germany, but New York City, where he was born in 1871 and where he lived until he was 16—a New York undergoing the birth pangs of a machine age—left an indelible impression that influenced much of his art. His father, a violinist of international fame, took the boy to Germany in 1887 to complete his study of music. There his parents separated.

The boy remained with his mother in Berlin and his interest turned from music to painting. Twenty years later he came to be acknowledged in Germany as one of the best painters practicing in that country, and his paintings were purchased by many of Europe's leading museums.

In the 1930s Feininger finally decided to return to his native land to escape a regime which both hated and feared foreigners and modern art. He was doubtful as to how America would receive her expatriate son, but he wrote, "I was met with kindness and good will all around. That helped a great deal, yet it took me some time to put forth new shoots. In Germany I was 'Der Amerikaner,' here in my native land I was sometimes classified and looked upon as a German painter—some have seen relationship to Chinese art in my work—but what is the artist if not connected with the universe?"

Today in America, more and more museums prize his works, among them the Detroit Institute of Fine Arts, Museum of Modern Art and Metropolitan in New York, Walker Art Center and University Gallery in Minneapolis, City Art Museum of St. Louis, and many others.

● *A street in an ancient town in Pomerania, 14th century. Today, after departed glories, the sleepiest, most neglected accumulation of brick walls and narrow, cobblestone-paved streets imaginable—but in the late afternoon these streets become submerged in their own deep shadows, leaving the summits of mellow brick capturing the glow of the declining sun and casting unexpected minor reflections on the walls opposite. This then was the hour of magical interplay of light and shadow which gave the artist his incentive.*

Lyonel Feininger

AFTERNOON LIGHT

by Lyonel Feininger

painted in 1932

Oil, 32 x 40 inches

41

ERNEST FIENE

Through the myriad phases of a versatile career, Ernest Fiene has been tagged Primitive, Impressionist, Abstractionist and painter's painter. He has, in all moods, been able to breathe into his work intensity of emotion and robust vitality. He rarely stoops to sentimentality and never permits morbidity to creep into his themes. Oil, water color, gouache and lithography are all equally facile mediums in his hands. His landscapes, flowers and figures are an aesthetic expression in sheer beauty, but he will turn completely around and just as skillfully and sympathetically paint industrial themes, as in his Pennsylvania series of miners and steel workers.

Born in Elberfeld, Germany, in 1894, Fiene came to America in 1912, giving up his earlier ambition to follow an engineering career. He studied painting at the National Academy of Design and the Beaux Arts Institute, lithography at the Art Students League.

He first exhibited with four water colors at the MacDowell Club in 1919. His first one man show was held at the Whitney Studio Club in 1923. Until 1928 his painting consisted of landscapes and figure compositions. In 1928 and 1929, after becoming an American citizen, he travelled in France. A Guggenheim Fellowship in 1932 took him to Italy to study the Renaissance masters and to take a course in fresco painting in Florence. From 1930 to 1935 his paintings were mainly of New York City and of the hills and villages of Connecticut. He particularly loves the snowbound remoteness of the New England hills.

A mural painted in 1936, depicting Paul Revere as an industrialist, was placed in the post office at Canton, Massachusetts. Soon after the Treasury Department Fine Arts Section commissioned Fiene to paint four murals for the new Interior Department building in Washington. His largest commission was awarded in 1939, that of executing two large frescos in the Needle Trades High School of New York City—allegorical in treatment, and with more than 200 figures.

In recent years he has designed several war posters and has completed a series of pictures for the Army Medical Department.

His works appear in the Whitney Museum of American Art, the Metropolitan Museum, the Museum of Modern Art, the Library of Congress, Washington, D. C., Phillips Memorial Gallery, Denver Art Museum, St. Louis Museum, Boston Art Museum, the Newark Museum, and other public and private collections.

● *"January" was painted in 1943. I had spent the year on my farm in Southbury, Conn. After the first snowfall the deer came out of the woods in search of food. They returned every afternoon at four o'clock to dig apples under the trees in back of my house. I watched them for weeks from an upper window and made studies. The old apple-tree in the foreground is fifteen yards from the house and the meadows and woods are typical of the hills in this section.*

Ernest Fiene

JANUARY

by Ernest Fiene

painted in 1943

Oil, 44 x 34 inches

42

J O S E P H   F L O C H

Joseph Floch is one of the noted European painters whom war has forced into American refuge. His addition to the American art world dates back only to 1941. Arriving in the United States in that year, Floch was given his first American showing in the Associated American Artists Galleries shortly thereafter. However, his work had been known to American audiences from the New York World's Fair exhibition, international exhibitions and an exhibit at the Art Museum of Toledo, Ohio.

Austrian-born, Joseph Floch had his first one-man show in Vienna, when he was 22 years of age. He studied at the Academy of Fine Arts in Vienna for three years and then went to Holland for further study. He lived in Paris for 24 years, where he became one of the outstanding artists with an international reputation. Throughout the continent, his work was invited for one-man shows—in the Museum of Winterthur in Switzerland, the Museum of Contemporary Art in Antwerp in Belgium, the Museum of Copenhagen, the Goudstikker Gallery in Amsterdam. He instructed a class in painting at L'École Industrielle Supérieure in Paris.

Floch's works were acquired for permanent collections in the museums of most European countries. In France he is represented in the Luxembourg and in the Jeu de Paume and the Museum of Grenoble. His works are also to be found in the Museum of Vienna and in the Museum of Mulhouse and in many others in France and England.

In the United States, his work has been acquired by the Art Museum of Toledo, and many private collections of note. Floch's work has been the subject of many articles and monographs by noted critics, including Roger Brielle's article on "L'Art et Les Artistes," Jean Cassou's article in *Art et Decoration*, Waldemar George's article in *Formes*, Professor Hans Tietze in *Deutsche Kunst und Dekoration*, and articles by Rene Hughe, Andre Salmon, Professor Max Eisler and L. Luzzato.

Early in 1944, Joseph Floch was honored by the receipt of one of the most important awards in the American art world, the Lippincott Prize given by the Pennsylvania Academy of Fine Arts, for his painting "Seated Woman."

● *When I arrived here from Europe my reaction was one of complete breakdown and deep depression, and to bolster myself I started to paint this picture. I had in mind a woman whose name was Marlene. She lived in a tiny one-room cottage with some sheep and dogs— all in the same room. She was part of the earth and her animals were like her children. Although I had her in mind, when I painted I put all my recollections of the French people in her. I tried to show their inner strength in the way she held her head, their defiance in the gesture of her arms, in her expression I tried to show a sort of courage which to me was symbolic of the France I knew in the war.*

J. Floch

FRENCH PEASANT
by Joseph Floch
painted in 1939
Oil, 36 x 30 inches

43

DAVID FREDENTHAL

During World War II David Fredenthal worked on two assignments as *Life's* war artist correspondent. Following V-E Day he went back to paint his impressions of postwar Europe. He has had a book of his war drawings published; three successful one-man shows are behind him; twice he has held a Guggenheim Fellowship. These are but a few of his achievements, and Fredenthal is still a young man.

Born in 1914 in a Detroit tenement, he has a background and heritage not unlike many other Americans. He has drawn from the time he was a child—drawing what he saw about him, from experience, from life. His parents encouraged him, though they had hopes of him becoming a professional man. At 14 David left home, becoming a true son of the depression, on his own and broke! Odd jobs kept him going and at 15 he graduated from high school. At Cass Technical High School he met Mary L. Davis, an exceptional woman and teacher. It was she who first suggested that he take art seriously, reminding him, however, that an artist must have "guts" and self-effacing humility.

At 19, a group of his sketches were shown at the Detroit Institute of Arts. In 1935, while on the assembly line at the Ford plant, he was awarded $500 by the Museum of Modern Art, making it possible for him to spend a summer in Italy, where he studied frescoes.

Returning to America, he met Zoltan Sepeshy, whose friendship and teaching were to contribute so greatly to his development. Sepeshy arranged for a fellowship at Cranbrook Academy, and at long last David was able to devote his full time to art. Until then he had never painted. He experimented concurrently with water color and fresco, and by the summer of his first year at Cranbrook he was able to assist Boardman Robinson on his Pittsburgh murals. This was a rich experience and the beginning of a great friendship.

Fredenthal then worked on murals of his own design. The first was for the Detroit Naval Armory; the second for the New York World's Fair—three huge panels in the courtyard of the Heinz Building. The next were for the post offices at Caro and Manistique, Michigan, the result of winning national competitions. He illustrated a special edition of Erskine Caldwell's *Tobacco Road*. Meanwhile his work was being hung in important exhibitions throughout the country. The war came and he was commissioned by the government to paint war production activity in the eastern defense plants. He became a member of the War Art Unit and was sent to the South Pacific, where he was attached to General MacArthur's command. The Unit dissolved, and *Life* put him under contract. His work does not focus on the terrible spectacle of war, but on the men themselves—our soldiers enduring the grimness of battle.

● *At the time this catalog went to press, David Fredenthal was off on another assignment as a* Life *artist correspondent in war-ravaged Europe. Under these circumstances it was impossible to secure a statement from him pertinent to "Mist in the Mountains."*

MIST IN THE MOUNTAINS

by David Fredenthal

painted in 1941

Oil, 30 x 40 inches

44

WILLIAM GLACKENS

Though he, too, was one of the famous "Eight," the "ash-can school," which back in 1909 rudely shook art out of its complacent coma, William James Glackens never quite went to the back alleys for inspiration. People, crowds of them, in parks, at the races, or at the seashore, wherever they went to have fun, furnished inspiration for most of his distinguished paintings. It was in such canvases that he possessed the rare ability to capture the glamorous festivity of the outdoors, the richness of nature, the atmosphere of contagious gaiety.

Of his technique John Sloan writes, "I have seen Glackens, that great painter and illustrator, make the same drawing over twenty times because he was never satisfied." Again Sloan says "Sometimes it is best to say something new with an old technique. Glackens had the courage to use Renoir's version of the Rubens-Titian technique and he found something new to say with it."

Quite at variance with the pictorial material he loved, Glackens, the man, was quiet and a bit aloof. He might talk about fishing or good food or vintage wines, of which he was quite a connoisseur, but painting was a subject that he kept locked up within himself. He cherished his peace of mind and preferred contemplation to argument.

Glackens was born in 1870 in Philadelphia where his ancestors had lived for many generations. After graduating from Central High School, Philadelphia, he began the study of art at the Pennsylvania Academy of Fine Arts, meanwhile doing newspaper illustrations for various Philadelphia newspapers. In 1895 he went to Paris to work independently, to study Renoir and Manet, and to exhibit in the Paris Salon and the Paris Exposition. Back in America, he worked again for the newspapers, this time in New York, and landed an assignment from *McClure's* magazine to cover the Cuban phase of the Spanish-American War. His finances continued to improve and he turned from black and white to painting in color.

He won any number of coveted awards and his work is represented in nation-wide museums—the Metropolitan and Whitney Museums in New York, the Chicago Art Institute, the Detroit Institute of Arts, the Phillips Memorial Gallery, the Corcoran Gallery and the Addison Gallery. He was also a member of the National Institute of Arts and Letters and the Society of Independent Artists.

(1870–1938)

MARCH DAY — WASHINGTON SQUARE

by William Glackens

painted in 1912

Oil, 25 x 30 inches

45

GRIGORY GLUCKMANN

Gluckmann would tell you that his paintings are not *a la page*. He has looked long and thoroughly at the old masters and the 18th century French masters, Fragonard and Chardin. Along the way he has even been called "the prince of all imitators." Gluckmann does not mind. It was part of the discipline of learning what to do with paint, oil and varnish. He would tell you further that he believes in beauty and his brush is dedicated to its creating. He paints brilliantly integrated figure pieces, shimmering landscapes, and nudes. In describing the latter, somehow one objects to the mincing word "nude." These are bodies, exquisite, unashamed flesh and blood bodies that call forth high praises from the discriminating critics. In reviewing a Gluckmann show, Arthur Millier of the *Los Angeles Times* wrote that "masculine tenderness toward women pervades his painting. Pale flesh tones shine at the core of his pictures and everything else is keyed to them. Shell-like ears and the napes of necks from which the hair is swept upward are treated by his brush with special care and affection. He evidently knows where women are most beautiful."

Gluckmann was born in Russia in 1898. He was educated at the École des Beaux Arts in Moscow. Later he spent three years in Berlin, studying languages and philosophy as well as art. Florence was next on his itinerary. After long and arduous years of study, he finally felt that his talent was fully developed and in Paris in 1924 he began to exhibit. From then on rewards came his way with gratifying frequency. He intended to make France his home and became a naturalized citizen, and served in the French army during the past war, escaping from Paris only six hours before Hitler's arrival there. He fled to southern France, and after a few months was able to get to the United States. That was in 1941. His response to America was warm and immediate, and he took out his first papers for citizenship. He is happy in America and something of his enchantment with life here is reflected in his later paintings. Added to his always superb craftsmanship there is new warmth and richness in his subtly related colors. Gluckmann works constantly and tirelessly, yet his output is not large. One senses that each picture is created with infinite care.

Among his many honors are the Gold Medal for Painting at the Paris International Exhibition, 1937, the Watson F. Blair Prize at the International Watercolor Exhibition, Art Institute of Chicago, 1938, and again the Watson F. Blair Prize for oil painting in 1945. His work is owned by the Musée du Luxembourg, Paris; Le Petit Palais, Paris; the Musée de la Ville du Havre; the Art Institute of Chicago, and many private collections.

● *In painting "Confidences," my first concern has been, as always when handling simultaneously several figures, to compose, to find an adequate balance in an integrated unit, as well as rhythmical sound. As for the technical problems, trying to create an atmosphere of feminine intimacy, I was searching for a subtle, transparent substance, avoiding brutality or violence in color oppositions, as I believe is required by this theme.*

Grigory Gluckmann

CONFIDENCES

by Grigory Gluckmann

painted in 1946

Oil, 23 x 18 inches

46

MARION GREENWOOD

In 1932 a youngster with long soft hair and enormous hazel eyes, who looked more like a glamour girl than a serious artist, went to Mexico and disproved the theory that mural fresco painting was too strenuous for a woman. At an age when most of her contemporaries were busy with boys and proms, she kept right on proving it for eight long years and proved that in addition to brains and beauty she possessed more than her share of courage. She lived alone for four years in Mexico, in mines and plantations and in primitive little villages among the natives, gathering material for her huge fresco (86 feet wide by 15 feet high) depicting the life of the Tarascan Indians for the University of San Nicolas Hidalgo. On this she painted steadily from early morning until dusk, high up on her scaffolding, for the demand of true fresco technique is swift, sure painting before the plaster dries. This won for her the public praise of Lazaro Cardenas, former president of Mexico, and of the press and was followed by the series of frescoes (covering 3,000 square feet) which she painted in the Mexico City civic center and market place, arousing the admiration of such men as Orozco and Diego Rivera. In 1940, back in the United States, Marion Greenwood turned once again to the easel painting which had been her first love. Of her exhibition at the Associated American Artists gallery in the spring of 1944, the critics were unanimous in their recognition of the humanity and rugged realism of her paintings and the highly personal style she has recently developed.

In 1943 she completed two magnificent and stirring war paintings which the government had reproduced as posters for the Fifth War Loan drive. In 1944 she was commissioned by the Army Medical Corps to paint a pictorial record of the reconditioning of the wounded.

Marion Greenwood was born in New York City in 1909. Her father was a painter, her mother a poet, and her sister and brothers are artists. She studied at the Art Students League and later an understanding mother took her abroad for further appreciation and learning to the Academie Collarosi in Paris.

She has exhibited at the Metropolitan, Whitney and Brooklyn museums, the Corcoran Gallery and the Carnegie Institute. She is represented in many collections and her painting "Mississippi Girl" is one of the few Americans hanging in Maurice Wertheim's collection.

● *One night in Harlem I made sketches at a rehearsal of a dance group, musicians and singers, who study the ancestral dance forms, chants and drumbeats of Africa—for recitals. In painting it later, I was interested mainly in organizing the composition in plastic terms on my canvas—the interplay of line and light and shadow masses, spatial and color relationships—and the mood and expression of the scene as I felt it.*

Marion Greenwood

REHEARSAL FOR AFRICAN BALLET
by Marion Greenwood
painted in 1944
Oil, 28 x 45 inches

47

W I L L I A M   G R O P P E R

Gropper is no self-indulgent painter of the beautiful—the fervor of a crusader burns behind his untamed pictorial epithets. His subjects are neither stuffy nor biased, his handwriting is bold and original, and he minces no words. For a lesser artist such tales might be dangerously thin ice, but in his case there is a daring, a freedom of speech that America understands and revels in. He ranks as a forceful commentator upon political and national affairs and in one-man shows from 1936 to 1944 has reached a high place in the group of nine America's Moderns.

His awareness of social errors very likely developed with the hardships of his formative years, for New York's Lower East Side learns life the hard way. At fourteen he was already working in a sweatshop —six days a week for six dollars weekly for four long years—meanwhile managing to study art at night. He attended the National Academy of Design, the New York School of Fine and Applied Arts, and later studied under Henri and Bellows. He finally landed a cartoonist's assignment for the *New York Tribune* in 1919 and also contributed to magazines that ranged all the way from *Spur* to *The*

New Masses. In addition, he has been the author of several books.

In 1927, with Theodore Dreiser and Sinclair Lewis, he went to Moscow and, as a guest, sat in on the Conference of Cultural Relations of Soviet Russia. He later published his *Sketches of Soviet Russia*.

Gropper's first exhibition of his paintings was held in 1936. He had been painting quietly without showing his work for fifteen years. At the present time he lives his busy and energetic life with his wife and two sons at Croton-on-Hudson, New York, and says he is concerned mostly with making this a peaceful, better world to live in.

His pictures are owned by the Metropolitan Museum, the Museum of Modern Art, Hartford Museum, the Museum of Western Art in Moscow, Duncan Phillips Memorial Museum, St. Louis Museum, Minneapolis Museum, Chicago Art Institute, and the Whitney Museum of American Art. His murals are in the Department of the Interior, Washington, D.C. and the post office in Freeport, Long Island, North-western Postal Station, Detroit, Michigan, and Café Society (Downtown), New York.

● *The U.S. Senate and the House of Representatives have had such an influence on American life, good and bad, that it has even affected the artist and the cultural development of our country. No matter how far removed from politics artists may be, it seems to strike home. Only recently one blasting speech of a reactionary representative resulted in not only doing away with the Section of Fine Art, but also dismissing the Graphic Division of the OWI and nullifying art reportage for the War Department. In my painting of the Senate, called "Opposition," I have portrayed the type of representative that is opposed to progress and culture.*

Gropper—

THE OPPOSITION

by William Gropper

painted in 1942

Oil, 28 x 38 inches

48

GEORGE GROSZ

The paintings of George Grosz will remain immortal even after time has dulled a little the motivating social context of many of them. Not that the context isn't potent—Grosz is a master of irony, he lashes out dangerously—but fortunately over the iron hand there is the velvet glove of magical paint quality.

He considers it a disgrace that he is the author of a series of bitter line-drawings which has been compared to the best work of Goya, Hogarth and Daumier. He is reluctant to speak of his past wherein he incurred the wrath of Hitler for his graphic attacks on Fascism. He calls the oils he has been doing for the past five years "Hell" pictures and, in addition to expressing the essential spirit of the age, he believes they are portraits of his inner self. "In 300 years, if there are still museums, they will look at my pictures and say, 'Look here! How troubled they must have been then!'" But he also loves less troubled subjects. Few artists enjoy painting the texture of a fabric, the sheen of fruit, the glint of water more than Grosz does and few can do it so well.

George Grosz was born in Berlin in 1893. He began drawing when he was five years old, imitating his father who went in for "doodling"

on tablecloths and cardboard beer coasters—only he started in by copying battle scenes. In 1909, when Grosz was sixteen, he enrolled in the art academy at Dresden. Later, he was awarded a scholarship which enabled him to continue at the Berlin Academy of Applied Arts. About this time he accepted commercial jobs, such as designing wallpaper, cigarette packages and book jackets, and began to sell his satirical drawings to the German magazines.

After World War I he began his attacks on Naziism, and in 1932 was compelled to flee to America. When he acquired his American citizenship in 1938 he said, "It is the fulfillment of a wish-dream that I've had since I was nine." To be called a distinguished American artist is his most appreciated compliment. A tense, complex man of moods, he lives with his family in Douglaston, Long Island, and believes that he has changed character since he has changed countries and that there is less of hell and hate, and more of warmth and beauty in his work.

Many American museums own Grosz' paintings. Among them are the Metropolitan, the Whitney and the Modern Art Museums, the Duncan Phillips Memorial Gallery and the Art Institute of Chicago.

● *"The Wanderer" is real and yet unreal at the same time. The old man is the everlasting human spirit . . . here once more he goes through a dark world—through an apocalyptic landscape—tireless and in deep, maybe grim, thought he wanders on until the dark day changes into a light and sunny day . . . the bird and the thicket of reeds and brambles symbolizing his thought. So he, the old man, is just a lonely reed, too.*

George Grosz

THE WANDERER

by George Grosz

painted in 1943

Oil, 30 x 40 inches

49

LOUIS GUGLIELMI

In a 1944 issue of *Magazine of Art*, Guglielmi wrote a beautiful and poignant article entitled "I Hope to Sing Again." In it, he permitted profitable glimpses of the sensitive character and mental processes of the man, which are also projected in his symbolic and smoothly wrought painting.

"It has been said that my work requires program notes. There may be some truth in that assertion. The mystification arises in the use that I make of fantasy in an otherwise orderly and objective representation. The method is as old as painting itself. Poets use it and call it metaphor and symbolism. I use it to express an idea, to invoke a mood, or simply for amusement. A painter chooses material suited to his genre of expression. For me a city landscape is an exercise in the abstract construction of forms, shapes of patterns and the rhythm of the angular. My painting has been called surreal, magic-realist, romantic and expressionist. I do not know what to call it. It has the elements of all these classifications."

Louis Guglielmi was born in Cairo, Egypt, in 1906. His father, a musician, brought the family to the United States in 1914, settling in New York. As an eager and impatient fifteen-year-old, he entered the National Academy of Design, where for five years he gloried in the life of the art student and the intense study of his craft.

The 1920s were years of cultural drought in America, from which many artists escaped to Europe, but Guglielmi remained here where the struggle for daily bread and the desire to continue to paint became an unequal battle. It was in the 1930s, when the government projects for artists began a cultural movement in this country, that he began to produce some of his best work. He began to show pictures in local galleries and national exhibitions, and in 1938 he held his first one-man show. He has been a consistent winner of fellowships and cash prizes and his paintings are included on the permanent collections of the Whitney Museum, the Museum of Modern Art, the Metropolitan Museum of Art and the Museum of Newark, New Jersey.

As a private in the army in 1944, Guglielmi's intense nature found the war environment not conducive to creative work, which needs solitude and reflection. But in the future he believes he will come into a renaissance of art and culture and of that day he says, "I hope for the familiar touch of the brush again. I hope to sing!"

● *The picture "Odyssey for Moderns" was begun in the early dark months of our travail of the present struggle. A lost people, crawling dream-like through the rotted timbers of a beached hulk, to win the beachhead for tomorrow. The soldier at the right, a segment of the bleached wood of the old world, contemplates the hurricane sun and the distant horizon. That is the suggestive meaning of the picture in a broad sense, and is the result of a persistent dream, caused by anxiety.*

Louis Guglielmi

AN ODYSSEY FOR MODERNS

by Louis Guglielmi

painted in 1943

Oil, 24 x 30 inches

50

ROBERT GWATHMEY

"Say it—don't hint at it—use simple language and make the statement a direct one." This might easily be the credo of Robert Gwathmey, who works in a paint medium wherein two dimensions are made potent enough to dispense with any chiaroscuro of the third. His paintings have been described as "the veritable skeleton of a picture for the observer to compose."

What he says has to do with the world he lives in, particularly the Southland where the plight of the Negro and the tenant farmer has caused him to use his brush as a castigating weapon.

This soft-spoken, gentle-mannered southerner was born in Richmond, Va., in 1903. That his painting expresses social commentary is quite natural, for Gwathmey began summertime vacation work at the age of 14. He worked in lumber yards, construction camps, newspaper offices, and department stores. After one year at North Carolina State College in 1924, he devoted the next five years to art via the Maryland Institute of Design and the Pennsylvania Academy of Fine Arts. He managed to study the art of Europe, first by shipping as a seaman aboard a freighter, and later by winning two Cresson scholarships. From 1931 to 1938 he taught art at Beaver College, Jenkintown, Pa., but at the end of this period he destroyed all of his work. "It takes ten years to wash yourself clean of academic dogma," he says. Since then his goal has been his own way of pictorial demonstration against the evils of society. In 1939 Gwathmey became instructor in the Department of Painting and Design at Carnegie Institute of Technology; and in 1941 he had his first one-man show at the A.C.A. Gallery. Critics said that his show "constituted a compelling vindication of the worth of the gallery's pioneering venture."

He has enjoyed diverse awards. As a winner in the Forty-Eight States Mural Competition he painted for the post office in Eutaw, Ala., a design descriptive of the community, of which someone remarked, "We are grateful that Athenian matrons, Roman nymphs, and blinded Justices with all their impedimenta are banished."

Gwathmey is represented in the permanent collections of Boston Museum of Fine Arts, Albright Art Gallery in Buffalo, Pennsylvania Academy of Fine Arts and San Diego Fine Arts Gallery. He won first prize in the National Water Color Show at San Diego in 1941 and is included in many important private collections.

● *I'm always disgusted by the usual chauvinistic depiction of the Negro, as if a people so victimized by discrimination should be forever happy-go-lucky, slapstick, etc. The painting of a man playing a guitar in a solemn mood is a simple truth often observed. One might react to a painting form as well as to sheer subject presentation. After a great fill of Impressionism at school, I've been interested in a greater flatness of color and a sparse use of images.*

Robt. Gwathmey

NON-FICTION
by Robert Gwathmey
painted in 1943
Oil, 29 x 24 inches

51

L I L Y   H A R M O N

West Tenth Street, in New York City, hums with the activities of its favorite artist. The Murphy family, Mrs. Feldman at the corner drugstore, the news dealer, carpenter and laundry man are all critics, admirers, friends and models. Their children pose for her while their parents stand by enraptured.

Miss Harmon's romantic and lyrical paintings stem from this warm environment. She admits to a poetic outlook, prefers to paint the more tender phases of life. She can't think of Nature and leave people out and says that if she were to paint a tree it would eventually end up with a little boy climbing it.

New Haven, in 1913, was her birthplace, and as a child mermaids were her first artistic delineations, usually drawn in old books which she found up in the attic. She studied two years at the Yale School of Fine Arts, then a year in Paris, and a final year at the Art Students League in New York.

In 1942, still obscure as an artist, she was working on two paint-

ings for the Artists for Victory show at the Metropolitan Museum when a troublesome appendix landed her in the hospital. She pleaded for time, managed to convince the doctor, and rushed home in time to finish the paintings—which were both accepted! Miss Harmon believes that her entire future hinged on that episode. She was sick, she was very discouraged, and the acceptance of the two canvases presented her with a beautiful new lease on life.

In appearance Lily Harmon is slender, dark and very pretty. She tells you, in her soft voice, that she is positively grim until a picture is completed—that she is a champion "worrier" but has a sense of humor and one of her burning ambitions is to justify the faith of the people who believe in her art.

In April 1944, she held a very successful one-woman show at Associated American Artists. Her paintings have been shown at the Carnegie Institute, the Pennsylvania Academy of Fine Arts and the San Francisco Museum.

● *"Strawberry Soda" was painted during a hot New York summer. I found Leora and Sue at the corner drugstore. Both girls worked in a nearby factory and sacrificed week ends for posing. At first I was fascinated by the pink flower glowing like an electric light in Leora's dark hair, and later by the beauty, love of color, and good taste of these girls. The difference in their faces—Leora's golden tone and Sue's rich, deep coloring—also inspired me. I painted them as I saw them, absorbed in conversation in a cool oasis among sweltering city streets.*

Lily Harmon

STRAWBERRY SODA

by Lily Harmon

painted in 1943

Oil, 29 x 34 inches

52

MARSDEN HARTLEY

"I have come to the conclusion that it is better to have two colors in right relation to each other than to have a vast confusion of emotional exuberance in the guise of ecstatic fullness or poetical revelation—both of which qualities have, generally speaking, long since become second rate experience. I had rather be intellectually right than emotionally exuberant, and I could say this of any other aspect of my personal experience . . . I am not at all sure that the time isn't entirely out of joint for the so-called art of painting . . . modern art must of necessity remain in the state of experimental research if it is to have any significance at all."

These were bits of Hartley's beliefs and—despite lack of recognition during four-fifths of his life—he held to them cheerfully and stubbornly. If a hill were more effective painted in terra-cotta against a sky and sea of deepest sapphire—if a cloud in rectangular form fitted the composition more to his liking—that was the way he painted it. He investigated every artistic expression from cubism to regional painting—constantly he travelled and studied. When he wasn't painting he was writing his many poems and essays.

Hartley was born in Lewiston, Maine, in 1877 and from the beginning art and literature were all-compelling interests. At 13, he was already doing precise drawings of butterflies and flowers for a professional naturalist. His art education—and a very thorough one it was—took him to the Cleveland School of Art, Chase School in New York, National School of Design and to all the important art centres abroad.

His first exhibition in 1909 took place at "291," that famous photo-recession gallery of Alfred Stieglitz, "which made a lasting impression on the art of America." Through the years Hartley carved out a distinguished career in literature. He was the author of some 22 volumes that had to do with poetry, philosophy and art. But, fortunately, painting always remained his first love.

Only in his later years did this pioneer for modern art receive full measure of success. His life was one of struggle, discipline and research; yet he maintained a happy nature, never indulging in any rebelliousness against hard times or the artistic blindness of his fellow men. Since his death in 1943, two memorial exhibitions have been held, by the Phillips Memorial Gallery in Washington and the Columbus Gallery of Fine Arts. During his lifetime he held 21 one-man shows and today his paintings are in the permanent collections of 23 of America's important museums.

(1877–1943)

END OF STORM—VINALHAVEN, MAINE

by Marsden Hartley

painted in 1943

Oil, 22 x 26 inches

53

CHILDE HASSAM

He had a discriminating yet full-bodied appreciation of music, laughter, light, color, movement, brave men and beautiful women. He enjoyed his prowess in boxing and swimming, he had an epicure's delight in vintage wines and choice viands. His Puritan ancestors had given him Spartan heritages as well, an astonishing capacity for work, a fighting attitude against hypocrisies and a headstrong belief in the rightness of his own course.

Childe Hassam has been named a dean of American painting. Until 1944 he had been the only artist for whom the National Collection of Fine Arts had broken an iron-bound rule. To be included in their collection no artist is eligible until the twenty years that have elapsed since his death have proven his worth. Hassam was included in 1943, only eight years after his death in 1935. Hassam has still another unique distinction. He is the only artist who has ever painted an entire series of flags. Between 1916 and 1919 he devoted most of his time to these symbolic silks, and the thrilling radiance and vigor of these pictures have caused many critics to unloose their most extravagant adjectives.

Frederick Childe Hassam was born in Dorchester, Massachusetts, in 1859, of English ancestry. In Dorchester High School he showed a definite aptitude for drawing, but football and swimming were attractions to be reckoned with, and he admitted "I could knock out any of the other boys with my fists." Something of the fighting instinct remained with him all his life. He never "gave in" once he had stated his case.

He began a business career in a Boston counting house, but realized within three short weeks that he had not the faintest interest in accounts. His next venture was a wood-engraver's office where his hand learned exquisite discipline and control. After three years of commercial illustrating, Hassam took off for Europe. In Paris he came face to face with the Impressionist teachings which were then the current rage.

Entering the historic Julian Academy he absorbed the teachings of Boulanger, Lefebvre and Doucet, but Hassam was too "American" to dally overlong. He brought home these new theories to try out on the scenes he loved.

In his art he mastered every medium including water colors, etchings and pastels. The list of his honors and achievements and the number of galleries which possess his work takes up an entire page in *Who's Who in American Art*.

(1859–1935)

AVENUE OF THE ALLIES

by Childe Hassam

painted in 1917

Oil, 36 x 28 inches

JOHN   EDWARD   HELIKER

In *Time* magazine for March 31, 1941, there appeared a list of very impressive names in the art world who had exhibited the previous week in the biennial show of Washington's Corcoran Gallery, for the biggest cash prizes ($5,000 worth) offered anywhere in the United States. The first prize ($2,000) went to a comparatively unknown painter, young John Edward Heliker, aged 31. Heliker's prize canvas, a hard-bitten, blocky Vermont landscape, had been put on sale in Manhattan the autumn before at $150, but, ironically enough, nobody had wanted it—then!

Heliker is young; his smile is slow to come but completely engaging when it happens; he would never be called loquacious, but if one is patient enough he gives his story. He particularly admires the work of Albert P. Ryder, John Marin, Marsden Hartley and Max Weber. He feels that he might rightly be termed an Expressionist, since he never works from Nature, only from the memories that record with the inner vision. He is extremely sensitive to the organization of a picture. The world he sees and puts down is his own world. Gently, he disengages it from its physical aspect and translates it, with the magic of his art, into some abstract interpretation of his own.

Heliker was born in Yonkers, New York, in 1909, of Dutch and Scotch parentage. He began to draw in early childhood, for it has always seemed a special sort of language to him. As a youngster, he developed an awareness of such men as Picasso, Van Gogh and George Grosz and he learned much from all of them. In 1929 he studied at the Art Students League with Kenneth Hayes Miller, Kimon Nicolaedes and Boardman Robinson. In 1936, Maynard Walker gave him his first one-man show, and in the *New York Evening Post* Jerome Klein remarked, "His landscapes are already masterful! His work should not be missed. It has a rich-bitter promise as impressive as anything that has appeared on our horizon in years."

Heliker spends most of his summer vacations on the farm, and much of the material for his pictures is gathered at this time—later to be recreated on canvas. He is represented in more than 20 private collections and in the San Francisco Museum, Addison Gallery, Denver Museum, Corcoran Gallery, Whitney Museum, Brooklyn Museum, William Rockhill Nelson Museum and others.

● *I have tried here to express something of the spirit of a place visited at Barton, Vermont, in 1943. It is a fairly naturalistic presentation; however, my concern was mainly with the organization of the plastic elements of painting. I have found the Vermont countryside especially hospitable to my painting activities; its blue hills and quiet villages, its magnificent rock formations, have given me the sort of material I like to work with. Not that I haven't found in cities a stimulating experience also, but somehow I find myself more at home in the "little world" of the farm—I feel free to work slowly there—where one is more consistently aware of fundamentals.*

QUIET EVENING
by John Edward Heliker
painted in 1944
Oil, 24 x 34 inches

55

R O B E R T   H E N R I

Robert Henri was the herdsman who goaded American art into her own adequate pastures. Critics have disagreed about his greatness as a painter, but all of them have agreed about his greatness as a teacher, and all of them acknowledge the debt due him as the leader of the "ash-can school." John Sloan writes that without Henri's inspirational encouragement he might never have painted seriously, that Henri was a great painter and had the ability to arouse the creative spirit in almost everyone. Saint-Gaudens pays handsome tribute, he writes: "Robert Henri, as the percussion cap that set off this uproar, came back from Paris in 1900, flushed with admiration for Manet and Goya. Henri, the racy, energetic, fluent technician, loved life, people and pupils. Henri held to the theory that painting in this country was a vehicle in which to express the life of this country."

He had an uncanny sense of putting the life around him onto canvas, and his followers were only too ready to discard the insipid prettiness then in vogue and replace it with the humorous, vigorous and sometimes squalid New York scene. He preached and admonished. His credo was "do not imitate, be yourself."

Robert Henri was born in Cincinnati, Ohio, in 1865. He studied first at the Pennsylvania Academy of Fine Arts under the instruction of Thomas Eakins and later became a pupil of Hovenden. His enthusiasm took him to Europe, where he absorbed the teachings of the old Julian Academy and the École des Beaux Arts. Back in America he went through a period of teaching at the School of Design for Women, in Philadelphia, but he was still seeking, still dissatisfied with the academic mandates. Once again he tried Europe; he explored Spain and Italy and wound up in France sharing a studio with Glackens.

Despite an extremely active life as a painter, Henri always found time to teach. For more than thirty years he helped to shape the destinies of thousands of young artists. He taught at the Chase School, the Art Students League and eventually in a school of his own establishing. Henri died in 1929 at the age of 64. The vigor and independence of his style brought him special renown as a portrait painter.

His paintings are represented in the Carnegie Art Institute, Chicago Art Institute, Metropolitan Museum, the Corcoran Gallery in Washington, D.C., and many others.

(1865–1929)

FISHERMAN'S BOY

by Robert Henri

painted in 1920

Oil, 24 x 20 inches

56

CLARENCE HINKLE

It is a fascinating experience to watch Clarence Hinkle weave colors together—deep tones and brilliant ones, interlaced with bold slashes of white. He lays on his pigments lavishly, his approach is sure, and gradually there emerge shapes of trees, craggy rocks, depths of sky and water, into landscapes that unloose new horizons for the imagination. At no time does he worry over literal transcription—but in a manner all his own creates pictorial themes that aim straight at the emotional reactions of the onlooker.

Probably it is this technique of his—apparently careless in his throwing on of hillocks of paint—that results in an almost third-dimensional feeling in his picture-making, a technique that few artists would dare to imitate. Like the great French artist Renoir, Hinkle has had no other major interest than painting. To him it is an interest so varied and so vital that he has painted seriously, steadily and daily.

An artist who has reached full and vigorous maturity before the glare of publicity has singled him out, Hinkle was born in Auburn,

California, in 1880. He studied with William Chase, Thomas P. Anshutz and Jean Paul Laurens. He has won many prizes and awards and has exhibited at many of the leading museums in America as well as in Europe. He has done more than his share of travelling and has found food for artistic thought in France, Holland, Italy and other European countries.

He has spent much time in research into the methods of the old masters, and as a teacher he has contributed greatly to the very distinctive art that is giving California a prestige of very high caliber today.

He has taught at the Chouinard School of Art, and in 1944 was teaching at the Santa Barbara School of Art. That same year he had a one-man exhibition at the Santa Barbara Museum which brought forth only tributes and no adverse criticism.

Clarence Hinkle is represented in the permanent collections of the Los Angeles Museum, San Diego Gallery of Fine Arts, Montpelier (Vermont) Museum and the High School in Springville, Utah.

● *The objects in "The Punch Bowl" were arranged for their color, glazed surfaces, contrasts and textures. A problem to be seen in paint. The following procedure seemed fitting: The pattern was first painted flat in white and gray tempera. The overpainting in varnish oil coverings was a matter of following through in warm and cool tones to the full colors and accents—the picture gaining in strength and luminosity.*

Clarence Hinkle

THE PUNCH BOWL
by Clarence Hinkle
painted in 1944
Oil, 36 x 30 inches

57

J O S E P H   H I R S C H

Joseph Hirsch keys his art to the tempo of the times. Fearlessly and vividly he makes his comments on a world of living realities. They are the broad views of an artist whose discerning eye and inquiring mind are tempered by a compassionate spirit. Sometimes his color is lifting, decorative, and again it will be muted and grim, ever associating itself with the mood of the picture. His pictorial structure is bold, sure and uncluttered.

Since 1941, Hirsch has channelized his talents into the war effort. He has painted War Bond posters, made pictorial records of the aviation activities of the Naval Air Base in Pensacola, for the Naval Medical Department in the South Pacific, and for the Army Medical Corps on the war fronts of Italy. Hirsch has put all of his energy and ability into these wartime assignments and makes a very beautiful statement when he says, "The cause of democracy is the cause of creative art and the artist who cherishes his cultural freedom will fight for that democracy in which it flourishes."

Philadelphia in 1910 was his birthplace, and at 17 he was awarded a four-year scholarship to the Pennsylvania Museum School of Industrial Art by the city of Philadelphia. He proved his right to that award by winning first prizes both in life drawing and illustration. Then came a period of study with George Luks in New York and later with Henry Hensche in Provincetown.

When he was 23 he compelled the attention of the art world by taking the coveted Walter Lippincott Award at the Annual Exhibition of the Pennsylvania Academy of Fine Arts for the "best figure painting in oil by an American citizen." In 1935, through the winning of a Woolley Fellowship for European travel, he spent a year and a half sketching and painting throughout Europe and the Orient.

At the New York World's Fair, by public ballot, he was awarded first choice for the best painting in the Exhibition of Contemporary American Art. In 1942 and 1943 he won two Guggenheim Fellowships, and a Treasury citation for his War Bond poster of 1943.

Hirsch's murals decorate the new Municipal Court Building, the Amalgamated Clothing Workers' Center and the Benjamin Franklin High School in Philadelphia. His work hangs in the permanent collections of the Museum of Modern Art, the Philadelphia Museum of Art, Whitney Museum, Addison Gallery, Boston Museum, University of Arizona, Corcoran Gallery and Library of Congress.

● *Guerrillas are heroic people. Their underground activity is so clearly a symbol of the fight for liberty, wherein good men kill, that I have endeavored to paint a monument to their nobility. These selfless men are armed with a great hatred, born of their love for the new life. The rebirth of the new in the very death toils of the old is nature's most sublime and constant law. It finds its epitome in these guerrilla fighters, who cherish the tomorrow in today's child, who kill because they love mankind.*

Joseph Hirsch

GUERRILLAS

by Joseph Hirsch

painted in 1943

Oil, 30 x 41 inches

58

EDWARD HOPPER

"My aim in painting has always been the most exact transcription possible of my most intimate impressions of Nature. If this end is unattainable, so, it can be said, is perfection in any other ideal of painting or in any other of man's activities. I believe that the great painters, with their intellect as master, have attempted to force this unwilling medium of paint and canvas into a record of their emotions. I find any digression from this large aim leads me to boredom" —that is Hopper's own lucid statement of his intent. By a method of sheer simplification and clarity of statement, his pictorial creations of the American scene are masterpieces of individuality. The distinguished artist Guy Pène du Bois comments: "Hopper is a painter who will make many artists of the past or present seem trivial. He will make them seem too talkative or too wasteful. He will make many of the 'great' moderns seem like funny little reciters of fairy tales. He will be shown in any comparison as a serious man, without patience for trivialities, capable of reaching majesty."

Far from pretty, his subjects include city streets on Sunday, mansions of yesteryear, lighthouses, and cheap hotel bedrooms peopled with lonely figures and painted with a hint of the satirical and an unmistakable American flavor. Nyack, New York, in 1882, was his birthplace and Nyack's shipyards were subjects for his first pencilled experiments. He studied at the Chase School in New York for five years with Chase, Henri and Miller. Paris, where he worked independently, was also included in his curriculum.

The famed Armory Show in 1913, which started American art on its upward surge, also put Hopper's feet on the first rungs of the legendary ladder but it was still not easy going, for he paints slowly and painstakingly. Another ten years rolled by before he scaled the top rung—and there solidly he remains today. In the same studio on Washington Square he has lived his simple philosophical life for the past quarter-century.

His pictures are in England's principal museums and in the collections of the Metropolitan Museum, the Whitney Museum, the Chicago Art Institute, the Pennsylvania Academy of Fine Arts, the Phillips Memorial Gallery and the Boston Museum of Fine Arts among others.

● *"Cape Cod Evening" is no exact transcription of a place, but pieced together from sketches and mental impressions of things in the vicinity. The grove of locust trees was done from sketches of trees nearby. The doorway of the house comes from Orleans about twenty miles from here. The figures were done almost entirely without models, and the dry, blowing grass can be seen from my studio window in the late summer or autumn. In the woman I attempted to get the broad, strong-jawed face and blond hair of a Finnish type of which there are many on the Cape. The man is a dark-haired Yankee. The dog is listening to something, probably a whippoorwill or some evening sound.*

Edward Hopper

CAPE COD EVENING

by Edward Hopper

painted in 1939

Oil, 30 x 40 inches

59

P E T E R   H U R D

Much has been written about the carefree lanky cowboy who has painted so many dramatic scenes of his beloved New Mexico—an artist, still young, who has come into his own and who by the force of his integrity and ability renews our faith in American art.

But it was in the years after 1942, as *Life's* war artist correspondent, that Hurd's career carried on to an even greater destiny. Hurd put his talent to work in a historic recording of World War II. His "Return from Rouen," wherein he paints the arrival of Fortresses from their first all-American raid on Europe, is a happy, hell-raising scene of irregular celebration. His "War and Peace" tells the tragic story of war—storm-clouds and bombers fill a tortured sky and below, in ominous shafts of sunlight, the peaceful activity of harvesting continues on an English countryside.

Hurd once said: "As for my philosophy of art, my credo is a simple one. It is to live as intensely as possible and keep my perceptions at a peak of sensitivity . . . It is hard to understand how, in an age so fond of science, we have so often ignored the learning of a sound technique. I do not refer here to flashy brush work or other tricks of the trade, but to the craftsman-like building of a picture from the physio-chemical standpoint. It is the duty of every serious artist to consider this, else how can we whose living must come from these works find a buying public."

Born in Roswell, New Mexico, in 1904, Peter Hurd's early ambitions were military, not artistic. He attended New Mexico Military Institute and continued on to West Point, but resigned after two years. He promised his father to complete his college course at Haverford, Pennsylvania, but while there he met the famous painter and illustrator, N. C. Wyeth, who recognized the boy's talent and by means of an eloquent letter won parental consent to forget college and concentrate on art. He studied for three years with Wyeth and continued at the Pennsylvania Academy of Fine Arts. In 1929 he married Henriette Wyeth, his instructor's artist daughter and after a few years returned to ranch life in his native New Mexico.

Hurd has painted fresco murals for La Quinta Art Gallery at Albuquerque, post office murals at Big Springs and Dallas, Texas. His easel pictures are owned by the Metropolitan Museum, the Art Institute of Chicago, the William Rockhill Nelson Gallery in Kansas City and the Art Center in Wilmington, Delaware.

● *"The Fourth of July" was painted from dozens of small studies and sketches made during the rodeos on two successive Fourths of July at Fort Stanton. My aim was to get all the color, the light and the glitter. I want the observer to see with me the contestants and the silvery dust; the cool cloud shadows gliding over the foothills; to hear the thunder of hooves, the cheering crowd, and the loud-speaker blaring the announcer's wisecracks—wry comments on those who miss their calves or get piled off their horses.*

Peter Hurd

FOURTH OF JULY

by Peter Hurd

painted in 1940

Oil, 30 x 36 inches

ERIC ISENBURGER

The year 1941 probably will stand out as most eventful in the life of Eric Isenburger. In June of that year he escaped the horrors of a concentration camp in France and fled to America. Four months later in New York he held his first one-man show at Knoedler's and sold twelve paintings out of an exhibit of twenty. In 1945 he held eight one-man shows in a twelve-month period—all of which would indicate that America and Isenburger have gotten along very well together.

The paintings he brought to America in 1941 were all executed abroad. At that time he seemed a true descendant of the French Impressionists. His landscapes, interiors, and figures emerged in thin, chalky tones in blotted outlines—very soft, very sophisticated pictures with a decided French flavor.

The paintings of 1945 and 1946 afford a quite exciting comparison. Juicy reds, blues and ochers have replaced the former pastel tones. There is still delicacy and subtlety—still the Braque influence—but there is an added power and assurance, the coming of age of a very fine artist.

Isenburger was born in Germany in 1902. A wealthy family would have preferred a banker's career for their son, but at seven young Eric was already busy with crayons, and at eleven serious study began. He studied at Frankfurt, Vienna, Barcelona, and Paris, and in 1925 he was winning recognition in the museums of Europe. Long before he came to America, Knoedler's were already measuring his artistic worth, which probably had much to do with his quick success upon arrival.

Isenburger tells his story simply and modestly and he makes one rejoice that America can still be the land of opportunity for at least one grateful refugee. He believes that in his art he has absorbed something of the spirit of America. He says that his earlier paintings were too soft, too charming . . . in the last few years he feels that he has improved in his handling of both color and design.

In looking at his pictures one knows that he speaks the truth, for they are so smoothly integrated that analysis of component parts comes only after a very long moment of enjoying a perfect whole.

His work is represented in the permanent collections of the Museum of Modern Art in New York, the Pennsylvania Academy of Fine Arts, the Thomas J. Watson Collection, and numerous private collections. In 1945 he won the National Academy of Design Prize for the most outstanding work in either painting or sculpture during that year. This prize was offered for the first time in 1945 at the 120th Annual Exhibition of Painting and Sculpture of the National Academy.

● *Our lives are represented in our paintings. All experiences and what we went through. We see and feel ourselves and the ones that surround us enclosed in a world. We sometimes draw the circle of the space close to us and, at other times, we widen it. Upon which we find it most important to touch the space to find our relationship to it.*

WINTER DAY
by Eric Isenburger
painted in 1945
Oil, 34 x 26 inches

61

J O E   J O N E S

Joe Jones likes wheatfields—with the wind rippling them, with the sun shining on them, when they're being harvested—that's why he paints them so beautifully. However, the yellows and golds of his palette lately remained untouched—the cold blues and grays very much in use, for as *Life's* war correspondent, bleak and barren Alaska was his pictorial assignment.

Jones is one of the vital younger artists who, in his eager seeking, has run the gamut from brutal social protest themes to sheer exuberant beauty. He has weathered his share of criticism, both favorable and stormy, but he is never ignored. He is exciting because he is young, not set in any mold, and his future is well worth gambling on.

"When a painting 'does' itself, unforced, not overworked, when the artist is plain drunk with the excitement of his subject, that's when he can't miss," thus Jones makes his honest commentary on art. His whole philosophy is to re-create on canvas his own very vital reflections on the subject involved.

This direct, headstrong young American who doesn't like "bunk," was born in St. Louis in 1909. He started with his father as an apprentice house painter and since, in the environment he knew,

artists were frowned upon as sissies or bar-flies, it was only to do better decorating that he finally enrolled in a vocational school. The temptations to experiment with still lifes and portraits were too much, however, and by the time he celebrated his twenty-fifth birthday he knew that painting—not house painting—was to be his career.

Joe Jones is one of America's successful young artists who made the grade without benefit of formal artistic education. He admits that he travelled a lot and found other artists very helpful along the way. In 1934 he organized art classes for unemployed youngsters, both white and colored, which he held in the old courthouse in St. Louis. Despite the disapproval of politicians in a Jim Crow state, and the continual battles that ensued and finally ousted him, the project stands out in his mind as one of the greatest satisfactions he's ever known.

Besides the easel paintings that represent him in many museums, including the Metropolitan, Whitney, Cleveland and Worcester Museums, he has done murals for the post office buildings in Seneca and Lawrence, Kansas, Charleston, Missouri, and Magnolia, Arkansas.

● *This is one of many paintings I did using wheat farmers as my main interest. Although I have a strong liking for the pictorial excitement of anything to do with wheat, my main aesthetic interest in the theme was the beautiful rhythm these men achieved in their work and their obvious enjoyment in this achievement—this always strikes me as an aesthetic fulfillment in any kind of work and adds up to a kind of beauty I believe in—the spiritual motive in painting.*

Joe Jones

WHEAT FARMERS

by Joe Jones

painted in 1936

Oil, 24 x 36 inches

62

M E R V I N   J U L E S

Mervin Jules uses his brush as a weapon with which to fight the social wrongs of our times. He pulls no punches and uses no delicate innuendo in his harsh condemnation of the plutocrat.

When he was only twenty-five years old, he held his first one-man show in New York. It included small tempera panels, somber in tone and masterful in execution, and a series of gouaches done in the coal-mining country of Pennsylvania. Although some of the critics deplored the irony and disillusion in the work of a man so young, they all agreed that here was an artist who felt strongly and painted ably, even though they didn't necessarily agree with his ideology or with his conclusion. In 1938 and 1939 critics commented on a more constructive tendency and philosophy in his later canvases.

Mervin Jules was born in Baltimore in 1912. His father owned a men's haberdashery store, and in true American fashion both parents sought for their son a more aesthetic and remunerative career. They decided on music and a 'cello was the chosen instrument. Jules endured six years of enforced practice before his parents gave in and decided that perhaps he wasn't "musical" after all.

In high school he associated with intellectual groups and pondered the problems of society, and it was not until he graduated from Baltimore City College in 1930 that he made up his mind to be a teacher of art. He enrolled at the Maryland Institute where he finished a four-year course in three years and then entered the Art Students League in New York under the instruction of Thomas Benton. Jules will never forget and will never cease being grateful for the instruction of Benton. In New York he designed silks, made picture frames and prepared gesso panels for artists. He lived on eight dollars a week and acquired first-hand experience at being one of the underprivileged—though only for a short time. He returned to Baltimore for a year and then came back to New York determined to conquer. It was through the recognition of Hudson Walker that he was given his first show. The critics were kind, collectors began to buy, and Jules began to breathe more freely.

He has had seventeen one-man shows and his paintings and prints are owned by many museums including the Metropolitan, the Art Institute of Chicago, the Baltimore Museum, Portland (Oregon) Museum of Art, the Library of Congress and the Museum of Modern Art.

● *An artist must be honest and paint what he feels. I try to express the intrinsic meaning of the things I feel most deeply. Ideas about people, about society, freedom, all the truths we value and love. In this painting of "The Conductor" I symbolized the wonder and power of music through the use of the orchestra and their leader blended into a composite whole in vivid interpretation of a composer's work.*

THE CONDUCTOR

by Mervin Jules

painted in 1944

Oil, 14 x 14 inches

63

MORRIS KANTOR

"He has a poet's way of drenching a picture in the mood which then becomes the substance of the picture more truly than the separate objects which fill up the canvas." The quotation in Harry Salpeter's article in *Esquire* seems a fitting comment on the painting of Morris Kantor.

Coming to America in 1911 from his birthplace in Russia, he later returned to Europe for study, painting independently, with a distinct sympathy for the French school. Nevertheless, this did not predominate in his work. Slowly, he dug his way into the American background and began to produce a delightful series of American scenes painted with the quality of the Colonial American primitives.

Another group, which is among his best known, are his interior-exterior pictures in which he shows the landscape through the door or window. One summer at Marblehead the Kantors discovered they had rented the "haunted house" of the community. He pictured the house in an inside-outside arrangement and it was awarded the Logan Gold Medal and a cash price of $2,500. The ghosts, if any, were friendly ones.

Kantor began to draw when he was ten years old. His mother encouraged his efforts, but his actual schooling took place when he came to America. He studied under Homer Boss at the Independent School of Art. The spirit of the school was insurgent rather than academic but Kantor does not recall any definite influence to which he submitted.

In order to study he worked at various jobs, meanwhile painting his nudes, still lifes and abstractions in all his spare time. He continued sending a painting annually to the exhibitions of the Independent Society from 1919 to 1927. Nothing happened. But in 1927 he spent a year in Paris haunting the Louvre and making critical analyses of his own work.

In 1928 his work began to click and in 1929 he had his first one-man show. He likes to paint and work in the country; reading and card games are favorite diversions, and occasionally he works with carpentry tools.

Today Kantor's work is represented in the major museums of the country, including the Metropolitan Museum, Phillips Memorial Gallery, Chicago Art Institute, Detroit Museum, Pennsylvania Academy of Fine Arts and the Whitney Museum.

● *"Girl in Yellow" was neither posed nor imagined. She just happened to sit that way. What interested me was her intensity and the relaxation of her flexible body, which gave the illusion of a plastic form suspended in space.*

Morris Kantor

GIRL IN YELLOW

by Morris Kantor

painted in 1940

Oil, 30 x 40 inches

64

BERNARD KARFIOL

Karfiol prefers the adventure in illusion to any anatomical inventorying. He then proceeds to prove his theories by anyone with a sophisticated eye for color and an appreciation for flawless draftsmanship. Landscapes, studies of nudes and children make up the bulk of Karfiol's work, but, whatever the subject, it is always the medium for the expression of his own distinctly personal emotion. An estimate of his work, written by a well-known critic as far back as 1917, was to the effect that Karfiol was consistently individual and scornful of any standards other than those based exclusively on the intrinsic value of the art expression concerned. Present-day estimates of the artist agree that he has a definite place in the heritage of painting, a place that is unique in American art. The quality of tenderness and intensity of feeling infused into all his work, and above all the nudes, by an extreme emotional sensibility, is the distinct contribution of Karfiol.

Karfiol reversed the usual procedure by getting himself born in Budapest in 1886, of American parents. They brought him to the United States as a child, and his father, an inventor and engraver, decided that the boy's budding artistry was worthy of all the encouragement he could give it. At 14 the youngster was already enrolled at the National Academy of Design in New York City. In the fall of 1901 he went to Paris and worked for two years at the Julian Academy. He exhibited at the Grand Salon in 1903 and 1904, lived a year in London and returned to America in 1907, where he remained, working in New York City and Ogunquit, Maine, with occasional trips to Cuba, Jamaica and Mexico.

His first work was shown at the Modern Artists of America Exhibition at the Brummer Gallery, then at the Armory Show in 1913. He exhibited at Hamilton Easter Field's gallery in Brooklyn and had three shows at the Brummer Gallery, and then an additional three at the Downtown Gallery, and with this latter gallery he is still connected.

Karfiol has been a consistent award winner; has shown at many important exhibitions throughout the country; is represented in many private collections and in the permanent collections of numerous museums, including the Metropolitan, Whitney, Museum of Modern Art, Addison Gallery, Baltimore Museum, Carnegie Museum, Corcoran Gallery, Phillips Memorial Gallery and many more.

● *It is difficult to explain to the layman that my first concerns in painting the canvas called "Two Sisters" were color, plasticity, movement. The human element enters in, of course, as it always does in my work, but gestures, contrast of draped figure beside nude, light against dark, the expression of a hand in relation to those of the other model, intensifying or understating as I feel a part essential to the complete statement—these, all of these, are necessary to express whatever personal feeling and emotion is found in my work.*

Bernard Karfiol

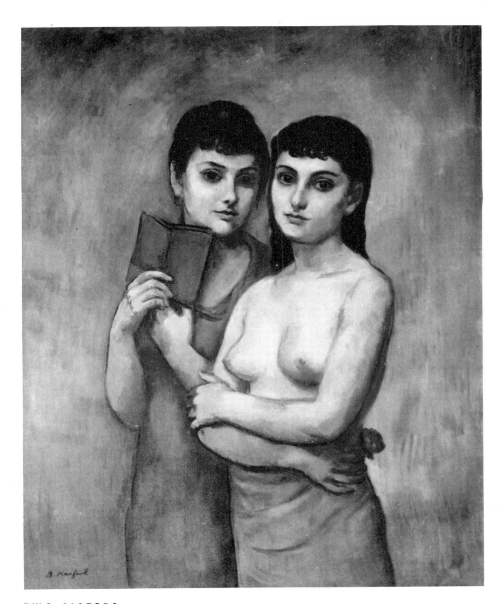

TWO SISTERS

by Bernard Karfiol

painted in 1940

Oil, 36 x 28 inches

65

H I L D E   K A Y N

Hilde Kayn's is the courageous and sympathetic story of an artist who struggled for recognition for years, with courage and perseverance holding her unfalteringly to her goal. After showing in important exhibitions in the United States for several years (including the Carnegie Exhibition in 1941) there came 1943, and like a bolt from the blue, against established name competition, Hilde Kayn won Second Honorable Mention in the Carnegie Exhibition and, immediately previous to that, one of her paintings, entitled "New Moon," was purchased for the permanent collection of the Toledo Museum of Art. This was followed by the Allied Artists Gold Medal and also by the acquisition of her painting "Consolation" by the Butler Art Institute, Youngstown, Ohio, for its permanent collection, as well as by her election to the National Academy of Design.

To hear her tell her story is a heartwarming experience. She tells you, with a charming accent, of her childhood in Vienna where she was born in 1903; of how she had two great yearnings, either to be a dancer or a painter. She studied for the ballet, but when she was thirteen lost both her parents within a year, and in the tragedy of Vienna, after the first World War, the family fortune was also swept away. Her childhood sweetheart, who later became her husband, made the decision to start life anew in the new world. He came to America in 1920 and prepared the way for her arrival in 1921. Immediately thereafter she entered the Art Students League, where Luks and Bridgman were her teachers. Luks especially was her idol and she still has hanging in her living room a treasured portrait head which she painted under his guidance.

Her canvases are usually group studies in which the rhythm of the figures is the outstanding characteristic. Her technique is loose and spontaneous, and shows a masterful control of lighting and design. Her palette ranges from singing tones to somber ones, in accordance with the mood of the subject. Her subjects go from the very gay to the very tragic, reflecting her own emotional moods—for she is a very intense person. She says: "You don't just talk to a person, or look at them, you look *into* them, you seek contact with the inner spirit. You feel their sorrows and their joys." She never uses models and feels that her early ballet training gave her an almost anatomical instinct for portraying the motions of the human body.

● *During my stay on a small island off the Atlantic coast, a young man among a group of frolicking young people, climbing the steep cliffs and rocks, lost his footing and fell to his death. This tragic and horror-stricken group of pale young faces, appearing more somber yet by the beards which they had grown during their vacations, so bewildered looking and so struck by the sudden tragedy, left a never-to-be-forgotten impression upon me.*

Hilde B. Kayn

SORROW
by Hilde Kayn
painted in 1940
Oil, 25 x 30 inches

66

ROCKWELL KENT

Louis Untermeyer wrote, "He is the most versatile man alive. I suspect that Kent is not a personality at all but an organization." Nor is this farfetched, for one time, Kent, in order to finance a trip to Alaska, hit upon the idea of incorporating himself as Rockwell Kent Inc., Art Products. The paintings and woodcuts he brought back were dividends on shareholders' investments.

Donald Ogden Stewart wrote, "He has honesty, integrity, humor and energy—there is something dynamic about the man which makes contact very close to what might be called inspiring." In a less serious vein he remarks, "To drive in an auto with him at the wheel is to want to be on good terms with God."

Homer Saint-Gaudens wrote, "Kent would hate to admit it yet he does strive to charm you into looking at his work, not to stun you on the back of the head by an unexpected rough-edged pictorial brick."

The Multiple Kent juggles a confounding array of activities, he is an artist, writer, architect, lecturer, explorer, politician, propagandist and dairy farmer, and no jack of all trades but a master of most.

Kent bows to no academy and dislikes the patter of the art world in general. He is a man of great talent and superb draftsmanship in every department of art. His lonely, majestic landscapes are worked in solid masses, architecturally constructed.

Kent was born at Tarrytown Heights, New York, in 1882. He started out to be an architect but changed his mind during his junior year at Columbia University. He studied art in New York under Chase, Henri and Miller and while still in his early twenties exhibited at the National Academy of Design. Kent was the youngest American artist to be represented in the permanent collections of the Metropolitan Museum.

Always restless, he has been a wanderer on the face of the globe and has discovered the beauty of adventure, loneliness, bleak reaches and barren outlines. Of his successful career as an author he says, "I am as much of a writer as a painter because I think in terms of art and in terms of literature."

He is radical and takes the obligations of citizenship seriously. He aligns himself with *labor*, of which he considers himself to be a part. He lives in Ausable Forks, New York, and admits that he is compelled to paint and write constantly to support his herd of Jersey cows in a fitting manner.

● *Looking down into the shallow grave as the coffin is placed in it stand five young Greenlanders. The earth and stones will rattle on the coffin's lid; a little mound will be heaped up on it; stones may be piled on top to keep the dogs away; little bunches of flowers, if it is early summer, or crudely woven wreaths of brush will be laid on the grave. Requiescat in pace. Amen.*

Rockwell Kent

THE BURIAL

by Rockwell Kent

painted in 1940

Oil, 35 x 45 inches

67

FRANK KLEINHOLZ

"Life begins at forty." The Kleinholz version should be even more of a best seller than the original volume, for his is the rare story of a man who, without juvenile precocity or adolescent floundering, came upon art in his maturity having already settled for a lawyer's career. He was searching for some form of creative expression and in 1937 while watching an artist friend paint he decided to try his hand at it. The very next day he bought brushes, paints and palette. He painted a little still life and a new career was born.

He now devotes his full time to art and no one is more amazed at the rapidity of his success and public recognition than he is. "Maybe," he suggests, "I've telescoped forty-three years into five. I feel like the lost wanderer on the desert who has found water— I'm lapping it up!" Despite his newness to art, he is unafraid of it. He puts down what he sees in spots of color, rich, lush and abundant; his second interest is design and to both ingredients he adds the final "fillip" which is the Kleinholz approach.

Called the "Brooklyn-born Gauguin," he is far more successful than Gauguin at a comparable age. He was born in Brooklyn, New York, in 1901 and went to work at odd jobs when he was fourteen.

He won a scholarship that admitted him to Colby College, Maine, where he tended the furnace and tables to further his tuition. Later he went to Fordham Law School and the career of lawyer was his fulfillment until Fate decided otherwise.

He was first discovered when his painting "Abstractionists" was chosen in the Directions of American Painting Exhibition, Carnegie Institute of Fine Arts, in 1941. Since then he has been invited to show his work at the Virginia Museum, Pennsylvania Academy, Art Institute of Chicago, Carnegie Institute of Fine Arts, Nebraska Art Institute, Whitney Museum, and to almost every important national exhibition. He was awarded the $500 purchase prize in the 1942 Artists for Victory Exhibition. He is represented in the permanent collections of the Metropolitan Museum and the Phillips Memorial Gallery of Washington, D.C.

His work has been acquired by John O'Connor, Acting Director of the Carnegie Institute, Alfred Hitchcock of Hollywood, California, and many other important collectors.

In 1944 he was conducting a weekly radio program over Station WNYC called, "Art in New York."

● *I love to paint children, particularly children of the city streets. I doubt if anywhere but in an American city can one find that pertness and independence that characterizes city kids. In "Bravadoes" I tried to catch that spirit. But to get the spirit is not enough—it must be implemented by color and design. I have used the shapes and symbols of the street to build a pattern in color against which the antics of the children could have free play.*

BRAVADOES
by Frank Kleinholz
painted in 1943
Oil, 24 x 12 inches

68

L E O N   K R O L L

Even as a little boy he haunted the corridors of the old Metropolitan Museum in New York City, so a father who looked upon art as a sure way to starve in a God-forsaken attic had little effect upon a son who was equally stubborn. With art as his beacon he set forth cheerfully and without misgivings. Being young, Kroll accepted the hardships enroute. He worked his way through the Art Students League, during which period he became a very proficient two-finger typist. His first teacher was John H. Twachtman. No less an artist than Winslow Homer encouraged him to continue, but there were the darker moments as well. He couldn't make the grade financially, and parental pressure finally drove him into making mechanical drawings for his brother's engineering business. For six months he stuck at it, meanwhile devoting all his spare moments to art. Eventually, and to his great joy, he won a travelling scholarship from the National Academy of Design that sent him over to Paris for two years of study with Jean Paul Laurens at the Julian Academy, and, so enthusiastically did he work, within four months he had won the Grand Prize for painting the nude.

He then came back to America, already confident in his future.

Soon he held his first one-man exhibit and a brilliant career began to get under way. His pictures began to sell, and he made many new friends, among them Speicher, Bellows, Glackens and Henri.

Kroll's work is usually gay and free, sunny and poetic, and always well balanced. Composition is the very strong virtue of Kroll as a painter. The artist is a first-rate colorist and usually sets objects under a rather high illumination, which, however, is never garish. Briefly, the artist brings to us an art of sound discipline, a painting that is grandly designed and always *soigné*.

Since 1912 Kroll has won awards with enviable frequency in all the important national exhibitions, including First Prize at the International Exhibition at the Carnegie Institute. He has taught painting in leading art schools, among them the National Academy, the Art Students League, Mills College and the Pennsylvania Academy of Fine Arts. He also lectured at various colleges, universities and the Chicago Art Institute. His pictures are owned by twenty-one museums and his murals decorate the new Justice Building in Washington, D.C., and the War Memorial Hall in Worcester, Mass. He was born in New York City in 1884.

● *The picture "My Model" was painted at Mt. Kisco during the summer of 1941. The girl, who is of Italian descent, had never posed before. She was sent to me by the village grocer who was on the lookout for possible subjects for my pictures. She impressed me with her simplicity, charm and dignity. I used a reserved color scheme to emphasize the design into which I co-ordinated forms representing the various objects, such as head, figure, drapery, rock and sky.*

Leon Kroll

MY MODEL

by Leon Kroll

painted in 1941

Oil, 28 x 37 inches

69

WALT KUHN

Walt Kuhn is another of those vital pioneering persons whose interests in art never remained within any smug realm of his own contributing. Other men's canvases—all art—are quite as absorbing to him, and away back in 1912 he helped organize the Association of American Painters and Sculptors. A year later, with the late Arthur B. Davies, he put all his energies into the planning of the Armory Show—that famed show which gave American art three constructive reactions, first shock, then food for thought, and finally a daring new impetus. It was he who rounded up Europe's moderns, such men as Van Gogh, Gauguin and Redon, and brought them to a bewildered American public.

Kuhn is a native New Yorker, born in 1880. At 19 he was already started on a career of picture-making, as a cartoonist on a San Francisco newspaper. For ten full years of a journalistic career he contributed his drawings and cartoons to magazines and newspapers all over America. Then Kuhn decided it was time to try a straight painting career. He went abroad. Holland, Germany, Spain and Italy were on his itinerary. He tried out various media—oil, water color, etching and lithography.

Back in America, he went for inspiration to that familiar world of the theater which he had known so well in his newspaper days; a world of clowns and acrobats and show girls, of grease paint and make-believe. He is a progressive and forceful artist who long ago cast aside dependence on borrowed idioms to give us forthright portrait themes of sound plastic construction.

Through the years Kuhn has given of his knowledge as an instructor to young white hopes. He has given time to devising and directing pantomimes and ballets. He has designed costumes, criticized manuscripts, sketched stage sets and acted as librettist.

In the spring of 1943 he held an exhibition of "Circus People" at the Durand-Ruel Galleries. He was for several years consultant and designer for the Union Pacific Railroad. The interiors of the club cars "Little Nugget" on the Streamliner City of Los Angeles and "Frontier Shack" on the Streamliner City of Denver, are his work, as well as some of the early planning for the famous Sun Valley resort in Idaho. His easel paintings are represented in an imposing number of collections and museums. Among the latter are the Addison Gallery, Brooklyn Museum, Denver Museum, Museum of Modern Art, Phillips Memorial Gallery, Dublin (Ireland) Museum, Columbus Gallery of Fine Arts, Detroit Institute of Arts, William Rockhill Nelson Gallery of Art and the Whitney Museum of American Art.

● *Walt Kuhn regrets very much that he is unable to comply with Encyclopaedia Britannica's request for a statement pertinent to his painting. He has made it a lifetime policy to abstain from any discussion of art, either personal or general.*

CLOWN
by Walt Kuhn
painted in 1943
Oil, 20 x 16 inches

70

YASUO KUNIYOSHI

New York atmosphere, a taste for French influence and the subtle oriental touch of his racial heritage are the unique blend which makes up the lyrical, sophisticated style of Kuniyoshi. Studies of women, restrained in color yet sensuously lovely, still lifes of un-related objects in a surrealistic arrangement, are painted from a palette of silky iridescent tones, and with a mastery of form that arouses in the beholder a powerful aesthetic reaction. With all due respect to Rudyard Kipling, East *has* met West in the person of Kuniyoshi who in his painting has shown us how fortunate such a meeting can be.

In his studies, which follow no other footprints, he starts from reality, stating the facts—then he paints from memory without the subject in view for a certain space of time, to combine reality and imagination.

Born in Okayama, Japan, in 1893, the son of a businessman, he was sent to America in 1906 to study methods of textile production. Once in Seattle, however, he honorably returned his father's money but determined to remain here to pursue art. He worked as a bus boy and fruit picker, and despite hunger and hard times managed

night classes at the Los Angeles School of Art and Design. Two years later he arrived in New York, and using as stepping stones the National Academy of Design and the Art Students League, with Kenneth Hayes Miller he set out upon a painting career. In 1925 and 1928 he travelled through France and Italy. Later, the winning of a Guggenheim Fellowship allowed him to visit Mexico and in 1931 revisit his native Japan.

Despite his thirty-eight years in America he is not permitted, be-cause of his Japanese birth, to become a citizen, but at the outset of the current war his student fellow-artists rose in accord and gave him a wholehearted vote of confidence. Among other war activities, he has painted posters for the OWI, and has written broadcasts for the Co-ordinator of Information.

He is represented in the permanent collections of the Whitney Museum, Museum of Modern Art, Columbus Museum, Brooklyn Museum, Albright Gallery, the Chicago Art Institute, Virginia Mu-seum of Arts, Santa Barbara Art Museum, Portland Museum, Phil-lips Memorial Gallery, Detroit Institute of Arts, Nebraska University Museum, Arizona University Museum and Cranbrook Academy.

● *Art is universal because people are universal. The stuff from which art is made—feeling, intuition, imagination—is a part of all people, everywhere. The roots of art are in our common human nature and great art is not something fallen from the sky, but humanity itself. I was quoted by an art critic as saying that I would dig trenches to do my share in this war. What I really said was that I would like to contribute and do everything I could as an artist, but if I were needed to dig trenches I would—and I can, too!*

Yasuo Kuniyoshi

SOMEBODY TORE MY POSTER

by Yasuo Kuniyoshi

painted in 1943

Oil, 46 x 26 inches

71

DORIS LEE

For the same reason that a bird sings—sheer joy of living—Doris Lee paints her exuberant and subtly humorous legends of the rural scene. In a sad world of too many complexities, one breathes a sigh of relief and feels free to admire, to enjoy and even to chuckle a little at the "busy" but delicious whimsy of her canvases.

Her pictures have that rarest of all gifts, charm, plus the fairy godmother gift of enthusiasm. She may sacrifice some detail of authenticity but she will replace it with a very beautiful and special kind of "imagining" which is far more satisfying.

She was born at Aledo, Illinois, in 1905 and confesses to a youthful tomboyish streak that did not always meet with parental approval. She recalls that her grandmother's hobby was woodcarving, and years ago her great-grandfather gave up farming for painting.

She attended Ferry Hall, a finishing school at Lake Forest, Illinois. Because the curriculum at Rockford College included an art course, she graduated from there in 1927.

In Rockford College she majored in philosophy rather than art and studied in Paris under Andre Lhôte. Obviously, Lhôte's abstractionist tendencies had little influence on her art. She worked at the Kansas City Art Institute under Ernest Lawson and was later a pupil of Arnold Blanch at the San Francisco School of Fine Arts.

She is good to look upon and most pleasant to talk to, and her gay, full life takes place between Woodstock, New York City and Key West, Florida. Gardening is one of her happy enthusiasms and springtime usually finds her engrossed in "growing things."

She has painted murals for the new Washington, D.C., post office and has won the Logan Prize at the Chicago Art Institute, the landscape award at the Pennsylvania Academy of Fine Arts, and other prizes. *Life*, *Vogue* and *Esquire* have all reproduced her work in color spreads. Most recent among them have been the brilliant and stimulating scenes of the current musical comedy *Oklahoma!* Her paintings hang in the Metropolitan Museum, the Art Institute of Chicago, the Rhode Island School of Design, Phillips Memorial Gallery, Washington, D.C., Buffalo Museum and others.

● *I enjoy enormously the variety of things in America and like nothing better than a leisurely sketching trip through the midwest, or the west or the south—to make many small, rough sketches of what I see, and then return to my Woodstock studio to paint pictures these sketches suggest. The pictures probably lack accurate documentation, but what one remembers is far more important, isn't it?*

Doris Lee

ARBOR DAY
by Doris Lee
painted in 1941
Oil, 22 x 34 inches

72

JULIAN LEVI

"I find it rather difficult to talk about my own painting. Briefly I am seeking an integration between what I feel and what I have learned by objective criteria; an integration between the tired, experienced eye and the childlike, simple perception." Julian Levi thus expresses his intent with the same sensitive clarity one feels in his painting.

His paintings for the most part are dedicated to the sea and those lonely beaches where fishermen work, mending their nets, careening their boats and repairing their buoys. Nostalgic scenes that evoke every memory, every smell and every sound of the sea for anyone who has come under its spell. His secondary interest is the human physiognomy, but he is suspicious of it when it represents mere beauty.

Julian Levi was born in New York City in 1900, and when he was seventeen entered the Pennsylvania Academy of Fine Arts, at a time when the academicians and the moderns had divided the academy into two hostile camps. Instinctively he sided with the latter group, mostly because they seemed more sympathetic, but later he found that his intuition had been correct for he preferred "the vigorous and progressive attitude toward life rather than adherence to outmoded form, and a turning away from life," as he expressed it.

Probably because in the early 1920s a post-war, 18th-amendment, Harding era of America was not yet ready for her own art, Levi took advantage of a Cresson Traveling Fellowship and set sail to a warm and welcoming Paris for the next four years. Later, in Philadelphia, he found that modern artists were still pariahs, accused of insanity for proclaiming Cezanne as a great and sincere artist, and in 1932 his return to New York was an exhilarating experience which brought about the final farewell to Bohemia.

Since Pearl Harbor, Levi has drafted his talents into the war effort. In 1943 *Fortune* published two color-spreads of his paintings of war psychiatry. The same year he did War Bond posters, pictorial records for the Army Air Corps Hospital at Coral Gables, Florida, and for the Medical Corps of the Navy in Norfolk, Virginia.

His paintings are represented in 14 museums, including the Metropolitan, the Whitney, and the Museum of Modern Art in New York, the Pennsylvania Academy of Fine Arts and the Albright Art Gallery in Buffalo. He works in oil, gouache, water color, silver point and lithography.

● *There was a time lag of several years between the first amorphous conception of the painting in the Barnegat Bay region and its final execution in Provincetown, Mass. Many compositional sketches intervened. The idea finally came to life early one morning on Cape Cod, when I saw a sky which gave me the clue to the movement of the whole picture. Up to that time, due to its geometrical structure, the design struck me as being too static. The rest was comparatively simple—three weeks of intense painting.*

Julian Levi

PREPARING NETS

by Julian Levi

painted in 1941

Oil, 20 x 24 inches

73

JACK LEVINE

There is a dark intensity in this moody young man whom Edith Halpert of Downtown Galleries in New York, and one of America's most-knowing appreciators and collectors of art, calls "a young Old Master." Levine is a crusader—savagely he denounces political and social systems and though the subject may lead to controversy, his painting ability leaves no room for argument. His deliberately distorted pictures are alive with nervous energy yet they never get out of hand—each one is composed into a unity, keyed to a somber palette and overlaid with brilliant flashes of color.

Jack Levine was born in Boston in 1915. He quit high school at the end of his third year, for he was already shackled with the burning desire to paint and already he was studying art under the tutelage of Denman Ross. In 1935, at the age of 20, he was subsidized by the WPA. Under this project he painted "The Feast of Pure Reason," a strong protest against "the hog at the trough" theory of government. This painting was reproduced many times in many publications and is now in the possession of the Museum of Modern Art in New York.

In 1939, when he was only 24, Levine had a one-man show at the Downtown Gallery. His paintings were scenes of Boston's South End. Plastic statements of the ugliness of life as he had seen it there —and these pictures made a profound impression on all who saw them. In 1942 the young man hit the jack-pot. His "String Quartette" won the 2nd Prize of $3,000 in the Artists' for Victory Show but, ironically enough, Levine was in the army and at the time painting had no place in his routine. Three-and-one-half years away from the thing he *had* to do. Levine rationalizes about it—he knows he is one of millions—he is willing to do his share—but can he make up for lost time? He says, "Every time I stand before Rubens' 'Queen Thomyris and Cyrus' I remember that Rubens was 56 when he painted it. It is a race against time if I am to be able to paint like that at the same age."

In the spring of 1945, Levine read in John Groth's interview with Picasso that he, Levine, had been put on the banned list of degenerate painters by the Nazi regime, and in that same spring of 1945 he won a Guggenheim Fellowship. Already he is represented in the permanent collections of many major museums—the Addison Gallery of American Art at Andover, Fogg Art Museum in Cambridge, the Portland Art Museum in Oregon, the University of Arizona in Tucson, the Metropolitan Museum, the Museum of Modern Art and many others.

● *After a lapse of three years, I am hesitant to summarize previous painting attitudes or to describe future courses. My point of departure which I myself had described as Expressionist, was in essence based on what I considered adult theater. I have never been interested in the abstract elements of painting in any "pure" sense. To me those elements were the means of presenting the human comedy or tragedy. That is, the redness of a nose was the symptom of a human condition; it was only secondarily a cog in a pictorial machine.*

Jack Levine

THE SYNDICATE

by Jack Levine

painted in 1939

Oil, 30 x 45 inches

74

L U I G I   L U C I O N I

Not for him the unfinished line, the something left unsaid—Luigi Lucioni gives us heightened realism, something more vital than a photograph. As Edward Allen Jewell puts it: "A kind of superclarity which drains every vestige of those softening qualities that seem inherent in 'atmosphere'."

Lucioni paints the American scene, particularly Vermont, with more love and realism than many a native-born artist. He once visited the Rockies but they were too austere, too remote, and back he hurried to the gentler hills of Vermont. Lucioni has achieved equal pre-eminence as a portrait painter. His flesh tones, hands and hair all testify to the qualities of old master portraiture. He lays on paint with microscopic care.

Malnate, a little town in the foothills of the Alps, in Italy, was his birthplace in 1900. When he was eleven his family came to this country and he grew up in Jersey City. At sixteen he entered Cooper Union where he studied for four years, meanwhile earning his living by doing commercial art work for an engraving house. The next five years he attended the National Academy of Design and it was as an etcher that he began his career in 1922. In 1924 the winning of a Tiffany Foundation Fellowship sent him back once again to Italy to study the Italian Primitives.

Since 1929 Lucioni has been spending his summers in Vermont and finally bought his own house in Manchester and reconstructed an old barn into a fine studio. He spends half the year there and the rest of the time in his Washington Square studio, where many amusing personalities of the world of opera and theatre drop in for friendly informal evenings of music. Disproving the legend of flaming Italian temperament, he keeps his emotions well in hand and is described as a careful, well-ordered person. He enjoys walking, reading and the companionship of dogs. He is quite a "maestro" in the art of cooking up huge batches of spaghetti.

Lucioni has taught at the Art Students League in New York. His paintings are represented in the collections of the Metropolitan and Whitney museums in New York, the Pennsylvania Academy of Fine Arts, the Atlanta Museum, Kansas City Museum, Denver Museum, Dayton Art Institute, Seattle Museum and many others. He paints slowly, his output is small but his work is popular alike with public and critics and finds a very willing market.

● *"Trees and Mountains" represents to me one of the most pleasant summers I ever spent . . . The particular spot of the painting had always fascinated me. The road was the familiar one that I went by every day and it was particularly lovely during the late afternoons. The two large trees made a striking design against the sky, and the rich pastures and meadows in the middle distance made a beautiful connecting link to Mount Mansfield beyond—the highest peak in the Green Mountains.*

Luig. Lucioni

TREES AND MOUNTAINS
by Luigi Lucioni
painted in 1936
Oil, 24 x 28 inches

75

GEORGE LUKS

The world at his door, the rugged, cheerful, commonplace world—until then considered unworthy of art which had grown very grand—was the challenge which George Luks accepted wholeheartedly and defiantly. Nor was he alone; he later discovered himself to be one of a group of "Eight"—the first artists who painted "American" and whose influence on art was to prove a vital and electrifying one.

Homer Saint-Gaudens, in his delightfully human fashion, sums him up neatly: "He lacked patience. He lacked restraint. He thrived on the ribald. There was nothing delicate about his personal or artistic stomach. He boasted, with reason, of his prize-ring prowess. He drank his share of liquor. He combined a *Hills' Rhetoric* of technical pictorial training with a love for Third Avenue art adjectives. He threw paint around with a muscular gusto, that at times produced answers of startling effectiveness, witness his portrait of Mrs. Gamley."

George Luks was born in Williamsport, Pennsylvania, in 1867, of American parentage. He commenced his education in art at the Pennsylvania Academy of Fine Arts. Later he continued his studies at Dusseldorf Academy, and in London and Paris.

Europe may have given him a patina of technical polish but there was no evidence of restraint in his complete Americanism, and he was overjoyed when the *Philadelphia Bulletin* handed him an assignment as artist-correspondent to cover the Spanish-American War. Sure enough, he was captured by the Spaniards and sentenced to death but his captors fortunately relented and sentenced him instead to return to America.

Upon his return, he accepted the job of staff artist and cartoonist for the *New York World*, and about this time began painting the goings-on of city life that had previously been let strictly alone.

One morning in 1933 George Luks was found dead in a doorway on Sixth Avenue, New York City—a tragic ending to a colorful character and a great American artist.

His paintings have been shown in all the important national and international exhibitions and have been accorded such honors as the Temple Gold Medal, the Logan Medal, the Hudnut Water Color Prize and the Corcoran Art Gallery Prize. He is represented in numerous private collections as well as in the permanent collections of many museums, among them the Metropolitan and Whitney Museums in New York, the Milwaukee Art Institute, the Detroit Institute of Arts, the Cleveland Museum and the Los Angeles Museum.

(1867–1933)

CABBY

by George Luks

painted in 1889

Oil, 27 x 22 inches

76

D A N   L U T Z

And out of the West comes a young man who has thrown away all the tired books of rules. He pays no heed to formulas. He has little interest in morals, reforms or sermons. Nor does he stoop to charm with the picturesque in any accepted or expected sense. At first glance, the untrained eye may become a bit wary but, given imagination, it will swiftly succumb to delight and stimulation.

Dan Lutz delves all the way into "Americana." Old streetcars at rest, deserted houses caught in the light of an eerie moon, interpretations of Negro spirituals, a gospel meetinghouse or a corner poolroom—these he will paint seriously, reverently or mystically, in accordance with the moods they evoke, and so honest is his own reaction that he is able to transmit it on canvas emotionally undiluted and integral. In his approach he is as direct as the Italian Primitives and as contemporary as a blues singer. He paints from within, individually, compellingly, with a disciplined resilient palette that accepts effortlessly the change from brilliant tones to somber ones.

Considering his accomplishment in the annals of contemporary American art, Lutz is surprisingly young. He was born in Decatur, Illinois, in 1906. His formal art education began at the Chicago Art Institute during the years 1928 to 1931. He wrested a B.F.A. degree from the University of Southern California, and in 1931 was awarded the James Nelson Raymond European Traveling Fellowship, which he used for study in various museums, art galleries and private collections.

Since 1932 he has been a member of the Fine Arts faculty of the University of Southern California, and became the head of the painting department there in 1938. During the latter year he was visiting instructor in figure, sketch and landscape at the Chicago Art Institute. From 1940 to 1944, he was visiting instructor at the Institute's summer school of painting at Saugatuck, Michigan. In 1944 he became instructor of landscape at the Chouinard School of Art, in Los Angeles.

Between 1933 and 1943, Dan Lutz was the winner of eleven national prizes and his work has been sought after by many museums and private collections. As for publicity and sincere critical recognition, his painting has aroused writers, reviewers and the American public, from coast to coast.

Among other galleries where the work of Lutz may be seen are the Wood Gallery, Montpelier, Vt., and the Vanderpoel Art Association in Chicago.

● *My purpose in painting is to reflect life in general and those of my own personal convictions which seem to have significance. In each picture I attempt to achieve a complete expression of the idea which I have in mind; it may be related to music, poetry or the ordinary life activity around me. "The Golden Chariot" is an expression of my emotional reaction to Negro spirituals.*

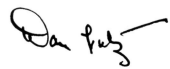

THE GOLDEN CHARIOT

by Dan Lutz

painted in 1944

Oil, 24 x 30 inches

77

HENRY LEE McFEE

McFee has no wish to reminisce on canvas but rather prefers the adventure in illusion. Yet his lush colors, brushed to exquisite textures and resolved into pictorial arrangements, are seldom beyond the realm of the visual. McFee would tell you that the resemblance is incidental. His aim is "to realize with color a plastic unit of design from the visual world." Whether he paints a still-life, a figure or landscape his approach is intellectual and the accent is on form. But always there is a fine collaboration between artistry and craftsmanship—and always there is leavening in his sensuous handling of color.

In his 36 years of painting, McFee has tried his hand at various kinds of picture making. In the early years cubism held his interest, and in this idiom few American painters have been so successful. In the 1930s, he painted a series of Negroes of Virginia. One of these, "Sleeping Black Girl," won the Temple Gold Medal and Arthur Millier said of it, "Time may even rate 'Sleeping Black Girl' the finest painting yet done on American soil, for it infuses traditional monumental grandeur with a modern feeling for the stuff of life, and its craftsmanship is superb." McFee says today, "I think in this series, and since, I have reached a body of richness and earthiness that my early work did not have."

A Missourian, born in St. Louis in 1886 of American parentage, he started out to be a surveyor but fortunately in his 21st year came into a modest inheritance which permitted him to follow his natural bent for art. He attended art classes at the Stevenson Art School in Pittsburgh in 1907 and a year later entered the summer classes of the Art Students League in Woodstock under the tutelage of Birge Harrison. He exhibited in 1912 with the Post-Impressionists at the McDowell Club in New York, and in 1916 at the Forum Exhibition.

All through the years McFee has been a consistent winner of important awards and is represented in the permanent collections of many museums, among them the Whitney Museum, Brooklyn Museum, Albright Gallery in Buffalo, Cleveland Museum of Art, the Corcoran Gallery and the Phillips Memorial Gallery in Washington, D.C.

● *My principal interest is in the* art *of painting. I endeavor with color and line to create an expressive unit of design from the things about me. Sometimes I am interested in the figure—sometimes it is the landscape that starts me working. But always the common objects about call me to make something living out of the commonplace. "Old Pine Branch" was painted in 1940 and 1941. I like the long leaf pine and the other objects I use, but my principal interest is to make an expressive canvas—a new and living unit.*

Henry Lee McFee —

OLD PINE BRANCH

by Henry Lee McFee

painted in 1941

Oil, 30 x 36 inches

78

PEPPINO MANGRAVITE

Mangravite's interest centers upon "the subtleties of human relationships, the everlasting fugitive implication between men and women," and it is with something of the psychologist's understanding that he captures these phenomena on canvas. Both as an artist and an instructor he has been termed an insurgent in art, but one remembers that America gratefully absorbed the earlier insurgents whom she viewed so apprehensively at the Armory Show in 1913.

Mangravite spends but one day on a canvas, which sounds like a staggering performance, but the rehearsal which leads up to it takes weeks of preparatory study and sketching. He works first with infinite care in gouache; he then makes a careful charcoal drawing the actual size of the canvas to be used, as a delicate outline; he matches his pigments to the tones in the gouache; he has his models all prepared and on the final day paints from sunup till sundown.

Mangravite was born on the island of Lipari, off the northern coast of Sicily, in a small penal colony for political prisoners, in 1896. His father, an Italian naval officer, was stationed there and the boy spent his impressionable childhood years in this strange environment of social exiles. They were men of intellect and they profoundly influenced his thought and character, and one of them, an artist, taught him the beginnings of a painter's craft.

His father retired in 1912 and the family moved to New York, but Mangravite returned to Europe again, to Paris and London. In 1914 he studied at Cooper Union and in 1917 entered the Art Students League with Robert Henri as instructor. During the summer Mangravite, his charming wife and two daughters live a happy outdoor life on their farm in the Adirondacks.

He has great personal charm and zest, and the true Latin's mercurial temperament. He is very positive in his opinions and believes that the gulf between the artist and the people is due to the artist's aloofness. "Not until he gets down among his fellows and tries to understand their spiritual needs can he hope to render that creative service which is his function in society."

He has executed murals for the Hempstead, Long Island, post office and the Atlantic City post office. He teaches at Cooper Union and the Art Students League in New York. His easel pictures are represented in Phillips Memorial Gallery, Corcoran Gallery, Toledo Museum, Whitney Museum and the Pennsylvania Academy of Fine Arts.

• *"Celebration" was painted in New York City in January 1944. During that month the abbey at Cassino had been destroyed; one of my relatives, a young pilot, was killed in the South Pacific; another returned from the same area with the Purple Heart. In January, no extraordinary changes were noticeable in the life of the great city—men were dying, children were being born—life went on. This picture conveys the message that whatever happens in our world nothing can destroy the creative spirit of man.*

Peppino Mangravite

CELEBRATION

by Peppino Mangravite

painted in 1944

Oil, 28 x 46 inches

79

HERMAN MARIL

It was once said of a certain painter that "he painted at the top of his lungs." By the same token one could say that Maril painted almost in a whisper—a clearly enunciated whisper that is very penetrable. Mind and mood are smoothly blended in his quiet, unspectacular scenes, that make no compromise to win easy applause. Like so many moderns, he makes use of the abstract theories, his conceptions are simplified, his color muted to a poetic minor key, still his pictures make that indelible impression that can only be made by good painting.

As far back as 1935 Olin Dows in the *American Magazine of Art* said: "Herman Maril has found himself at 26. He has digested from a number of sources a personal and subtle language that is sophisticated and simple. It is not only fluency and talent. It is a mature point of view." That same year he won first prize in the Exhibition of the Work of Maryland Artists, held at the Baltimore Museum of Art. In 1942 he was inducted into the armed forces, serving until September 1945, during which time he was able to carry on with his art only in spare time. In 1945, however, he held an exhibition of gouaches at Macbeth Gallery in New York, of which Hudson

Walker wrote, "I sense in them a new warmth in his attitude toward people; in his handling of color; and a greater sense of spatial design."

Maril was born in Baltimore, Maryland, October 13, 1908. He attended Baltimore Polytechnic Institute and Maryland Institute of Fine Arts. During the earlier years he supported himself by painting signs and show cards for department stores until he established a place for himself among the younger group of American artists. From 1935 until the outbreak of World War II, he was an instructor in painting at the Cummington School in Massachusetts.

As a muralist he decorated post offices at Alta Vista, Va., and West Scranton, Pa. His easel paintings are represented in the permanent collections of the Metropolitan Museum in New York; Phillips Memorial Gallery in Washington, D.C.; Baltimore Museum of Art; Municipal Art Society of Baltimore; Peale Museum of Baltimore; Howard University Gallery of Art, Washington, D.C.; Cone Collection, Baltimore; Crane Collection, and in other collections of Europe and America.

● *"Playing Soldier" was made (on a furlough) from a gouache which I did in "spare" time while training with a tank battalion in the state of Kentucky. The land about me attracted my interest. I felt a closer contact with interior sections of our country. I intend to develop one or two more of the sketches of that period now that I am back to civilian life, and hope to keep the spontaneity and richness of these when they become larger and more fully organized compositions.*

Herman Maril

PLAYING SOLDIER

by Herman Maril

painted in 1944

Oil, 24 x 30 inches

80

J O H N   M A R I N

Marin never pads his stories with superfluous passages. He caters to the imagination of the onlooker and refuses to hamper it with obvious and boring details. Ofttimes he repeats his joyous tales of ships and seas, of skies and trees, but always the version is new, exciting and unburdened. Nature, herself, might well approve the charming liberties he takes.

Though he is extremely proficient in oils, Marin's great love is water color—a medium which permits of no fumbling, no revision—and his mastery of it has led critics to proclaim him to be the greatest water-colorist of his time. Normally such an extravagant statement would lead to all sorts of controversial harangues, but in Marin's case there seems to be only the sweetest accord.

John Marin was born Dec. 23, 1872, in Rutherford, N.J. As a youngster the desire to paint was relentless, insistent—there were also the relentless parents, frowning on an artistic career. A carpenter, a bartender—such vocations would not have been nearly so shocking—but Marin refused to give in. The vision remained unclouded, even as his art today remains unclouded. Reluctantly, the family packed him off to art school. Two years (1898–1900) yielded neither good nor bad, but even then Thomas B. Anschutz, one of his instructors, recognized a great talent in embryo. He studied at the Pennsylvania Academy of Fine Arts and the Art Students League in New York, and in the next five years he absorbed much of the art of Europe.

It was not until 1909, via the clairvoyant vision of Alfred Stieglitz, that he found a life-long friend and champion. Stieglitz held Marin to a high level of creative distinction, whereon his achievements in more than 30 years of nonderivative expression are scarcely less than magnificent.

He has had one-man shows of sea and landscapes annually in New York since 1909—including a one-man show at the Museum of Modern Art in 1936. Marin's works are represented in many major collections, including the Metropolitan Museum, the Museum of Modern Art, the Brooklyn Museum of Art, San Francisco Museum of Art, the Phillips Memorial Gallery in Washington, D.C., and in numerous private collections.

● *To get to my picture, I must for myself insist that when finished, that is when all the parts are in place and are working, that now it has become an object and will therefore have its boundaries as definite as that the prow, the stern, the sides and bottom bound a boat. And that this my picture must not make one feel that it bursts its boundaries. The framing cannot remedy. That would be a delusion and I would have it that nothing must cut my picture off from its finalities.*

John Marin

MARIN ISLAND—SMALL POINT, MAINE

by John Marin

painted in 1931

Water color, 16 x 21 inches

81

REGINALD MARSH

Of the painters who have taken New York City for their inspiration, Reginald Marsh and John Sloan are two great names. There is a profound history of the city in their work. In the Sloan pictures, the busy animation of the street was expressed in flowing rhythmic lines and undulating but firm surfaces, while the whole texture of Marsh's painting of the city some thirty years later is pitted and pockmarked and the line is nervous and jittery. Marsh admits of one strange pattern that he repeats increasingly in his pictures. Always his lush young girls step forth with confidence, almost too assertively and then, inevitably, there will appear the shadowy uncertain figure of a tattered hobo, a hopeless cripple, or the drunk asleep in a doorway. Marsh ponders over it. In his mind it becomes a disturbing element because he cannot define the implication behind it.

Born in 1898 in an apartment over the Café du Dôme in Paris, of American parents, both of them artists, he took his first steps balancing precariously between his father's and mother's easels. During his childhood in America—for the family returned to Nutley, New Jersey, when he was two years old—he absorbed much of the conversations of Bellows, Sterner and Haskell who were prone to drop in informally at his father's studio.

It was at Yale, despite a father who warned, that he decided upon art as a career and began as a cartoonist for the Yale *Record*. Newspaper cartooning and magazine illustrations followed, with spare hours spent at the Art Students League studying under Sloan, Luks and Miller. He became interested in the theater and began "doing" sets and curtains for John Murray Anderson's *Greenwich Village Follies*.

After several trips to Europe, to look around, he returned to New York and took a studio near Kenneth Hayes Miller whose painting interests were also focused on the parks, beaches and sidewalks where New York ignores the formalities.

Concerning a show in 1941, the critics stated that Marsh had reached a high-water mark in easel painting; that he was painting with more vigor and was using a cleaner palette. He has done murals for the Post Office Building in Washington, D.C. and the Custom House in New York City. His easel pictures have been acquired by the Metropolitan Museum, Whitney Museum, Addison Gallery, University of Nebraska, Springfield Museum, the Pennsylvania Academy of Fine Arts, Lenox Art Association, Art Institute of Chicago, Hartford Athenaeum, the Boston Museum and many others.

● Regarding "Wooden Horses," I painted this on a gesso panel in egg yolk and powder color in 1936. It represents one of the fast wooden race-horse rides in George Tilyou's famous Steeplechase Park in Coney Island. Eddie Tilyou, himself a collector of American paintings, permitted me to stand and sketch this scene. I painted the picture from sketches in my studio without the use of models.

Reginald Marsh

WOODEN HORSES

by Reginald Marsh

painted in 1936

Oil, 24 x 40 inches

82

FLETCHER MARTIN

Fletcher Martin's paintings place him in a second generation of the American Naissance. He is one of those younger "re-evaluators" who have taken the trouble to penetrate the American scene to its underlying essence and instead of painting the thing seen, he interprets the experience felt.

Martin recently took this talent of his to war. As war artist correspondent for *Life* magazine he witnessed the bombing of Algiers from a hotel balcony on the water front. His thrilling paintings of the fight on Hill 609 in Tunisia gave readers an unforgettable account of the war. But his paintings were not always the brutal scenes of combat, in passing he sketched the ironic, the pathetic and sometimes humorous angles of war.

The son of an itinerant newspaper man, Martin was born in Colorado in 1904. His father began when he was 12 to teach him the printing trade, but young Martin rebelled and when he was 16 decided to face the world "on his own." He learned life the hard way but he bought a lot of memories. He worked as a harvester and lumberjack, took up boxing and became a top-notch boxer, and from 1922-26 he served a four-year enlistment in the U.S. Navy.

After that, in California, while he was working as an assistant to a mural painter, he began to take art seriously. He landed some federal mural jobs and made good. He began to win museum awards and he had one-man shows both in San Diego and Los Angeles.

His only formal art education had been a correspondence course in cartooning when he was ten years old but in 1939 this husky, slow-speaking man, whose drooping red mustachios give him a glum and sardonic expression, succeeded Grant Wood as art instructor at the University of Iowa. His theories on teaching are worth repeating; he said: "I don't believe in teaching art. It isn't something you can teach. The only thing I can do is keep students in a state of excitement about their work, to tell them the worst thing they can do is to study in the formal sense."

He paints horses, steers and cowboys with a flair that is eloquent of his years in Idaho and his love of riding, and he has an amazing knack for stopping-down action at its top speed. His work is included in private collections and several museums including the Metropolitan Museum, the Los Angeles Museum, and the Museum of Modern Art in New York.

● *This picture, "Tomorrow and Tomorrow," is a comment upon the drab, imprisoned life of the ordinary prostitute and the great sadness she must feel if she ever allows herself to think of tomorrow.*

Fletcher Martin

TOMORROW AND TOMORROW

by Fletcher Martin

painted in 1938

Oil, 48 x 30 inches

83

HENRY MATTSON

After Henry Mattson has not painted for awhile some inner conscience begins prodding and nagging, urging him back to his easel and, as he puts it with charming whimsy, "So there I stand before a fine, clean white canvas. It is impervious, it does not argue with me but I argue with myself and eventually with it. I have no plan, not a thing to go on, but I begin. So I put a stroke here, a deeper blend of color there and gradually some form takes place and I say 'Oh, yes! Maybe that's a bit of land jutting out—that looks like an angry sky up there'—thus almost subconsciously a picture insists upon its own creating."

That is Henry Mattson's mystic approach to his poetic painting. Of his seascapes—which are favorite pictorial material—he says the sea has always held for him fear, awe and fascination. He will look at it for hours, but he will paint it from memory. It is not the visual beauty he longs to convey but the sense of power, the ominous quality, the spirit and not the substance—not from the surface but from the very depths of the ocean floor, its weight, its mysterious content.

All this he explains in a soft voice which still carries the trace of his native Sweden. There is something very fine and sincere and heart-warming in this tall, gentle, blue-eyed man who does not fit into any stereotyped category of art but brings to mind another famous American master, Albert Pinkham Ryder, who long ago gave us the same mystic poetic qualities in painting.

Henry Mattson was born in Gothenburg, Sweden, in 1887. At eighteen, on this side of the Atlantic, he worked as a mechanic in Worcester, Massachusetts, and most of his earnings went to pay for his courses at the Worcester Museum. Later he went back to Sweden, but there an unimaginative professor saw little merit in his work so back to America he came for a second time. He worked as a machinist at the International Harvester Company in Chicago, devoting all his spare hours to painting. In 1916 he went for three months' study with John Carlson at Woodstock, N.Y., and there he has remained ever since.

He has done two murals for the Portland, Maine, post office and won a Guggenheim Fellowship in 1935. He is represented in the Metropolitan Museum, Whitney Museum, St. Louis Art Museum, Detroit Institute of Arts, Newark Museum, Phillips Memorial Gallery and many more, and has a picture in the White House at Washington, D.C.

● *Now about the painting "The Bayou"—I spent the last winter in Florida on the west coast, and painted a few pictures—I thought the picture looked like the bayous so I called it that. It does not represent any special place, I painted for two months on it before I succeeded in conveying my impressions of Florida on this canvas. Later I worked it out in my studio as I do all of my paintings.*

THE BAYOU

by Henry Mattson

painted in 1944

Oil, 26 x 34 inches

84

FRANK MECHAU

The furor caused in 1937 by his mural "Dangers of the Mail," painted for the Washington, D.C., post office, must in retrospect delight Frank Mechau. Historians rose in wrath at the idea of unclothed ladies being scalped by Indians who, according to the painting, had already overturned the stagecoach and had wrought considerable havoc upon the rest of the party. Irate citizens gave out interviews to the newspapers—one wag even went so far as to call it "mural turpitude." But Mechau retorted, "No artist ever cared or wished to be considered an archaeologist or an ethnologist. My intention was to create an imaginative reconstruction of a massacre."

The hullabaloo eventually subsided, but the dashing, bearded Mechau must have gloated just a little, for the bitterly disputed mural catapulted him to fame, and Edward Bruce, head of the Federal Art Project, said regarding his work, "Frank Mechau's paintings alone would have justified the entire PWA program."

Mechau is one of America's best known Western painters, and quite properly, since he lives in Colorado, horses have a way of dominating most of his canvases—but these are not the kind of horses one would find on any tour of the West, or East for that matter. These are mythical, untamed creatures, wild, imaginative and bursting with energy. They do not bear the patient, humble stamp of man's mastery. Tumultuously, yet in beautifully ordered organization, they whirl and play in an untouched world of their own. Something about them appeals to the wildness latent in all of us.

Frank Mechau was born in Wakeeney, Kansas, in 1903. He began his art studies at the University of Denver and continued at the Art Institute of Chicago. Then came Europe—Paris, Florence, Munich and the other art-fabled cities were part of his itinerary. Upon returning to America he became associated with Boardman Robinson in mural work at the Colorado Fine Arts Center. He was twice awarded Guggenheim Fellowships. As an instructor, he taught at the Colorado Fine Arts Center, the Kirkland School of Art in Denver and in his own school—the Mechau School of Modern Art. After 1939 he was head of the departments of drawing, painting and sculpture at Columbia University. In 1943 he made a 20,000-mile trip as artist-correspondent for the Army and *Life* magazine. His easel paintings are in the permanent collections of the Museum of Modern Art, the Detroit Institute of Arts and the Metropolitan Museum.

● *From the subjective angle, one man represents the multitude of men who took over the West's toughest role, the cowboy-prospector. They knew no home and rarely stayed in one place long enough to make friends. For the few who accidentally "struck it rich" to become political powers and builders of ostentatious mansions, there are thousands still working on ranches and doggedly prospecting the high ranges, eking out an existence—a wonderful group of forgotten men of Lincolnesque character.*

Frank Mechau

TOM KENNEY COMES HOME

by Frank Mechau

painted in 1943

Oil, 30 x 47 inches

85

SIGMUND MENKES

Menkes, in his gentle, unselfish manner, would rather talk about America than to make any personal observations about himself or his value as an artist. He feels very deeply that America at this time has accepted the heritage of the world's art; that it is a great honor but a graver responsibility, and that the artist and the American people alike must share the responsibility to hold the gift a precious one.

When pressed further for a more personal attitude toward art he will explain that for him there is great beauty in painting which he desires to translate into "coloristic melodies." He does not consider himself a popular painter—as one must have an ear for certain kinds of music, so it is with his kind of painting. In a one-man show at Associated American Artists in May 1944, however, he stood by and listened with grateful wonderment when enthusiastic comments, not only from critics but from a layman audience, indicated he was quite wrong.

Menkes was born in Poland in 1896, and studied at the Cracow Academy. When he was 23 years old he went to Paris and held his first successful exhibition. He did religious murals for many of Poland's old cathedrals, the restoration of old frescoes, and painted new frescoes of his own conception.

His paintings were shown in America eight years before he came here. He has a great love for America but admits that during the first three years a strange language and a different gear of living were pretty hazardous obstacles to overcome.

Recently he has been working on a series of compositions which he likes to consider as "Monuments of Our Time." The theme of these is the heroic resistance of the Polish Underground—and particularly the tragic happenings of the Warsaw ghetto.

Since his arrival in America, in 1935, he has had three one-man shows in New York. In 1941 one of his landscapes won a prize at the Corcoran Art Gallery in Washington, D.C.

Menkes was represented in the Art for Victory show and his paintings hang in the permanent collections of the Metropolitan Museum, the Museum in Wichita, Kansas, the Albright Gallery in Buffalo and the Jeu de Paume in Paris.

● *The painting "Peaches," which has become a part of the Encyclopaedia Britannica Collection, represents an example of a new conception which I have been developing in recent years. It consists of a brighter chromatic key in the creation of light through color. It also shows the fundamental constructive approach in most of my paintings. My work, being essentially abstract at the start, is becoming humanized in the process of realization through close contact with life. This, in my opinion, is the first condition of every work of art, without which a painting is nothing else but a mechanical ornament, more or less pleasing to the eye.*

Menkes

PEACHES
by Sigmund Menkes
painted in 1943
Oil, 32 x 22 inches

86

GEORGE L. K. MORRIS

His is an art of omission, simplification, and intelligible essence—it is a variety of modern art dedicated to the complexity of modern life. For many its appeal is not at first glance, but in art as in music one remembers that too often the catchy tune wears thin. Morris is a pioneer for an artistic expression attuned to the times. His results make no deprecatory compromise, but if openmindedness were permitted an "I told you so" what about the Wright brothers, Fulton, Whistler or Van Gogh?

This intensely serious, sincere artist admitted that at first it was amazing how reluctant he was to break with literal transcription—the desire to hang on to faces and objects was a strong one—but once the break was made, the sense of relief, of freedom and adventure were liberating to a rare degree. Morris, today, is preoccupied with the war. Commando raids, invasion barges, house-to-house fighting, night bombing—these subjects he has reduced to their essential drama, stripped from their forms all their superfluous details, and applied to the task all his skill in cleancut coherent plastic organization. Technically, they could be termed cerebral abstractions, but the fact is that they are full of the impact of war.

New York City in 1905 was his birthplace. When he graduated from Yale University in 1928 art was already beckoning insistently in his direction. He supplemented Yale Art School with courses at the Fontainebleau Art School, and later at the Art Students League. Between 1930 and 1934 he studied with Leger and Ozenfant in Paris, and travelled around the world.

His literary powers parallel his artistic ones, and he is the author of numerous articles. He was, in turn, editor of the *Yale Literary Magazine*, the *Miscellany*, the Museum of Modern Art *Bulletin* and *Partisan Review*. In 1944 he was teaching at the Art Students League in New York. He has exhibited in museums and galleries throughout the country as well as in London and Paris, and has had several one-man shows. He has done frescoes in private residences and has sculpted in bronze and marble.

Morris is represented in many distinguished collections and in the Berkshire Museum, Philadelphia Museum, Whitney Museum, Phillips Memorial Gallery and the Yale Gallery of Fine Arts.

● *My method began with evolving a realistic sketch of the scene—and I would then go to the other extreme and work out an abstract picture. At some point the two would begin to merge. In its early stage "House to House Fighting" was a scene in France. As it emerged from the abstract state a trapezoid would become a face, parallel lines would fall on an opened shutter, rifles or machine guns might evolve from cylinders. Chinese characters seemed to fit the design more congenially than French print in the shop signs, and many of the trapezoid-faces had become undeniably Japanese. Of itself, the scene shifted to the Orient.*

George L. K. Morris

HOUSE TO HOUSE FIGHTING
by George L. K. Morris
painted in 1943
Oil, 26 x 32 inches

87

DALE NICHOLS

"The old swimming hole; the warm dusty road we trod barefoot; the thrills of Halloween; snow battles and kid parties. It is perhaps as a subconscious yearning for a return to these happy days that I, after ten years of fighting for a place among the designers of Chicago, have turned to painting farms and the countryside."

But Dale Nichols goes right on fighting, for he is a man of theories, and a crusader to boot. He crusades for better art in advertising and commercial illustration and refuses to permit his painting career to tremble at the snobbery of academic criticism. He rebels against having to accept all the "unfounded confounded rules" and believes that art can serve its purpose in industry, and that advertising is a great educational force. "It doesn't matter whether one is designing waste baskets or murals, the same sort of satisfaction will accrue to the artist if he has made his work be true to himself."

In 1935 he was able to prove his credo and furnish a delightful "I told you so" to the scoffers when his "End of the Hunt" took first prize in a contest of several thousand middle-west painters, sponsored by the Art Institute of Chicago. Grant Wood was one of the three judges, and later the painting was purchased by the Metro-

politan Museum in New York. The magazine *Coronet* describes him as a champion of beauty who deplores modern concentration on back-alley scenes.

He was born on his father's grain and livestock farm in Nebraska in 1904. His mother first noticed he had a knack for drawing things when he was four years old, but there wasn't time on a farm to pay much attention to it. At school, his teachers encouraged him and by the time he was nineteen his mind was made up. He went to Chicago and studied at the Academy of Fine Arts and later at the Art Institute, meanwhile making layouts for a calendar concern.

Nichols works in water color, pen and ink and oils, changing mediums with equal mastery and winning honors in all. He has lectured at the University of Illinois as Carnegie Visiting Professor of Art and was at one time a member of the *Chicago Tribune* art staff. He holds frequent one-man shows and his paintings are owned by the University of Illinois, the Art Institute of Chicago and the Metropolitan Museum in New York. In recent years Nichols has divided his time between his "rancho" in Arizona, his beloved Nebraska, Alaska and Mexico.

● *Axle grease is a boon to the farmer, for it permits him to store his machinery in a snowbank. A generous application of axle grease to the machine's perishable metal parts will keep it free of rust in any weather. Of course, the paint peels off, and the wooden parts crack. But who cares? A farmer buys a corn harvester for the sole purpose of harvesting corn. Only an artist would think of the danged thing as an ornament.*

Dale Nichols

WINTER STORAGE

by Dale Nichols

painted in 1945

Oil, 30 x 40 inches

88

GEORGIA O'KEEFFE

The better to intensify their mysterious beauty, her flowers are prodigious. The better to evoke living creatures she will paint their bones—the underlying structure of their being. Landscapes she will abstract to an unforgettable essence. Her language is exotic but uncluttered, and in it there is no hint of collaboration with any other paint language.

O'Keeffe would feel no offense if one called her a "woman painter." She would know that her painting is "Woman"—tender, subtle and sensory, on more intimate terms with Nature than man could ever be.

In Texas years ago—away back in 1916—a very young O'Keeffe who had struggled with all the rules of art and already had turned her back on illustrating and advertising commissions, began to put down things in her own way. She sent these sketches to an intimate friend, Anna Pollitzer, with the admonition that they were not to be shown to anyone. But Anna Pollitzer thought otherwise and took them to Alfred Stieglitz who recognized the vital, the new and uninhibited in these sketches. He said, "Finally, a woman on paper."

Later, on Dec. 11, 1924, Georgia and Stieglitz were married, and through the years Stieglitz has stood guard over the destiny of O'Keeffe. His genius for steering art safely through uncharted seas has been like a bulwark, keeping her free, direct—a pure artist.

Georgia O'Keeffe was born Nov. 15, 1887, at Sun Prairie, Wisconsin, of an Irish father and a Hungarian mother. At ten years of age she copied flowers and announced serenely that she would one day be an artist. As a youngster she attended convent school. After courses at the Art Institute in Chicago she continued on to the Art Students League in New York, where William Merritt Chase and F. Luis Mora were instructing. Years later she was awarded the Chase Scholarship there. For a time in Chicago she worked as a free-lance commercial artist. These were the years of struggle—breaking with the teaching of others, even teaching art herself—always seeking her own way of expressing.

Finally, in Texas, she began to draw and sketch—obeying some insistent formula of her own. These were the sketches which, in the hands of Anna Pollitzer and Alfred Stieglitz, began the true career of Georgia O'Keeffe. In 1939 she was chosen as one of the 12 most outstanding women of the past 50 years at the New York World's Fair.

Today her paintings are represented in the permanent collections of the Art Institute of Chicago, the Phillips Memorial Gallery, the Museum of Art in Brooklyn, N.Y., the Cleveland Museum of Art, and in the Whitney Museum, the Museum of Modern Art and the Metropolitan Museum in New York City and many more. In 1943 O'Keeffe was given a retrospective exhibition at the Art Institute of Chicago.

● *I found that I could say things with color and shapes that I couldn't say in any other way—things that I had no words for.*

Georgia O'Keeffe —

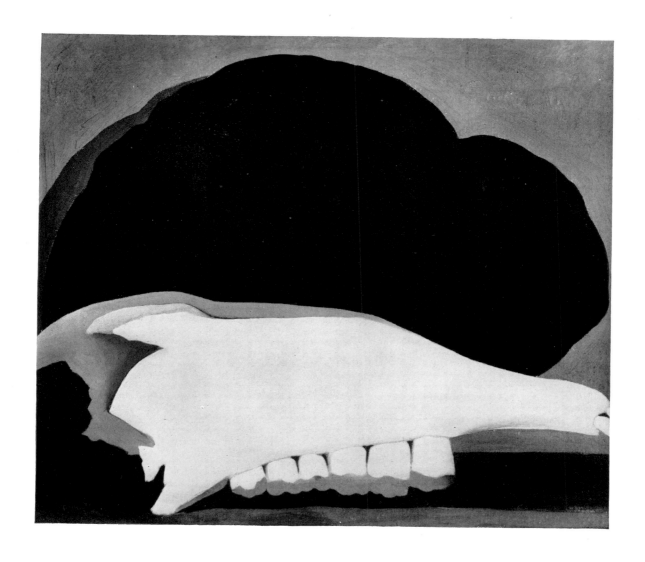

JAWBONE AND FUNGUS

by Georgia O'Keeffe

painted in 1933

Oil, 17 x 20 inches

89

W I L L I A M   C .   P A L M E R

His is no story of empyrean temperament scaling the heights with roughshod and undisciplined insistence; it is instead the more human story of the boy without expansive ego, who got there by steady and quiet endurance.

It was the depression of 1929 that shaped Palmer's career. At that time he was doing very nicely with his interior decorating for the top-drawer set of Park Avenue, when one fatal day in October his wealthy client returned from a panicked Wall Street without money enough to pay any bill. Discouraged and almost broke, Palmer went home to Iowa and later to Canada. He turned once again to art. He painted and studied constantly and four years later, in 1933, he had his first one-man show at the Midtown Gallery.

Palmer was born in Des Moines, Iowa, in 1906. In 1924 he came to New York and enrolled in the Art Students League and then he really began to wrestle with Fate. He wasn't good enough for Frank Bridgman's life class so he changed to figure drawing with Boardman Robinson and later with Kenneth Hayes Miller. He was shy and self-effacing, the least promising of pupils, and the most comforting advice he could get from each instructor was a dubious "work-like-the-devil" formula. He did, too, and with each new season he conquered timidity and discouragement. Later he went to the École des Beaux Arts de Fontainebleau and studied fresco painting with Paul Baudouin.

In 1933 he worked for the PWA project, and murals became his first claim to fame. In 1936 he painted fourteen panels for the Queens General Hospital in New York depicting the development of medicine. He did mural decorations for the new Post Office in Arlington, Massachusetts, and the Post Office Building in Washington, D.C. In his easel paintings, which are owned by many museums, his chief concern is with the stormier aspects of Nature, of wind-swept clouds creating forms almost mystically dramatic.

In 1944 he was on leave as director of the Munson-Williams-Proctor Institute School of Art, in Utica, New York, serving in the armed forces.

● *Painting to me is not the development of a message or a technique—it is the art of painting which interests me. "Fish Story" was developed from sketches and drawings made at my summer home on the northern shore of Lake Ontario in Canada. My work has been called Romantic—this, I presume, is such a Romantic picture. However, it is not a concoction, but is something which I had seen and experienced. The dynamic movement of the forms presented moved me to paint the canvas. I really am interested in producing paintings which have substance, integrity, and which through time continue to interest the spectator. All I ask is that the paintings be enjoyed and that the spectator realize that there is a beautiful art of painting which has a great tradition behind it.*

William C Palmer

FISH STORY

by William C. Palmer

painted in 1939

Oil, 30 x 36 inches

90

WALDO PEIRCE

The trouble with Peirce is that the man in him dominates the artist, and no matter what writer or critic starts out with an analysis of his work, sooner or later the Peirce personality becomes the subject with even greater enthusiasm. Perhaps it is because his art mirrors his spirit so perfectly. A paragraph of Harry Salpeter's is still worth repeating. He says, "To look at a roomful of Peirce's paintings is a physically exhilarating experience. It may be winter outside but it's spring and summer indoors. His are not studio paintings. They should be hung on the branches of trees. They are liberating and unashamed. They say that it's good to be alive."

Peirce, who looks like a genial, bearded giant, was born in Bangor, Maine, in 1884. Young Peirce was sent to Harvard to be "gentled," but the Harvard culture had little conventionalizing effect. His talents for literature and art were eclipsed by his flair for football and conversation. The latter has ever flowed freely. Elizabethan and robust in tenor, an unmitigated joy to all but the left-over Victorians, if there are any.

He studied for a while at the Art Students League in New York and then went abroad to the Julian Academy. He journeyed to Spain, and with the Spanish painter Zuloaga worked in an old church which had been transformed into a studio. He absorbed Goya and Matisse and later a certain Renoiresque feeling began to appear in his canvases. During World War I he enlisted in the ambulance corps of the French forces. After the war he returned to Spain and further travel with his good friend Ernest Hemingway.

After more than twenty turbulent years of adventuring and misadventuring, painting and wandering, Peirce came home to America. He had married for the third time, and his young and pretty wife Alzira, his three young children, especially the twins, were beloved material for his many paintings of family life.

He found in them all the inspiration he needed: he began growing roots in his own country and with this new phase Peirce acquired a new and tender depth in his art. He is included in the permanent collections of many important museums, including the Metropolitan, the Addison Gallery of American Art, the Pennsylvania Academy of Fine Arts, Brooklyn Museum and the Whitney.

● *"Alzira and Anna" was painted from a one-minute drawing of Anna in a tub in the farm kitchen . . . . Alzira knelt down to dry her off. In case of doubt I always am inclined to put in the Maine background or shore—preferring a living sea to a blank wall—I don't mind a good kitchen wall though. In this picture I think I let the tide come in and go out several times before I quit . . . painting in the rocks and then covering them with ocean again. I enjoy painting my kids for they insist upon keeping on living and moving instead of assuming the rigor mortis of studio models . . . it's like shooting wild duck sometimes . . . or at them . . . I never shoot ducks myself, or anything except with a paint brush.*

Waldo Peirce

ALZIRA AND ANNA
by Waldo Peirce
painted in 1940
Oil, 43 x 31 inches

ROBERT PHILIPP

"Painting is a distressing profession—it's a bit like having a temperamental mistress whom you love and hate at the same time. I suppose, for the most part I would be called a figure painter with a leaning toward the romantic, but once in a while I have to paint a brutal or ugly picture—have to get it out of my system—otherwise there is the danger of getting in a rut, of painting potboilers."

There seems little danger of Robert Philipp's falling into any rut; he is far too versatile. In 1941, at Associated American Artists, he held an exhibition of twenty-five paintings of the American scene. Before that he had gone to Hollywood to execute portraits of movie stars and social notables. He has had portfolios of paintings reproduced in color spreads in *Life*, *Esquire* and the *Magazine of Art*. One critic says of him: "It has been characteristic of Philipp not to be satisfied with a formula, however effective. Rather, he has continued to enlarge his technical scope and widen his aesthetic horizon. His fluent brushwork, richness of texture, and beauty of pattern are sustained by sound drawing, firm structural design and unfailing tact in the use of color."

Philipp was born in New York in 1895. As a boy he absorbed a musical comedy atmosphere under the influence of his father and uncle who, working together, produced such hits as *Alma, Where Do You Live?* and *The Midnight Girl*. Philipp discovered that he possessed an excellent tenor voice and for a while considered a singing career. He toured with the road company of the *Student Prince* but, although he met with a favorable reception, turned once again to art. He wonders, however, where the musical career might have led him. He studied for four years at the Art Students League under DuMond and Bridgman and for another two years at the Academy School. He traveled in Europe but did not study there. Henry McBride, the noted art critic, mentions Philipp as one of America's six best painters.

Philipp and his petite and attractive wife, who is also his favorite model, live in a Manhattan penthouse. She plays the piano and writes songs and is now completing a play that the Shuberts plan to produce. Philipp has been a repeated award winner and his pictures are included in the permanent collections of the Brooklyn Museum, the Whitney Museum, the Museum of Fine Arts in Houston, Texas, and in innumerable private collections.

● *There are all sorts of ways of getting inspiration. Some have to starve, some over-eat. I happened to have slipped my shoes off in the box, feeling delightfully comfortable, and looking perfectly respectable from the waist up. The theatre was the Henry Miller. The play—"Harriet." The star—Helen Hayes. The inspirational idea came to me in the last act which really was a corker in color and lighting effects.*

HARRIET
by Robert Philipp
painted in 1944
Oil, 25 x 30 inches

92

HORACE PIPPIN

In the procession of down-to-earth painting, Horace Pippin deserves a very special niche. Considered the first important Negro painter to appear on the American scene, he has a fresh insight into Nature and tells about it in a language all his own. It is a language of homely poetry with the charm, simplicity and sincerity of all authentic folk art. One looks in vain for any characteristic technique, color or composition of any old or modern master. He says "Pictures just come to my mind and then I tell my heart to go ahead." He loves to paint, and he paints the things he loves. He's been doing it for 40 years without benefit of any formal painting knowledge. Praise to Lincoln, hymns of honor, the charm of southern plantation life, flowers and lace—in each instance he selects a special color harmony to tell the story, from a riot of reds and purples and yellows to a symphony in white, black and gray.

Originally considered a Primitive painter, his growing sophistication has gradually eliminated that label. His work remains completely uninhibited, free, fanciful and delightfully individual, but with no loss of charm he has added a fine sense of design, the quiet aware-ness of aesthetic principle, and the growth of his own personality.

Horace Pippin was born in West Chester, Pennsylvania, in 1888. At an early age he moved to Goshen, New York. There he attended public school and supported himself doing odd jobs. He worked as a junk dealer, iron moulder and hotel porter.

During World War I, a bullet hit Pippin in the right shoulder. Since then he has not had the ability to lift his right arm to a horizontal position. Consequently, he has to push his painting arm along by means of his left hand. Even this handicap could not kill his love for painting—he kept on for years, satisfying his tremendous inner urge, and it was not until 1937, at the Chester County Art Association's exhibition, that he was discovered.

Since that time he has had several one-man shows throughout the country. His paintings in full-color reproduction have been reproduced in *Life*, *Time* and *The New Yorker*. He is represented in the permanent collections of the Pennsylvania Academy of Fine Arts, Albright Art Gallery, Philadelphia Museum, Phillips Memorial Gallery, Whitney Museum and Rhode Island Museum.

● *I do not know what to say in regards to my painting. Sometimes I think I'll never know painting for there is so much to know. "Holy Mountain" came to my mind because the whole world is in such trouble, and in reading the Bible (Isaiah XI 6) it says that there will be peace in the land. If a man knows nothing but hard times he will paint them, for he must be true to himself, but even that man may have a dream, an ideal—and "Holy Mountain" is my answer to such dreaming.*

H. Pippin

THE HOLY MOUNTAIN
by Horace Pippin
painted in 1944
Oil, 30 x 36 inches

93

HOBSON PITTMAN

There is a mysterious quality in Hobson Pittman's dreamy interiors that gives one a little guilty feeling of being an intruder gazing uninvited on someone's intimate premises. One reviewer says, "Hobson Pittman is the poet-painter of the empty room. His profoundly felt and hauntingly brushed interiors—lighted from without by moon or sun and from within by lamp and moon as conspiring protagonists—vibrate with news of the presence that is withheld. There is a sense of immanence . . . that would be understood at once by men such as Maeterlinck and Poe, Debussy and Albert Ryder."

Most of his scenes are at eye-level or below, to further the illusion of intimacy—of looking *into*. The shapes of the objects are subtly placed to permit exquisite structural organization and his palette diffuses to tones of luminous reflections.

Pittman was born on a farm near Tarboro, North Carolina, in 1900. When he was ten the family moved to Tarboro, into a large rambling post-Civil War house with high ceilings and long windows opening onto spacious verandas and filled with fascinating Victorian *objets d'art*. All the houses he visited were similar in type and, as his canvases attest, all of them made a profound impression on the boy who was later to paint them with such nostalgic tenderness.

When he was 14 he began his formal art education in the private classes of Miss Molly Rouse in Tarboro. There he studied for four years, and to Miss Molly's teachings he still looks back with fondness and gratitude—she introduced him to great painting. Later he attended Pennsylvania State College, the Carnegie Institute of Technology and Columbia University. From 1928 to 1935 he made several trips abroad, absorbing art in all the great museums—and museums he considers the greatest teachers of all. Though he is a prodigious painter he finds time to teach, and there again he proves his greatness. He rarely permits students to see his work lest their own individuality be influenced. Most of his freshness of outlook he owes to their eager, enthusiastic, and always searching questions. He teaches at the Pennsylvania State College and at the Friends' Central Country Day School in Overbrook, Pennsylvania.

Pittman has won many coveted awards and honors, and is represented in various private collections and in 11 major museums, including the Metropolitan Museum, Whitney Museum, Pennsylvania Academy of Fine Arts, and the Phillips Memorial Gallery.

● *The painting "The Studio" was developed from the Attic Scene of* La Boheme. *There is a smaller painting of the same subject which was done after seeing the opera, but less intricate than this canvas. This scene has always impressed me with its brooding light and desolate atmosphere, and finally, after seeing it a number of times, the painting was started. This larger version has any number of changes and additions such as the table with still-life arrangement, the open door with seated figure and the transparent blue curtain.*

Hobson Pittman

STUDIO INTERIOR

by Hobson Pittman

painted in 1940

Oil, 30 x 40 inches

94

HENRY V. POOR

That unequivocal thing called quality is the very essence of the painting of Henry V. Poor. This man looms a large figure in the world of contemporary American painting—an unbiased participant who chooses to record the variety of things that interest him, in beautifully composed and dignified paint language.

With rare simplicity he says, "I used to be full of paint philosophies. Now I just believe in painting. What you see with your eyes is rich and varied and beautiful to the point of heartbreak, and in your medium of paint you try to create something whole and perfect in this image, partaking of the beauty of the world you see and know."

Poor stems from a pioneering family—Kansas in 1888 was his birthplace. There he learned to fish and hunt and ride and grew up in a friendly world of loving relatives. His aptitude for art manifested itself at an early age and even in grade school he was the outstanding blackboard artist. During high school years drawing was taboo—by parental edict—"It wasted too much time." But during his sophomore year at Stanford University he decided to major in art, meanwhile supporting himself in an astonishing variety of odd jobs. After college came a year at the Slade School in London, studying with Richard Seckert, and later in Paris where the revolutionary painting of Cézanne, Matisse, Gaugin and Picasso furnished him a brilliant guiding star. Back in America he taught art at Stanford, did his part in World War I, had a one-man show, and then for ten years perfected himself in the more remunerative career of ceramist: this being a question of economics. Nine years later, in 1929, he returned to his easel painting and it was in 1937 that Edward Alden Jewell, in commenting upon his one-man show said, he "would pit Henry V. Poor against any living artist anywhere!" In addition to his enviable reputation as easel painter and potter, Poor has also distinguished himself for his fresco works—among them a series of 12 panels for the Justice Department building in Washington, D.C. His easel paintings are represented in an impressive list of museums—the Whitney and Metropolitan in New York, Addison Gallery, Cleveland Museum—and in many of the more important private collections.

● *What you see and understand imposes itself on you, and you impose on it your particular sensibility, your will, your concept of perfection and the personal instinct of your eye and hand, and out of this conflict or this accord comes a painting—a portrait or landscape or still-life—which is a reflection, an interpretation of life, but has its own life. A slender girl, full of intelligence and the moodiness of a creative person, standing, with her pallid skin slightly contrasted with a white shirt against a slightly less lighted ground. These relations of such similar light surfaces are what you might call the theme of this portrait.*

Henry V. Poor

CARSON McCULLERS

by Henry V. Poor

painted in 1944

Oil, 36 x 24 inches

95

A B R A H A M   R A T T N E R

Rattner's mystical, symbolic and geometric compositions are usually based on the human dilemma—the conflict between spiritual ideals and material desires. A rebel against the academic mandates, he prefers to evoke emotion rather than to baldly state a fact. He explains feelingly "Here on this earth in our time, in order to paint beauty one would have to maintain a degree of complacency utterly incompatible with the ugly and unbeautiful manifestations that are taking place. The emotions aroused by the unbeautiful must find expression. They are the goings-on within the soul of the artist, and when projected in crystallized form become plastic representations of his emotional and spiritual complexes." In a painting, Rattner says, the elements such as line, color, shapes, etc., are the realities with which the artist must build, rather than with the reality of an object in nature.

Abraham Rattner was born in Poughkeepsie, New York, in 1895. His love for drawing and painting led him to abandon his architectural studies at George Washington University and to enter the Corcoran School of Art. He was awarded a scholarship to study at the Pennsylvania Academy of Fine Arts. His studies there were interrupted by the outbreak of World War I. He served in the first American camouflage unit to go overseas, and took part in three major engagements.

After the war he returned to the Pennsylvania Academy to continue his art studies. He won a scholarship for study abroad, and in 1920 went to Europe. In Paris he studied at the École des Beaux Arts and at the Ransom Academy. He returned once more to the United States when World War II swept across Europe in 1939.

Rattner's work was exhibited in Brussels, Paris and London, and was hung in the Musée de l'Orangerie in Paris and the Musée de Grenoble, being purchased by the French government. He is also represented in important private collections in Europe. In America he has exhibited in New York, Chicago, New Orleans, San Francisco, Los Angeles, Santa Barbara, Dartmouth University and Philadelphia. His canvases are owned by the Museum of Modern Art, the Phillips Memorial Gallery, the Pennsylvania Academy of Fine Arts and by numerous private collectors.

● *Within—on the inside—not what the eye sees on the outside—nor measured: the interior the reality, of all things and men. A window. Fruit. A woman reading a newspaper—objects—appearances of little importance—analogies incidental to the symphony form of an invisible interior because to the painter, color, line, shape, measure, texture, the oblique, vertical or horizontal, etc., are as real as bricks and mortar to the builder. Out of these are formed his equivalent for sacrificed appearances seen by the eye on the outside of things to build his world of the interior for all men.*

Rattner

INTERIOR

by Abraham Rattner

painted in 1944

Oil, 20 x 26 inches

96

ETIENNE RET

He has a way with paint much as a poet has with words, and, like good poetry, each turn of his fancy charms by surprising. As though his mind were swept clear of all immediate events and influences, Etienne Ret abides in a timeless dream world—a world heedless of reality. It is as though he alone had caught some fragment of its song and improvised upon it in his own way. Mystery, poetry and flights of the imagination abound there, oblivious of any conventional standards imposed upon the artist.

The way Etienne Ret does this—the tools he employs, both of the intellect and the painter's craft, his method of organizing a canvas, his imaginative weaving of opalescent color and his exquisite taste—beguiles the eye and frees the imagination. Since his technique is entirely personal and has never been a matter of mechanics, nobody else is apt to produce paintings such as his.

Etienne Ret was born in Bourbonnais, France, in 1900. His childhood home was the famous house of Savigny-sur-Orge, where the Vicomte de Chateaubriand wrote *Mémoires d'outre-tombe*. He attended the College of Mesnieres. His family had hoped that the boy might be interested in farming but after completing his military service in 1924 he entered the *atelier* of Maurice Denis and Georges Desvallieres, the latter of whom, in company with Georges Roualt and Henry Matisse, had been a pupil of Gustave Moreau. Desvallieres was a muralist, so that it was on a ladder that Etienne Ret learned to paint. He was also influenced in his vision of art by the poet Max Jacob, whom he met in Brittany. He also studied at the Beaux Arts School and at the École des Arts Decoratifs in Paris.

In 1929 Ret published his own book of poems, *Blindman's Bluff*; he won the Florence Blumenthal prize and did the scenery for a new presentation of *La Damnation de Faust* at the Paris Opera. Later, he exhibited in London and Paris. He visited Tunis and Algeria and made pictures of the natives. He studied El Greco in Toledo, Goya in Madrid, Memling in Bruges and Brueghel in Antwerp. Since 1934 he has been living in southern California, becoming an American citizen in 1940. The rare quality of his work has been constantly enriching the thriving, vital art of the Pacific coast. He is represented in many collections, both in France and America.

● *Long ago, as a young apprentice, I moulded iron in the flame of the forge; and as a gardener I knew flowers and trees by their first names. Perhaps I have kept the love of manual labor, of clarity and of simple things. Does not every artist cry "Simpler, simpler! Clearer, clearer!" . . . Chardin and Renoir . . . The pursuit of light . . . With the colors of earth to create the sky and capture the fragility of the flesh . . . As the angel of Reims smiles* la joie de vivre *with a frank heart and without egoism, the true artist sings of the love of daily things which a long time ago began to build the eternal reality. This I have tried to do in "Came Rosy-Fingered Dawn."*

Etienne Ret

CAME ROSY-FINGERED DAWN

by Etienne Ret

painted in 1942

Oil, 29 x 23 inches

97

UMBERTO ROMANO

Since 1928, when Umberto Romano's work first appeared in American exhibitions, he has been considered one of the foremost modernists in figure painting. His work may be divided into three periods. In the period 1928–33 his work was strongly influenced by the style and technique of the Italian Primitives. In the second period, 1933–40, critics have said that his work showed a kinship with the Renaissance painters. In the present period, after 1940, Romano has achieved a highly personal art expression. He expresses with great emotional impact the intensities of life. In this way his work belongs to the tradition of the great humanists, such as Rembrandt, Goya, Daumier and Roualt. One is moved by the almost savage-like treatment of pigment and the use of somber, haunting color, combined with an underlying sensitivity.

In the field of portraiture he holds an important position. He has painted many notable portraits of socially prominent people, among them Sara Delano Roosevelt, whose portrait was accepted by President Roosevelt for the collection of the Hyde Park library.

Romano was born in Bracigliano, Italy, in 1905 and came to the United States in 1914. His art education included four years of study at the National Academy of Design. He received the Pulitzer Prize in 1926 and travelled for a year in Italy, studying the methods and techniques of the Primitive and Renaissance painters, making his headquarters at the American Academy in Rome.

For six years, from 1934 to 1940, Romano was head of the art school of the Worcester Art Museum. In 1933 he established the Romano School of Art in Gloucester, Massachusetts, and the unique Gallery-on-the-Moors, where the classes were conducted, became the mecca for advanced students of figure, portrait and landscape painting.

Romano has been the recipient of many awards and honors, including the Peabody Prize of the Art Institute of Chicago, the Crowninshield Award, the Tiffany Foundation Medal, the Atheneum Prize, and others. Among the many collections in which his works hang are the Worcester Art Museum, Rhode Island School of Design, Fogg Art Museum, Smith College Museum, Springfield (Mass.) Art Museum, the Addison Gallery, and many private collections.

● *I have always wanted to paint the "Knockout." The crowds at a prize fight—the hot, harsh, glaring lights, the heavy blue smoke— the yells, the jeers and the tense restlessness of thousands of people. People of different races, of different nationalities, of different status. I have been stirred, moved, aroused by the hot, sensuous light on human bodies in the ring, by the powerful savagery of two taut, brutal forces in combat, by two violent bodies—at times human, at times animalistic, prancing, pacing, calculating, waiting, waiting for that one great climactic moment, the opening for that punch, that terrific, murderous punch—the Knockout!*

THE KNOCKOUT

by Umberto Romano

painted in 1944

Oil, 31 x 38 inches

98

I V E R   R O S E

As though he knew some secret formula for melting light rays and blending them with his palette tones, Iver Rose's paintings are aquiver with a new kind of excitement. In these paintings light and color spill freely over contours—ofttimes blurring forms but always translating them to a more eloquent interpretation. This is a man who really paints the sound of things and the feel of things. It is emotional painting which must jolt even tired critics from their routine summarizing—and which permits ordinary folks like you and me "to let ourselves go" in sheer enjoyment.

Rose says of his credo, "I believe that the understanding and application of the abstract in painting is all-important but I do not believe in making abstraction a conclusion in itself as the abstractionists and non-objectivists are doing in spite of their protestations to the contrary, for what they are accomplishing is the creation of a modern academy that has within it the same germ of stagnation as the past and present academies had and still are afflicted with, nor do I believe in making the abstract elements so obvious that one's work becomes a blueprint of 'How to paint a picture'—rather I hold instead that the abstract should be a method of approach toward the beautiful." His painting attests the sincerity of this credo.

Iver Rose was born in Chicago, Illinois, in 1899. There he studied at the Chicago Art Institute night school and Hull House art classes. Between the ages of 19 and 29 he did free-lance illustration and layouts. In 1929 he chucked all commercial work overboard and soon became the perennial artist.

He says, "My little savings seemed to be in constant flight . . . I lived in lofts, holes and shacks . . . became intimately acquainted with eviction laws and the cheapest grease joints . . . I was sustained by a keen desire to paint and a mirth that well matched my girth . . . the girth stood me in good stead for I could go on long, forced diets without harm to myself . . . I tipped the scale at 300, more or less, and it wasn't all muscle."

His first easel painting was completed in January 1930 and since then he has had four one-man shows. He has been represented in numerous national and international exhibitions throughout the United States, and is permanently represented in the Andover Museum, Cranbrook Museum, American Academy of Arts and Letters and in a number of private collections.

● *"Sharp Drummer"—you saw him at high-hat balls in Harlem, you saw him at juke-box hangouts and jitterbug halls—he was there whether you saw him or not. He was there low, high and sharp—he swung in rhythm from a deep purple beat to a high brassy yellow —he was sure sharp.*

SHARP DRUMMER

by Iver Rose

painted in 1944

Oil, 22 x 30 inches

99

S A M U E L   R O S E N B E R G

One of Pittsburgh's foremost artists is Samuel Rosenberg; and of Pittsburgh, where he has spent most of his life, he says, "Its very ugliness is beautiful. When I go to the Hill district I come home with my head full of ideas for paintings: the rivers, the people, the houses perched at precarious angles on the hills, the whole covered with the smoke of the steel mills making opalescent lights and transparent blacks, laying color over color, letting each one play its part in the final mood."

When asked which of his paintings he liked best, he said, "Always the one I am working on. This time I will surpass anything I've ever painted!" Which is reason enough for his work to continue to grow. He never stays within boundary lines. He is never afraid to experiment, but always there is continuity in the change. He is a mature artist who handles social comments without indulging in soap-box posturings.

Born in Philadelphia in 1896, his family moved to Pittsburgh when he was 11 years old. He studied at the Carnegie Institute of Technology, and later for a year at the National Academy of Design. He began to exhibit his work at the Associated Artists of Pittsburgh when he was 17, and at 21 was given Second Honor. He continued

winning every award offered by the Association as well as the Carnegie Prize in 1935. He has shown in national exhibitions at the Corcoran Gallery, Pennsylvania Academy of Fine Arts, Whitney Museum, Chicago Art Institute, Butler Art Institute, Museum of Modern Art, the Albright Gallery, the Golden Gate Exposition and many others.

Not only is Rosenberg a creative artist, but he contributes greatly to the training of others. In 1917 he founded the art school of the Irene Kaufmann Settlement, and in 1944, besides being its director, was also assistant professor at Carnegie Institute of Technology, director of art at the Pennsylvania College for Women, and director of art at the Pittsburgh Y.M.H.A. and Y.W.H.A. Since his teaching is adequately remunerative, he has never tried to live by the sale of paintings, which has kept him free in every sense of the word.

Since 1940 Rosenberg's interest has been a gradual development toward abstraction—using great saturation of color and aiming at the expression of an emotional release. His continual research has made him an acknowledged authority on the use of tempera. His art is democratic, substantial and honest, and his subjects he finds within his own environs.

● *In "Out in the Night" I have used the wall as a symbol of the barrier, physical or spiritual, which exists among us humans. In this case, the barrier shuts the family out, forcing the group to travel in space, searching for an opening which will let it in to home and comfort and warmth. As is my custom, I have allowed the mood to dictate to me the technique, the color and the composition.*

Samuel Rosenberg

OUT IN THE NIGHT
by Samuel Rosenberg
painted in 1944
Oil, 20 x 24 inches

100

DORIS ROSENTHAL

The much discussed good neighbor policy finds a sincere and sensitive exponent in the art of Doris Rosenthal, who brings to America all the intimate charm of Mexico, and to Mexico the compliment of finding within her populace the most fascinating pictorial material. Not that they are in the least like travel posters, but these Rosenthal canvases make you yearn to see the country. They give you Old Mexico, its color, its people and children and landscape with intriguing intimacy. More of an explorer than a tourist, Doris Rosenthal goes beyond the beaten path for her material and catches the still unexploited spirit of Mexico. Her husband, in describing her activities there, remarked, "I see her dousing herself with mosquito spray and rushing into far places no American has gone before. Doris wouldn't do it any other way."

Born in California, Miss Rosenthal graduated from the Los Angeles State Teachers College and Columbia University. Her art training took place at the Art Students League where her instructors were such men as Bellows and Sloan. Later she made an extensive tour of Europe before beginning her own teaching career at Teachers· College and the James Monroe High School, both in New York City.

Her first trip to Mexico, made possible by the winning of a Guggenheim Fellowship, was followed by a second trip when the fellowship was renewed. Again, in 1940, she made a third expedition. When not pioneering in Mexico, Miss Rosenthal lives in New York with her producer-playwright husband Jack Charash.

An earlier period of her art was devoted to painting the sleek, sinewy stevedores of Louisiana's levees. Another period she concentrated on "back stage and theater scenes" and her husband, who is very proud of her work, hopes that one day she will go back to the theater period. In discussing art, Miss Rosenthal resents the ever-qualifying expression "woman artist." She believes that art is either good or bad and never male or female which seems a perfectly reasonable and legitimate statement.

She has had one-man shows at the Baltimore Museum of Art, the Slater Museum, the New York Galleries and at Teachers College. In 1932 she was included in "Fifty Prints of the Year," and in 1935 was awarded the first lithograph prize at the Western Print Makers Exhibition in Seattle. Her painting "Sacred Music " is owned by the Metropolitan Museum in New York.

• *The Tarascan girl in the center of the picture lived in Patzcuaro. I had been on a two-weeks' burro trip into the state of Michoacan with a party of ten Mexicans. The dress of the Tarascan Indian women is quite beautiful and strange and rather costly. The pleats of the skirt are so heavy and so set that the skirt sticks away out in back. The other girls are Indians who came in to the Friday market in Patzcuaro, and they posed for me. I had quite a session with the girl's mother who feared I was sketching the girl for an ulterior purpose.*

Doris Rosenthal

BY THE SEA

by Doris Rosenthal

painted in 1943

Oil, 32 x 40 inches

101

ANDRÉE RUELLAN

"My work can be no better than I am myself as a person and no deeper than my understanding of life as a whole. It is true that I paint some landscapes and still lifes, but from the earliest drawings, my deepest interest has been for people at work or at play. It seems to me that it is in the most everyday surroundings—a subway entrance, a market place or on the street—that one finds the unexpected in situation and aspect." Charming petite and brunette Andrée Ruellan thus conveys her deep, sincere, artistic philosophies. Although she is young enough to feel that most of her achievement lies in the future, her work to date has been impressive. She has won the praise of critics for her fine craftsmanship and superb sense of composition. Her New York street scenes are among the best of her canvases.

Andrée Ruellan was born of French parents in New York City in 1905. She attended the Art Students League, studying sculpture with Leo Lentelli and drawing with Maurice Sterne.

In 1922 a scholarship sent her to Rome for further study with Sterne. From 1923 to 1929 she lived and studied in Paris. In 1929 she married John W. Taylor, the painter, and they returned to America to make Woodstock, New York, their permanent home.

"In my formative years," says Miss Ruellan, "it was my good fortune to meet three fine people. The first was Robert Henri, who made a lasting impression in spite of my very young age. The second was Maurice Sterne, a most stimulating teacher. And in 1927 when I met Carl Zigrosser in Paris and he asked me to have an exhibition at the Weyhe Galleries in New York, began a fine friendship."

She exhibits regularly at the Kraushaar Galleries in New York and her drawings, prints and lithographs prove her artistic versatility. She is represented in the permanent collections of the Metropolitan Museum of Art, Fogg Museum, Phillips Memorial Gallery, Whitney Museum, University of Nebraska, Rockhill Nelson Gallery in Kansas City and many private collections.

An impressive artistic documentation, this, to a slender young woman who still holds the future in her hands. She lives happily with her husband and mother in an old house built into a hillside just below Cooper Lake. She and her husband work in separate studios near by, and the neatness of her studio speaks eloquently of the well-organized serenity of her life and her ambitions.

● *"Market Hands" depicts the corner of a market on a winter's day, when the work is nearing an end. I first came to know my love of markets and their outlying districts, and for the people who work there, at the great, bustling Les Halles when I was a student in Paris. I still find much in common with those early impressions, whether I am on New York's East Side, in the ornate building in Savannah, once the city slave-market, or in Charleston's rambling passageways near the port.*

Andrée Ruellan

MARKET HANDS

by Andrée Ruellan

painted in 1943

Oil, 24 x 20 inches

102

PAUL SAMPLE

There is something very comforting about getting acquainted with the art of Paul Sample, for here is no mystic, brooding over vague subtleties and complex messages. His are the fresh, clean-cut, untortured pictures by a man who absorbs the richness of living and lets it flow from his brush, literally, simply and freely in all its myriad phases.

As *Life's* war correspondent in 1943, he made a patrol aboard a submarine, painting the life of the sailors who live in the closest confinement of all our fighting men. He painted patrol and carrier planes and lived aboard a carrier on a wartime cruise. In 1937 he did a superb set of paintings for *Fortune*, a series of eight of the country's principal seaports, for an article about competitive commerce. Whether he paints "boxing" pictures or his charming Vermont landscapes, he portrays the human side of the American scene.

Sample's is a typically American "success" story; he never fought an indifferent world, and he never starved in a garret; a pretty neat arrangement that instinctively one approves of. Louisville, Kentucky, in 1896 was his birthplace, and because his father was a construction engineer his childhood years were spent in practically every section of the United States.

In 1916 he went to Dartmouth where his contact with art consisted of sleeping through an "art appreciation" course. He won an intercollegiate boxing championship, played football, basketball, and brought forth hot notes from a saxophone. His college career was interrupted by a year of service in the navy and shortly afterward Sample was threatened with tuberculosis. Followed four years of recuperation in the Adirondacks and during this unhappy period "he had opportunity to reorganize the trend of his life and had some maturity to prompt such reorganization." He began his actual artistic erudition at the age of thirty under the teaching of Jonas Lie and, almost from the beginning, honors and awards came toward him with delightful frequency.

He is married to a Vermont girl and, although their home is at present in Vermont, they lived for some years in California. No family group is complete without their 5-year-old son Tim and their Irish setter Lucy. He has been a prolific award winner, and his easel paintings are owned by the Metropolitan, Boston, Springfield and Brooklyn Museums, the Chicago Art Institute and other institutions. He has taught at the University of Southern California and is artist-in-residence at Dartmouth College.

● *Sketches for this picture were made in the vicinity of my home in Norwich, Vermont. It pictures a typical sugaring scene and brings together elements from various places and experiences in connection with sugaring. These were recorded in the form of studies and sketches and the finished painting is thus a summing up or composite of these.*

Paul Sample

MAPLE SUGARING IN VERMONT

by Paul Sample

painted in 1944

Oil, 30 x 38 inches

103

GEORGES SCHREIBER

"My Americanism is not just a piece of paper—I am passionately and by choice an American." Georges Schreiber, who lived through and was sickened by the tragedy and bankruptcy of Europe, who as a child of ten experienced four years of German occupation in a bleeding Belgium during World War I, makes no pompous statement, for this dynamic, vital young man proved his love and enthusiasm by a lonely two-year tour of the country capturing the characteristic Americanisms of every state—a monumental task that few artists would attempt. These he exhibited at Associated American Artists—so successfully that they were all sold before the show closed. Schreiber terms himself a social painter, for in his canvases the projection of humanity—the worker, farmer or fisherman—is his first desire, but he is an emotional painter as well who puts on vibrant color with daring and drama that compels the least responsive eye.

Born in Brussels, Belgium, in 1904, he was a mere five-year-old when drawing first intrigued him, and ever since art has remained his one magnificent obsession. He studied for two years at the Arts and Crafts School in Elberfeld, Germany.

He admits that at the age of twenty-four, he was quite a successful and arrogant young man. This arrogance, which he admits with a humorous youthful grin, stood him in good stead when he arrived at that age in New York. With it he succeded within six months in contributing his cartoons and drawings regularly to most of the New York dailies.

Schreiber painted the War Bond posters "Keep Them Flying," "Back the Attack," and the 5th War Loan poster "Fire Away!" He was also the creator of the "Back the Attack" slogan. Late in 1943 Schreiber returned from a week's cruise on a submarine during which he gathered material for a series of paintings showing the activities of a submarine on patrol. He is represented in the permanent collections of the Whitney Museum, Metropolitan Museum, Syracuse Museum, Museum of the City of New York, Swope Art Gallery of Terre Haute, Indiana, and many other collections.

● *"Brass and Strings" was painted in the Spring of 1945. With this subject I have gone back to an old love of my young days, the circus. The picture was directly inspired by several paintings of the same clowns which I finished 15 years ago. They were the Fratellini brothers of Paris. In contrast to the earlier paintings the present one is a liberal interpretation of the famous brothers, it is more concerned with textural values and imaginative composition. It is the more ambitious effort in a series of five paintings executed during the year on a clown subject.*

Georges Schreiber

BRASS AND STRINGS

by Georges Schreiber

painted in 1945

Oil, 36 x 46 inches

104

W I L L I A M   S.   S C H W A R T Z

One day a student at the Art Institute of Chicago painted a large nude in violent blues and greens. His classmates were convulsed, but his instructor did a bit of judicious thinking. Here was a student who already had shown mastery of conventional technique, who possessed an amazing facility for getting a likeness, suddenly going overboard for some inner urgency of his own. The instructor fortunately capitulated, and Schwartz was permitted to have his own way with art.

He believes that to copy a natural appearance is a misconception of art and foolish pride on the part of the artist to compete with the opulence of Nature. Schwartz therefore rejects literal transcription and through the prisms of his imagination prefers to translate it into a unity of harmonious forms in color. He paints America in singing reds and greens, purples and orange.

William Schwartz was born in Smorgon, Russia, in 1896 of a humble family. As a youngster of eleven he set forth for Vilna and begged admission to the Art School. He passed the rigid entrance examination and a free scholarship was the reward. Unfortunately the scholarship did not include bread, and hunger was a constant companion. His schooling was completed at fifteen, and an older brother already

in America arranged for his passage. He recalls that the first months in New York, the rhythm of the American scene, was a bewildering and amazing phenomena. He worked in Omaha as a house painter and Chicago was next on his itinerary. He arrived there with ten dollars in his pocket and a dream in his heart. In 1916 Schwartz entered the Chicago Art Institute and worked for sixteen hours a day. He waited on table, ushered in theaters and sang in concerts and operas. Schwartz was also a student of music and his lyric tenor voice helped him deflect occasional financial crises.

By the time he graduated from the Institute he had already had a canvas included in the annual exhibit of Chicago artists and was ready to begin working for himself.

Schwartz is constantly at work. If he is not painting he is sculpting clay or handling a lithographer's crayon. His works are represented in forty-five public collections including the Universities of Nebraska, Missouri, Illinois, Wyoming and Minnesota, the Art Institute of Chicago, Library of Congress, the Detroit Institute of Arts, the Art Alliance of Philadelphia and the Public Art Gallery of Dallas, Texas.

● *For twenty-five years in Chicago my neighborhood has been the city's near north side. I have painted the buildings, the people, and the activities which are the life of the area. In this particular painting, I have tried to combine a number of buildings with certain typical street incidents. At the time of painting, I was working on the problem of achieving a unity of line, form and color. This painting is, therefore, my own reaction to my own characteristic American environment.*

William S. Schwartz

NEAR NORTH SIDE—CHICAGO

by William S. Schwartz

painted in 1935

Oil, 36 x 40 inches

105

ZOLTAN SEPESHY

In his art, Sepeshy is no limited propaganda painter, since he believes that social significance finds its most valid expression when an artist honestly paints all that he sees and feels without dogmatic selection. He seems content to translate his reactions to nature into the idiom of pigment with clarity and elegance. He has been called an etcher in paint and his "wire brush" technique in tempera, with which he achieves the smoothness of his surfaces, has caused many in the art world to buy a ticket to Cranbrook to quietly watch over his shoulder.

Sepeshy is an American artist of Hungarian birth and the American father of two American children, so he accepts his status as a matter of course with no denial or protest against his native land. In 1921, when he was 23 years old, he left a bloody and destitute Hungary which had become, because of the Treaty of Trianon, the victim of civil wars. He came to America with an education, an ability to paint pictures and a diploma qualifying him to teach art. He had already studied at the Academy of Fine Arts in Budapest and with his father had absorbed much cultural travel all over Europe.

Sepeshy arrived during the money-mad era of the 1920s. He went to Detroit and tried to peddle his pictures, but he ended up by stacking lumber in a lumber yard, painting billboards and dressing windows. In 1926 an old friend gave him a round-trip ticket to New Mexico where for four months he painted, the native Indians for the most part, and upon his return to Detroit he sold every picture and shortly after was given a teaching assignment at the Society of Arts and Crafts. Mural commissions followed, for the General Motors Building in Detroit and the Fordson high school in Dearborn. In 1933 he held his first one-man show in New York, and became associated with Cranbrook Academy at Bloomfield Hill, outside Detroit. That same year he married and established a home, and the homesick immigrant became an important American citizen.

Sepeshy's paintings may be found in many public collections: the St. Louis Museum of Art, the Nebraska Art Association, Detroit Institute of Arts, Chicago Art Institute, Toledo Museum of Art, Albright Gallery of Buffalo, Wichita Museum, San Diego Museum, Youngstown Museum, Terre Haute Museum, University of Arizona Collection, International Business Machines Collection, Flint Museum, *et al.* In addition he has been awarded many important prizes.

● *I am happy that "The Pod Gatherer" should find its place in the Encyclopaedia Britannica Collection, for I consider it to be one of my best paintings. Not only did it mark the realization of long experimentation with a new approach in tempera, but it has sentimental significance for me as well. Although it is not a portrait, the subject is my wife, whom I had really seen gathering pods near our north Michigan hangout and who thereby inspired the painting.*

Zoltan Sepeshy

POD GATHERER

by Zoltan Sepeshy

painted in 1941

Tempera, 27 x 32 inches

106

CHARLES SHEELER

Charles Sheeler is mainly concerned with man's inventiveness. As an artist, he is willing to forego the fanciful liberties which are his prerogative, to give you, instead, an integral recording of the things that man does in his world. But Sheeler's interpretation goes far beyond such a prosaic statement. He gives you a factual painting—whether it be a waterwheel, an airplane, a locomotive or a maze of machinery—but he gives you a bright and shining conception at its moment of utter and immaculate perfection; at that precise moment when the slanting shafts of a benevolent sun put things in their very best light. "Not strange, inhuman masses of material, but exquisite manifestations of human reason. As the artists of the Renaissance reflected life by picturing the human body, so he reflects life through such forms as these; forms that are more deeply human than the muscles of the torso because they trace the pattern of the human mind as it seeks to use co-operatively the limitless power of nature."

Born in 1883, in Philadelphia, of Welsh and Irish origin, Sheeler started out with three years' study at the Quaker City School of In-dustrial Art, followed by an additional three years at the Pennsylvania Academy of Fine Arts. His summers were spent abroad studying what most appealed to him in the art of the old world.

He returned for a time to Bucks County, Pennsylvania, where the old barns, buildings and Colonial handicraft satisfied his bent for American structural form. In 1927 he spent six weeks photographing the Ford plant at River Rouge, and through the years, made paintings of the scene. To the ordinary eye, his delicate precision of line and brush seems almost miraculous without benefit of slide rule and compass.

Sheeler's paintings are owned by the Museum of Modern Art, Phillips Memorial Gallery, Fogg Art Museum, Boston Museum of Fine Arts, Cleveland Museum of Art, Columbus Gallery of Fine Arts, Detroit Institute of Arts, Chicago Art Institute, Worcester Art Museum, Metropolitan Museum, Wichita Art Museum, Whitney Museum and many more. His erudite work is frequently to be seen reproduced in *Fortune*.

● *Of the many approaches to painting I have preferred that of a design planned in advance of the final work, to include as its first principle a structural framework within which the elements of the picture are co-ordinated. With this structure established, the final work may be as stark or elaborate as one may desire. This structural design includes a consideration of three-dimensional composition as well as two-dimensional pattern. A diversity of subject matter has been of interest to me, to which these basic principles are applicable. "Winter Window," included in this collection, interested me as a subject because of the combination of indoor and outdoor aspects of nature within the frame.*

Charles Sheeler

WINTER WINDOW
by Charles Sheeler
painted in 1941
Oil, 30 x 24 inches

MILLARD SHEETS

"Instructions in oil, sermons in paint, monitions in fresco—all meant to remind us that art is a mission and that our reform is its affair—all these flourish. But, for you and for me, is there not a place too, and a bit higher on the wall, for the art of a young man who has never gotten over the joyous fact of having been born into a world full of charming surprises that he would share with us? 'Day is here!' his pictures cry, 'with life, color, beauty.'" Thus does Dr. Hartley Burr Alexander sum up the work of Millard Sheets.

In May of 1944 Sheets returned from India, where, as *Life's* war correspondent, he spent more than a year making an official water-color account of the activities of the Far Eastern theater of war. The water colors and drawings he brought back are unforgettable emotional experiences.

Sheets lives in California, in an architecturally perfect ranchhouse which he himself designed and built in the beautiful Pomona Valley. The magazine, *American Home*, in June 1944, showed its approbation of his skill as an architect by picturing the ranch house in full color, complete with blueprints.

Sheets was born in Pomona, California, in 1907 and attended the Chouinard School in Los Angeles. During his final school year his work attracted the attention of Dalzell Hatfield, who arranged for his first one-man show in Los Angeles. At the same time he entered the Davis Competition at the Witte Memorial Gallery of San Antonio. Despite a mistake in shipment, by which the wrong painting was entered, he won the prize of $1,750—this with the picture "The Goat Ranch." Meanwhile, his one-man show was so successful that he was invited to exhibit by some twenty museums all over the United States. Sheets arranged for his traveling exhibit and then set off for Europe to study the old masters in the museums of France, England, Germany and Holland.

Back in America, he was asked to teach at Chouinard, at Scripps College in Claremont, California, and he also accepted the director-ship of the art department of the Los Angeles County Fair. He holds one-man shows every year, and during the summers of 1935 and 1936 he taught at the University of California and the University of Hawaii. His works are represented in the Whitney Museum, Brooklyn Museum, Dayton Art Institute, San Francisco Museum, Los Angeles County Museum, Seattle Museum, San Diego Gallery of Fine Arts, and many others, as well as in the White House, in Washington, D.C., and in some 300 private collections.

● *To me the occurrences of everyday life are often filled with dramatic and emotional grandeur, as well as effective decorative values. In "The First-Born" I tried to set down on canvas a decorative scheme which an act of nature had endowed with intense dramatic force and meaning. The picture was painted on my ranch in the Padua Hills of California.*

Millard Sheets

THE FIRST-BORN

by Millard Sheets

painted in 1939

Oil, 40 x 50 inches

108

EVERETT SHINN

Everett Shinn, one of the distinguished survivors of the "Ash-Can" school, refuses to be subdued by the turning leaves of a relentless calendar. In November 1943 he once again held a one-man show—a new edition of his tales of three cities, Paris, London and New York. Some of the landmarks are gone, spires and commerce have taken their places, but Shinn is no conservative objecting to the rebuilders of cities. If they make their changes, Shinn, chameleon-like, changes too—and applies his brush with fidelity to the present.

The stage and tent, dancers and carnival performers, the streets, slums, cafés and alleys—their gaieties and somber moments—have always caught his unjaded eye and imagination. For more than five decades he has been the romantic recorder of those three great cities—their moods and spirits and essences—which to future generations may be more revealing than all the history books.

Shinn was born in Woodstown, New Jersey, in 1876 of Quaker parents. He studied at the Pennsylvania Academy of Fine Arts, but for a time, while a student at the Spring Garden Institute, he considered building locomotives as a career. He secured a job in the Baldwin Locomotive Works but, fortunately for art, was fired for defacing the neat detailed drawing of an intricate valve action by parading hansom cabs and gay crowds over the precision of a piston stroke. He worked for Philadelphia newspapers, for the New York *World*, *Herald* and *Journal*, for *Harper's Weekly* and other magazines. Then came his one-man shows in all the leading galleries, with pictures of the docks, theaters, slums—all the activities that make up the story of a great city in repose or gaiety. Stanford White, Elsie de Wolfe and Elisabeth Marbury were his promoters. He decorated theaters and did murals for the fabulous mansions of yesteryear. A decoration for the city hall of Trenton, New Jersey, depicting the industries of that city, was executed on a canvas measuring 44 by 22 feet. He illustrated books, did scenic designing and worked as a motion picture art director and as a playwright.

Shinn's pictures rarely come up for public auction. In all the great museums his work is cherished—among them the Chicago Art Institute, the Whitney Museum, Brooklyn Museum, Detroit Institute of Fine Arts and Phillips Memorial Gallery in Washington, D.C.

● *This picture, "Ballet," is to me time off from depicting cluttered slums, dejection and the wrangling weave of a drab humanity. It is the wish to move in the fragrance of grease paint and a lighter sphere of existence—to watch bodies free themselves from earthy obligations and believe in their strapped-on tinsel wings. There is soul nourishment in the sweat and stress of labor, yet, like one from the slums who eats a cream puff, I too hunger for the sweet, light flavor of the stage, where for the hour of painting the taste holds until I glimpse a crumpled human on a park bench.*

Everett Shinn

BALLET

by Everett Shinn

painted in 1944

Oil, 21 x 31 inches

109

MITCHELL SIPORIN

Not until he himself began to wield a brush, did Mitchell Siporin realize that to his mother he was indebted for his artistic ability. In his case he reversed the usual procedure by launching her career. His mother used to watch him work, making comments and suggestions, and one day young Mitchell handed her some brushes and said, "Go ahead! Paint!" She did, too. Critics call her "primitives" wonderfully exciting and imaginative work by a comparatively inexperienced artist.

In expressing his own views, Siporin says, "Art that is important to me should have social significance, but the painting must be built up to be plastically sound. Good painting should be as important to the onlooker as it is to the artist who created it. Every artist who is worth his mettle desires and needs an audience. Artists should be an important link in every civic enterprise and become an important part of society." Siporin lives up to every word of this statement. His entire interest is on the social scene surrounding him, and always there is time given to research and authority before committing it to his masterly and individual draftsmanship on canvas.

Born in New York City in 1910, Siporin has lived in Chicago from the time he was a year old. After graduating from Crane Junior College, he went on with his art training at the Chicago Art Institute, and later studied privately with Todros Geller. In his art he has entered many fields—he has done book illustrating, cartoons for *New Masses* and *Esquire*, book jackets and stage designs.

Under the sponsorship of the Federal Arts Project he did the "Stockyards" series of 30 gouaches; a mural "Steel" for Bloom Township High School; three murals in Lane Technical High School —one of Jane Addams, who had greatly influenced his life and outlook, "Lincoln and Altgeld" and the "Prairie Poets." Siporin is a great admirer of Carl Sandburg. He entered the Army in December 1942, and as technical sergeant in the U.S. Army Engineer Corps he was stationed abroad. His portrayals of the Italian war scene appeared in *Yank* (the Army weekly) and in *Fortune*.

His frescoes decorate many buildings in the Middle West and his easel paintings are in the permanent collections of many museums, including the Metropolitan, Whitney and Museum of Modern Art in New York, University of Arizona and Smith College Museum.

● *"Night Piece" is one of a series of paintings of refugees, a subject I was deeply moved by at the outset of the war, and with which I was to gain an intimate personal knowledge as a soldier in Africa and Italy. Daumier's paintings of the homeless, and paintings of refugees such as Rembrandt's "Rest on the Flight from Egypt," have always had an appeal for me because of their sympathetic emotional statement of the plight of the dispossessed . . . The people in "Night Piece" stand in the dusk, luminous in the last glow of light.*

Mitchell Siporin

NIGHT PIECE
by Mitchell Siporin
painted in 1940
Oil, 30 x 24 inches

110

JOHN SLOAN

The days of plush and bric-a-brac, when art was prim and high-flown and evasive, were receding into an outmoded past—it was in 1908 to be exact—a handful of artists, who were partaking wholeheartedly of the uninhibited life of Greenwich Village, McSorley's bar and Petit-pas' restaurant, revolted against the hypocritical aspects of art and suddenly staged a rebellion. They were called the "eight," "the black gang," "the ash-can school," and John Sloan was one of the leaders. He battled against academic painting—he helped in bringing Modernism to America, and his pictorial material was America.

Honest, ironic and an exceptional draftsman, he painted the back alleys and barrooms, characters of questionable virtue, bringing to art the beauty of realism, to become a heroic figure in contemporary American art.

The most rabid of critics eventually subsided, rose-colored glasses were thrown aside, but Sloan stood up—"for beauty is in honesty and in truth" and Sloan had conditioned them to substance, not affectation.

Of American parentage, he was born in Lock Haven, Pennsylvania, in 1871. His study of art began at the Spring Garden Institute and later at the Pennsylvania Academy of Fine Arts. He worked as illustrator for Philadelphia newspapers and in 1905 went to New York, did magazine and book illustration, and finally "joined such other young illustrators as Glackens, Luks and Shinn, all with keen noses for the scent of the human scene."

About that time he began to paint seriously and it was at the Armory Show three years later that Sloan was to begin his career of electrifying the staid critics of the day. His importance does not end with his own career, for as a teacher he has guided generations of young painters who now at the peak of their career pay sincere tribute to his inspirational guidance. He taught at the Art Students League for sixteen years. Very recently he wrote a book, *Gist of Art*, which has great value to the artist but it is so beautifully written, so permeated with his rich philosophy, that its appeal in literature is universal. Sloan is represented in the Cincinnati Museum of Art, Carnegie Institute, Metropolitan Museum, Phillips Memorial Gallery, Corcoran Gallery, San Diego Gallery of Fine Arts, Addison Gallery and almost every important museum and collection in America.

● *"Chinese Restaurant" was painted in 1909, on Sixth Avenue, in this New York in which I still preferred to feel a stranger. The girl is feeding her boy friend, before taking him home, in one of the many Chinese restaurants of that day, where only Chinese food was served. Graphic expression and resonant in color.—Excerpt from comment in* Gist of Art.

John Sloan

CHINESE RESTAURANT

by John Sloan

painted in 1909

Oil, 26 x 32 inches

111

LAWRENCE BEALL SMITH

He has a quick eye to see a story, and the humorous perspective with which to tell it tenderly and dramatically. The artist himself, lively and enthusiastic, deals in the human side of the story, and there is about him the quality of a star reporter. Whether it is the delightful antics of youngsters or the grim business of men at war, Smith's pictures are alive. This is at least part of the reason why *Coronet* finds his future worth watching.

Lawrence Beall Smith is the artist who created the War Bond poster "Don't Let That Shadow Touch Them" which was reproduced and distributed by the U. S. Treasury Department during the First War Loan Drive. He then went overseas as artist war correspondent aboard an aircraft carrier to do a series of paintings and drawings on naval aviation. Later he spent six months in England and Normandy gathering material concerned with the work of the Army Medical Corps in the field.

On his return from a war theater overseas in 1944, Lawrence Beall Smith wrote, "I have just returned from a six-months' stay in the European theater, and since my return from that weird world I have been up to my ears in the business of readjusting to the pleasant life with my wife and two kids in this flying-bombless land of milk and honey, or I should say *eggs*."

His birthplace was Washington, D.C., in 1909, and his childhood was spent in the Carolinas, Kentucky, Illinois and Indiana. While he was an undergraduate at the University of Chicago, from which he graduated in 1931, he spent his evenings studying at the Chicago Art Institute. He took additional training under Thurn in Gloucester, Massachusetts, and under Hopkinson and Zimmerman in Boston.

Smith added lithography to his repertoire and was honored with an invitation to exhibit in the International Exhibition of Lithography and Wood Engraving at the Chicago Art Institute. He taught for several years at the Child-Walker School in Boston. His paintings have been shown in every major museum exhibition throughout the length and breadth of the country.

His work is permanently hung in the collections of Harvard University in Cambridge, the Addison Gallery of American Art, the University of Minnesota, Herron Art Institute of Indianapolis, Sheldon Swope Art Gallery in Terre Haute, and in many private collections.

● *"Corner in Carolina" was painted in Cambridge, Massachusetts, from notes taken on the subject six months before while in Wilson, North Carolina. In company with Aaron Bohrod, Peter Hurd and Paul Sample I had been sent south by a tobacco company to see the tobacco country and industry. I have always felt a strong pull toward Negro subject matter, and this Saturday afternoon dress parade before a freakish bit of southern architecture caught my eye after a day spent in the tobacco warehouses nearby.*

Lawrence Beall Smith

CORNER IN CAROLINA

by Lawrence Beall Smith

painted in 1942

Oil, 20 x 30 inches

112

RAPHAEL SOYER

Probably from his Russian forbears comes the melancholy strain that typifies Soyer's work. Painted with subtle form and rich texture that stem from realism, his poignant tales go far beyond the underlying social protest theme. The seamy side of life, the pathos of the needy, their unfulfilled dreams, their elemental fears, come to life in his canvases.

Born in Tombov, Russia, on Christmas Day in 1899, Soyer says that he and his brothers (one of them his twin and all of them today well-known artists) looked longingly toward America from early childhood and had already adopted its heroes and its legends.

Their interest in art was stimulated by their father's drawings, primitive yet alive, of people, birds and animals. Encouraged by their parents the walls of their home were decorated by their childish art. Upon arrival here when he was ten years old, the entire family found themselves stymied with economic conditions and a strange language to conquer. The wisdom of their parents, however, kept the home a warm, safe haven from which they could view without rancor the realities of a somewhat hostile world. Raphael sold newspapers and worked in factories, but with quiet, gentle insistence, managed to pursue his interest in art by way of Cooper Union, the National Academy of Design and later under the tutelage of Guy Pène du Bois at the Art Students League.

Around 1926, Soyer exhibited a painting in the Salons of America show, and there he met Alexander Brook who helped him to start selling his work. In 1929 he held a one-man show at the Daniel Galleries. The press was enthusiastic and ready sales followed. In 1932 he began teaching at the Art Students League.

He is an expert lithographer and in this field has received his full share of honors. He has greatly distinguished himself by the work he has done in art projects for the United States government. In appearance, Soyer is slender to the point of fragility, his eyes are tired and brooding and his voice little more than a husky whisper.

His work is represented at the Whitney Museum of American Art, the Phillips Memorial Gallery, the Metropolitan Museum, New York Public Library, Baltimore Museum, Addison Gallery of American Art, Columbus Gallery of Fine Arts, Corcoran Gallery, Buffalo Art Association, Brooklyn Museum and many more. He has also done a mural in the Kingsessing postal station in Philadelphia.

● *I was often intrigued by the tawdry window displays of staring mannequins and colorful hats, as well as by the girls and women attracted to them. I made some sketches of the store fronts and of the people looking into the windows. Later on, as the composition evolved and took definite form, a few models posed in the studio as the window shoppers. I also obtained two mannequin heads. My idea was to paint frankly and directly a casually composed picture of women in their everyday dress and characteristic mien.*

Raphael Soyer

WINDOW SHOPPERS

by Raphael Soyer

painted in 1938

Oil, 36 x 24 inches

113

EUGENE SPEICHER

Speicher's painting is at once vital, subtle, well-made and fresh in spirit, whether he paints a young girl, a simple landscape or a bouquet of flowers. It is a tonic to stir the imagination, a pleasure to the eye and reflects his sense of quality in life.

His birthplace was Buffalo, New York, in 1883 and his first venture into art took place as a precocious four-year-old when he executed a "Tomatoes and Basket" composition in colored chalk on a blackboard to the complete consternation of a teachers' convention.

Sports, however, put art out of the running during most of his school years and it was while he was working ten hours a day as a lumberjack and relaxing before dinner by means of a stiff game of basketball that he still found time to study evenings at the Albright Art Gallery. The winning of a scholarship enabled him to study at the Art Students League in New York under William Chase and Frank DuMond, and while he was still a student galleries were beginning to show his work. To make additional money he made "quick" portraits for $25, and eventually attended the Henri School of Art.

When he married and settled in Woodstock, Speicher's financial status was still so low that he even made furniture out of old packing cases. The years between 1910 and 1915 were not easy but by 1920 he was considered one of America's most successful portrait painters. Speicher could be a very wealthy man but he will refuse to accept uninspiring commissions and prefers to paint only what pleases him.

"There was never a man of such famed imagination provided with so orderly and calculated a life. His tidy flat in New York, his meticulously managed home in Woodstock, his handsome, upstanding wife who spreads her sheltering wing over his studio hours and welcomes you otherwise with her marvelous cooking, his golf score so enviably low that it is never mentioned, all speak for the reason that he heads his craft"—such is the honest tribute paid by Homer Saint-Gaudens.

"The only museums," writes a critic, "which have not Speicher's paintings are: first, those which are going to get them, second, those which cannot afford the luxury." Every five years Speicher holds a one-man show. His paintings are owned by twenty-seven museums, among them the Metropolitan Museum, Albright Gallery, Cleveland Museum, Corcoran Gallery, Detroit Institute of Arts, the Museum of Modern Art and the Whitney Museum.

● *"Head of a Young Girl" was painted in Woodstock, N.Y., in 1940. The subject is Miss Jean Murray of Saugerties, N.Y. She is a charming and simple girl, and a close friend of ours. I liked her forthright look. She has a well-shaped skull and rich complexion— like a piece of ripe fruit. Her eyes are dark and set well in her fine oval face, which is framed by her dark brown hair—thick and luxuriant. She seemed the personification of young girlhood.*

Eugene Speicher

HEAD OF A YOUNG GIRL

by Eugene Speicher

painted in 1937

Oil, 20 x 19 inches

114

FRANCIS SPEIGHT

Francis Speight employs all the subtle ingredients of the true artist—mind and heart and hand all in serene collaboration. Each picture is the result of something he has seen and to which he has reacted strongly. If his type of painting *must* be labelled it might be called modern realism, but discarding labels the important thing is that it is good painting—so good that one can stand before a Speight picture and be lifted, both eye and mind, from the ruts of everyday mundanity.

There are art connoisseurs who know and love "painting" who would tell you of the greatness of Francis Speight, but it is what he himself says that is beautifully relevant of the modesty and "grass roots" common sense of the man behind the artist. "The thing to paint is that toward which you have a real emotional response," he says. He suffers at exhibitions if he is asked to talk about his work or make "explanations" of his technique. He says, "I cannot find any reviews of my paintings. . . . Some have been lost, others have been mistakenly burned with trash. . . . I do not believe that my work is widely enough known and approved to warrant a detailed, intimate or newsy biography. If I do write anything I usually find it embar-

rassing when I see it exactly as I wrote it in print." So, instead, he quietly paints the country towns and stone and stucco houses around the Pennsylvania countryside and refrains from any commentaries beyond those warranted by his eloquent brush.

Speight was born in 1896 on a farm near Windsor, North Carolina, where the first Speights had settled some 200 years earlier. Both his father and uncle were Baptist ministers. While a student at Wake Forest College he began taking art lessons from Ida Poteat at Meredith College. He served in World War I, and later, in Washington, studied at the Corcoran School. Later he attended the Pennsylvania Academy, where Daniel Garber was teaching, and while there he won two Cresson Travelling Scholarships. He has won awards for his paintings at the exhibitions at the Chicago Art Institute, the Corcoran Gallery, the Pennsylvania Academy and the National Academy of Design. Since 1925 he has been teaching at the Pennsylvania Academy of Fine Arts. He is permanently represented in the collections of the Metropolitan Museum, Pennsylvania Academy of Fine Arts, the Ranger Fund of the National Academy of Design, and the Toronto (Canada) Art Gallery.

● *I first began painting around here in 1925. I always liked the tone, simplicity and weight of the houses. While I tried my hand at painting railroad tracks as far back as 1921, for a long while I usually left out all poles and wires. But I have come to use them more and more, and in this picture, if I recall correctly, the same care was given to the shapes and variety of the spaces bounded by the high tension wires and poles as to all the other forms and spaces.*

Francis Speight

TRACKS IN WINTER
by Francis Speight
painted in 1942
Oil, 30 x 36 inches

115

JACK GAGE STARK

Diffused in soft patternings of flickering light, painted daringly with a magnificent disregard for punctual details and sharp edges, the pictures of Jack Gage Stark propel the mind and eye swiftly from a mundane world to an enchanting sphere of spiritual and emotional beauty.

His pictured tales are personal confidences, dedicated to the special delight of a sensitive spectator. They are filled with the excitement of living. They have taste, selection and restraint. His models do not seem to have posed in other studios. His colors—and he promotes alliances quite against the rules—adjust to the sweetest harmony and often rise to quite magical crescendos. Critics, when they look at his work, are reminded of Watteau, Lancret, Boucher and Fragonard. They like his sense of humor, the delicate gestures, even the element of caricature that he applies in a special manner all his own.

Stark was born in Jackson County, Missouri, in 1882. He began to draw and paint before he could write, and despite many unwelcome interruptions he has continued to do so ever since. His first serious instruction came from Van Horne Millet, who later urged him to go to Paris, where it was his good fortune to spend his formative years (from 1900 to 1907) working in the Academie Delacluse and in La Pallette with Jacques Emile Blanche. He says, "It was my further good fortune that that was a high period to be in Paris, and I knew and was helped by many fine painters."

Returning from Paris, he lived for many years in Silver City, New Mexico, where he worked alone in a beautiful country. In recent years he has divided his time between Silver City and Santa Barbara, California, with several odd years spent in France.

However, California today claims him for her own, where he is an intrinsic and integral part of that delightfully refreshing art which is fast compelling attention from the art world at large.

Jack Stark's work is represented in many private collections, including those of Joseph T. Ryerson and Channing Peake, and in the Santa Barbara Museum of Art and the Chicago Art Institute.

● *"Sulky Star" is not only a picture of circus performers, behind it is a method of work learned from the performers themselves—long, patient preparation for one brief, flashing moment of presentation—that followed many trials, many failures, many revisions of thought. The first version was painted in Paris in 1930–31. The notes were made in the Cirque Medrano and the models I was using at that time were an Italian acrobatic dancer and a Russian girl from the circus. In many subsequent versions, the arrangement of the picture underwent changes of design, coloration and posture of the figures. The gesture of the first figure, the characteristic open pose of those who live by balance, remained much the same. I painted this final version in 1943–44.*

Jack Gage Stark

SULKY STAR

by Jack Gage Stark

painted in 1944

Oil, 32 x 24 inches

116

MAURICE STERNE

Sterne adds to the variety and emotional happiness of the pictorial craft. A wanderer on the face of the globe, he has kept himself from wearing thin and has kept his painting ability limber enough to adapt itself to whatever pictorial adventure has come his way. He believes that by cultivating not only technique but also vision art escapes from conventional channels. He has been called one of the greatest draftsmen among modern painters. He is also important as a sculptor, note his Rogers Kennedy Memorial in Worcester, Mass.

Sterne was born in Libau, Russia, in 1878. His early youth was spent in Moscow, and he and his widowed mother came to New York when he was about 12 years old. As a youth he sold newspapers, worked in factories, was apprenticed to a mapmaker and even took a turn at bartending. He studied at Cooper Union, and in 1894 entered the National Academy of Design, where Thomas Eakins was instructing anatomy. For the next ten years Sterne studied art in this country, and his first canvases were shown in New York in 1902, at the old Country Sketch Club on Broadway.

In 1904 the winning of a travelling scholarship started Sterne on his years of wandering—in Italy quattrocento Italian art, Piero della Francesca and Antonio Pollaiuolo in particular, had a profound influence on his future development. In the fall of that year he settled down in Paris, where he exhibited at the first Salon d'Automne. The eminent critic Roger Marx was very enthusiastic about his work at that exhibition. But Italy and Greek sculpture lured him back—so in 1907 he went to Greece where he spent about a year, mostly in a monastery on Mt. Hymettus, where he concentrated on painting and the Greek classics.

Following three more years in Italy, in 1911 he was enabled to fulfill his dream of visiting the Far East—stopping in Egypt, then on to India, Burma, Java and, going to Bali for two weeks, he stayed two years! Here was done some of his finest work—dozens of paintings, hundreds of color studies and thousands of drawings. Returning in 1915 to America, he settled in New York and New Mexico, but after World War I returned to Anticoli in Italy, and has since divided his time between the old world and the new, painting, sculpting and teaching. He has exhibited his work in various galleries throughout the world, and is represented in the permanent collections of most of America's museums and many in Europe.

● *"Village Performance," painted in 1927, has for locale the little village of Anticoli-Corrado in the Sabine Hills, Italy, where life is primitive but the people are cultured and highly civilized . . . Arguing with a friend, a surrealist who considered only dreams and nightmares as suitable material, I chanced to look out of my window and there was the performance on the piazza—so I painted it. It is not what one paints but how. It is not how one feels but what. This, as I see and feel it, is important.*

Maurice Sterne

VILLAGE PERFORMANCE — ANTICOLI

by Maurice Sterne

painted in 1931–34

Oil, 40 x 40 inches

117

A L B E R T   S T E R N E R

In 1943, when he was 80 years old, Albert Sterner held a one-man show in New York of 14 paintings he had done since 1941, and Edward Alden Jewell, the knowing critic of the *New York Times*, headed his column: "80-Year-Old Artist Proves a Modern." Mr. Jewell went on to say, "There is no getting around it. Albert Sterner has the most youthful spirit of any artist his age that I have ever known. He is alert, active, enthusiastic, vital. And right now he is painting top-flight pictures. He has perhaps never painted better."

Sterner has ever held to his creed that the artist must paint for the people—not for himself or for other artists. "It is the easiest thing in the world to be different—for the charlatan can be original because he will resort to tricks that an honest workman would scorn. The works of the great masters of the Renaissance owe much of their wonder to the required purposefulness of their endeavor."

Albert Sterner was born in London, England, of American parents, on March 8, 1863. From his earliest childhood he drew, and is known to have spent most of his pocket money for boxes of water colors. When he was 11, his nomadic family moved to Birmingham. There he was admitted to the celebrated King Edward's public school. His examination papers placed him at the head of 700 applicants. Soon

he was also attending the Birmingham Art Institute School. Financial misfortune caused the family to return to America, while Sterner was sent to an uncle in Germany and earned his living in the office of a large agricultural implements factory in Baden. In 1879 he rejoined his family in Chicago. At 19 Sterner became an instructor in the original Chicago Art Institute, then a tiny tin-roofed building on the barren lake front. After three years in Chicago he went to New York, where the main part of his career has been spent.

From New York he went to Paris to study at Julian's and the Beaux Arts. He traveled in Italy and later, about 1904–05, had a studio in Munich. Mention should be made of Sterner's noteworthy work in black and white during his middle and recent years. He was a pioneer of artist-lithography in the United States.

Albert Sterner's work is represented in the Metropolitan Museum, Brooklyn Museum, New York Public Library, Library of Congress, Toronto Museum, Andover Museum, Art Collection of Yale University, Fogg Art Museum; in the South Kensington and Victoria and Albert museums in London, England, and in many private collections.

● "Fruit and Wine" was painted one winter in a highly lighted conservatory overlooking the East River, in Astoria, N.Y. It looked out across Hell Gate to the concrete railway viaduct (seen through the window in background). The painting is attacked alla prima, *boldly, with special attention to color. There is, for me, no set way to paint. Each subject is a new adventure. From the earliest days of my practice I have been, and still am today, a constant technical experimenter in many media. I believe that the acquisition of more and more means, of varying character, equips the artist to express himself more and more lucidly.*

Albert Sterner

FRUIT AND WINE
by Albert Sterner
painted in 1934
Oil, 41 x 30 inches

FREDERIC TAUBES

Frederic Taubes began to paint when he was three years old, took up serious art studies at four, and at ten was ready to receive his A.N.A. His grandmother was concerned over his precocity, but his mother mentioned complacently that there had been a good many freaks in the family—musicians, playwrights, actors and adventurers—despite the solidity of papa's banking business.

Taubes defies any ordinary descriptive phrasing—new adjectives would have to be invented to set him down in black and white, his honesty and his personality are both devastating and soul-satisfying. He admits that he is quite pugnacious and truculent, probably because he is way under six feet tall. He is unafraid to voice opinions, militantly if need be, and he is conscious of his other erudite accomplishments, but in art he prefers to be termed a craftsman. He thinks he paints exceedingly well, but he says: "What's the hurry? Let's wait a hundred years or so before we determine my status as an artist."

Born in Lwów, Poland, in 1900; at fourteen he was a follower of Cézanne; at sixteen he indulged in Dadaism; at eighteen he was painting abstractions, and entered the Bauhaus in Weimar at nineteen. His wealthy family lost their fortune in the inflation in Austria around 1920, and, as a consequence, he became in succession: sign and poster painter, magazine and newspaper illustrator, professional ski-guide in Switzerland, and then toured for several years all over Europe as an itinerant painter. Meanwhile he had acquired three citizenships and spoke five languages, all with a foreign accent. Consequently, he felt that he belonged nowhere, so he came to America.

He has been a professor of art at four universities, lectured all over the United States, is the author of *Technique of Oil Painting* and two other important books on paint techniques and one on aesthetics, and writes his own column in the *American Artist*. He grinds his own paints, makes his own oils, varnishes, canvases and even frames. "But," says he, "I do not pluck the bristles from the pigs' backs to make brushes."

Taubes has had eight color-spreads in *Life* magazine and his paintings are owned by a dozen galleries, including the Metropolitan Museum of Art in New York, the Fine Arts Gallery of San Diego, the San Francisco Museum of Art, Mills College in Oakland, California, and the Art Association of Bloomington, Illinois, among others.

● *"Portrait of a Painter" represents a likeness of the greatest painter of religious subjects in our time: Fred Nagler. One of Nagler's paintings is indicated in the background. In painting the portrait my chief intention was to establish rhythmic sequences of forms, upon which the entire composition is built. The range of colors is narrow, for their sole purpose is to support the structure of the painting.*

PORTRAIT OF A PAINTER

by Frederic Taubes

painted in 1940

Oil, 36 x 30 inches

119

WILLIAM THOENY

A deep understanding of craftsmanship is the solid foundation on which rests the aesthetic inventiveness of William Thoeny. His scenes of New York are the singing "Thank you's" of a man who finds the new world a livable place. For Thoeny is another European who has come to America to add his own very individual lyrics to the art of America.

Only a seasoned and disciplined talent could blend the emotional and the abstract to such articulate expressions—as though he painted with eyes and ears, mind and heart, all in the sweetest accord.

Thoeny, the son of a prominent and cultured family, was born in Austria in 1888. He was educated at Graz, Austria, and later at the Munich Academy in Germany. At seven he showed a decided aptitude for drawing, but music was equally absorbing. It was not until he was 19 that he made the decision in favor of painting. The rhythm and grace of his painting would certainly indicate that the years of musical study were an enriching influence.

Thoeny was one of the contributors at the beginning of a new movement which was later to include such revolutionaries as Klee, Kandinsky and Miro. In 1923 he founded the Secession in Graz. He enjoyed outstanding success throughout the cities of Europe with his sparkling and colorful description of the local scene and through his engravings illustrating the works of Balzac, Dostoievsky and others.

In 1938, finding Europe utterly incompatible with his way of living, Thoeny came to America. In less than two years he was winning plaudits from the New York critics, one of whom wrote: "W. Thoeny is the name of an artist new to America. But it's a name that ought soon to become familiar. For Thoeny is extremely gifted, a painter's painter, who manages to be technically very sophisticated and at the same time emotionally very impressionable . . . The whole effect of his work is very gay and spirited . . ."

Since living in America he has had several one-man shows and has been invited to exhibit in many important exhibitions. In addition to ten European museums, he is included in the permanent collections of the Museum of Newark, New Jersey, the Metropolitan Museum, the Pennsylvania Academy of Fine Arts. the De Young Memorial Museum in San Francisco, the Detroit Museum, the Mills College Museum in San Francisco, and in many private collections.

● *In all my New York pictures I never cared to paint in a purely realistic sense, but to find a pictorial form to convey the fascinating impression of this gigantic city. If I have sometimes succeeded in this intention, it is the result of detailed studies which I have worked at for many years, by doing drawings and water colors which were essential to find the right form. Most of them are now in museums. Since I have always considered the East River to be one of the most interesting surroundings of the city, it is a great satisfaction to me that the picture "New York, East River" now belongs to the* Encyclopaedia Britannica.

W. Thoeny

NEW YORK, EAST RIVER

by William Thoeny

painted in 1943

Oil, 25 x 30 inches

120

BRADLEY WALKER TOMLIN

Somehow one shies away from the term "abstractionist"—and actually dislikes the word—when one looks at a Tomlin translation in pigment long enough to sense the rare qualities behind it. There is a sort of subconscious "lady in the dark" revelation in his picture-building far more meaningful than the average put-it-on-canvas painting.

All the essences of dream, conscious thought and psychology conspire together to an unobvious but strong emotional definition of a given theme. Perhaps it takes the combination of both cerebral and spiritual qualities for its fullest appreciation, but even a surface eye may delight in its color and inventiveness of design. Arranged arbitrarily in subtle relationships he paints such still lifes as "Outward Preoccupation," "Burial" and "To the Sea." In all of them there are symbolic suggestions, whispered implications, in a potent language all his own.

Tomlin works slowly and with great concentration. He has limited himself to a somewhat restricted field and yet he manages to create a wide variety of expression. There is neither repetition nor carelessness, nor adherence to a pattern in any of his canvases. Bradley

Walker Tomlin was born in Syracuse, New York, in 1899. He graduated from Syracuse University in 1921 and won the university's Hiram Gee Fellowship for European study, and in 1922 he became a member of the Louis Comfort Tiffany Foundation.

Between 1923 and 1927 Tomlin spent most of his time abroad, where he studied at the Academie Colarossi and the Academie Le Grande Chaumiere, and worked independently in his own studios in France, Italy and England. His first one-man show was held at the Montross Gallery in New York in 1924.

After returning to America Tomlin taught art, and from 1932 to 1941 he was a member of the faculty of Sarah Lawrence College, but since 1941 he ceased teaching in order to devote his entire time to his painting. He is a member of the Federation of Modern Painters and Sculptors, and has done mural decorations for the Memorial Hospital in Syracuse, New York.

Tomlin's work is represented in the permanent collections of the Brooklyn Museum, Pennsylvania Academy of Fine Arts, Whitney Museum, Metropolitan Museum and the Duncan Phillips Memorial Gallery in Washington, D.C.

● *This painting, "To the Sea," was painted during the period throughout which the toll of sinkings of Atlantic shipping had been particularly heavy, and I have endeavored to put down on canvas some of the thoughts which I had at that time.*

B. Tomlin

TO THE SEA

by Bradley Walker Tomlin

painted in 1942

Oil, 30 x 37 inches

121

FREDERICK J. WAUGH

The sea and its rolling surf was adequate material for a whole lifetime of painting, and Frederick Judd Waugh will probably go down in art history as America's most popular academic painter of seascapes.

When, for the fourth consecutive year, he won the Carnegie International popularity prize, Waugh wrote that it would have given him pleasure had a good ultra-modern picture captivated the public interest. He said, "I am greatly in favor of Modern pictures and am keen about Surrealism, as my own experience in dreams lives up to it completely." But Waugh never got around to experimenting with these ideas. He remained faithful to the sea and his consistently beautiful, realistic canvases brought him international fame, as well as prizes and a more than substantial income.

Waugh was born in 1861 in Bordentown, New Jersey. His father was a portrait painter, but he discouraged the boy from following in his footsteps and not until young Frederick ran away from home in protest was he permitted to study at the Pennsylvania Academy of Fine Arts where Thomas Eakins was instructing. Later he continued at the Julian Academy in Paris, and finally at the Grez and Barbizon.

For 13 years during the early 1900s he remained in Great Britain, and upon his return to America he settled in favor of a cozy house and garden in Provincetown, Massachusetts, facing the sea and harbor and ships he loved so well. He once remarked, "None of my pictures has ever completely satisfied me. I hope that some day I can paint one picture of which I can say 'This is the sea.' "

Waugh was a quiet person who was never comfortable in crowds and rarely attended the openings of his own art exhibits. Occasionally he went in for "hobby" painting and highly skillful wood carving, but these were done for his own diversion. He also turned his hand to writing, being the author of *The Clan of Munes*.

He received the National Academy of Design's Palmer Memorial Marine Prize of $1,000 for a painting in 1929 and was a consistent winner of prizes at the Carnegie Institute in Pittsburgh.

The art of Frederick Waugh is represented in many of the major galleries of the United States, including the National Gallery at Washington, D.C., as well as in the Bristol (England) Academy, the Walker Art Gallery in Liverpool, England, and the Durban Art Gallery in Durban, Union of South Africa.

(1861–1940)

MARCH—NORTH ATLANTIC

by Frederick J. Waugh

painted in 1933

Oil, 32 x 48 inches

MAX WEBER

It was 1909. Hardly anyone in America had seen the work of Cézanne —Rousseau was an unknown—the Armory Show was still five years in the future. Thus unheralded, modern art made its "controversial" debut via the paintings of Max Weber. Today, long after the storms and censure and bigoted intolerance dissolved into triumphant applause, Max Weber is still painting with augmented power and eloquence.

Max Weber was born in Bialystok, Russia, in 1881, and when he was ten his family migrated to the United States, to settle in Brooklyn, N.Y. For three years he studied art at the Pratt Institute, and in order to save money taught at public schools in Lynchburg, Virginia, and at the State Normal School in Duluth, Minnesota.

Then came Europe for further study. Spain and Italy, studying the Italian Primitives and Renaissance painters, then to France and the gripping influence of Cézanne which made him a pioneer for modernism and a foe of academic formulas.

The adverse years he accepted calmly with an age-old heritage of philosophy and patience. Eventually there began to appear on his canvases Biblical characters and legends, and as one critic put it "It was with the entrance of this Hebraic quality into his art that his destiny as a great modern religious painter moved toward fulfillment." Meanwhile, he has written several books on art subjects.

For more than thirty years he has been exhibiting works that are an intrinsic part of the history of American art. Of a recent show which drew 22,000 people and was held over for three weeks longer than originally scheduled, he said: "I thank God I am here in America and can have this exhibition and show these bearded rabbis. Only, Hitler should see this!"

Weber is represented in the permanent collections of the Metropolitan Museum, the Whitney Museum, Los Angeles Museum, Newark Museum, the Museum of Modern Art, Brooklyn Museum, Phillips Memorial Gallery, Washington, D.C., etc. He has taught art at the Art Students League for four years. With his wife and two children he lives in deep contentment in Great Neck, Long Island.

● *I find a living spiritual beauty emanates from and hovers over a group of Jewish patriarchal types when they join in the study of the Torah. Their discussion is inspired and ecstatic, serene and meditative, and their gestures and attitudes are indicative of a subconscious trancelike mood and suspense. Their eternal quest and interpretation of the ethical and spiritual significance and religious content of the Torah is most inspiring, austere and picturesque. The three standing patriarchs in "Discourse" are placed in an interior that lends plastic architectural strength and ecclesiastical character to the picture. The color-gamut of gray and sombre but rich and luminous tints augments the life and the almost indefinable mystical environment and mood of the scene.*

Max Weber

DISCOURSE

by Max Weber

painted in 1940

Oil, 27 x 22 inches

123

GRANT WOOD

Grant Wood's father was a factual man. It is said that in his youth he returned a copy of *Grimm's Fairy Tales* to the giver, saying, "We Quakers can read only true things"—and "as the twig is bent," perhaps it was this natal inheritance which, like a good conscience, guided the son through the will-o'-the-wisp bypaths of art to his distinguished destiny as America's most famous painter of the American scene.

For Grant Wood, too, in his youthful Paris phase went Bohemian. He grew an astonishing "pink" beard, read Mencken and was almost convinced that the midwest was culturally barren and inhibited. He began to paint the "sleazy artifices of impressionism" only to realize, unhappily, that these canvases might have borne the signature of any number of his contemporaries. For him, they said nothing! He went on to Germany to study the early German masters. He began to analyze what it was that he really knew and he realized that it was Iowa. "Suddenly I realized that all the really good ideas I'd ever had, came to me when I was milking a cow. So I went back to Iowa."

When he began to paint the homespun American scene, Wood was quickly acclaimed the most celebrated white hope of 100 per cent Americanism in art. In brittle, clean-cut and objective style, he told his ungilded homely tales. Thomas Craven said of his "Woman with Plants"—"In draftsmanship and sheer control of medium, this picture of Wood's mother is superior to Whistler's mother and in vitality, endurance and substance it reduces the Whistler tribute to a fragile silhouette."

Wood was born in 1892 in Anamosa, Iowa. After the death of his father, when he was only ten, he moved with his mother and sister to Cedar Rapids. For the next nine years, he mowed lawns, milked cows, worked as a truck gardener, house painter and carpenter, meanwhile teaching himself to draw in his leisure time. Later, he studied at the University of Iowa and the Chicago Art Institute. After World War I, during which he had served in the Camouflage Division, he continued his studies in Paris at the Julian Academy. For many years he taught art at Iowa State University, trying not to teach any special style but only to help young artists paint the things they know about in whatever way they see them. His death in Iowa City in 1942 was a tragic loss to the art world, for the paintings he left were comparatively few. Precisely meticulous in detail, he painted on the average of two pictures a year. His pictures are represented in the Whitney Museum, the Art Institute of Chicago and many others.

(1892–1942)

PORTRAIT OF NAN
by Grant Wood
painted in 1936
Oil, 37 x 32 inches

CARL WUERMER

Carl Wuermer has no quarrel with Nature. He asks nothing better than to make some lovely scene come alive on canvas just as Nature planned it originally. He is an intent observer and no minute detail escapes his meticulous brush, but more than that there is a personal, lyrical quality as though he loved the scene he painted and wanted to capture it complete.

His smooth limpid surfaces, the delicately restrained tones, are eloquent of an artist, who is interested in sensitive realism and uses no short cuts to achieve perfection.

Wuermer, who was born in Munich, Germany, Aug. 3, 1900, came to America in 1915 and became a citizen shortly thereafter. His art education was entirely American and he says of it, "The period of 1918 to 1925 was perhaps the most fortunate time for an alert student of art in America, particularly in Chicago. It was a time of becoming aware—of the great architecture of Frank Lloyd Wright; of the literature of Carl Sandburg and Sherwood Anderson; of the great exhibitions being brought to the Chicago Arts Club of the latest in European and American painting and sculpture; of new music by John Alden Carpenter and Leo Sowerby. Together with the rigorous technical training at the Art Institute, it was indeed, to my mind, a privilege to be an art student in Chicago."

Wuermer "caught on" without undue struggle. His paintings began to appear at national exhibitions, and before he was twenty-five he held his first one-man show, at the Anderson Galleries in Chicago. He has won prizes and awards consistently since 1926, among them being the First Popular Vote Prize at the American Autumn Exhibition at the Grand Central Art Galleries in New York City in 1944.

Carl Wuermer is represented in the permanent collections of the Municipal Art Collection of the City of Chicago, the Buck Hill Falls Art Association, and numerous private collections in the United States, Canada and England.

In his hours of relaxation Wuermer chooses as his hobbies gardening; listening to music; the study of architecture; and reading books on music, art, history and science.

● *This Catskill Mountain subject, which inspired me to paint "Winter Solitude," is very familiar to me. I made the acquaintance of this little valley about twenty years ago and the landscape I painted of it is really a recent portrait of an old friend. As with all my paintings, all problems of rendition—such as color, pattern, character of line, etc.—have been carefully solved before any work was begun on the canvas.*

Carl Wuermer

WINTER SOLITUDE

by Carl Wuermer

painted in 1941

Oil, 25 x 30 inches

125

KARL ZERBE

All the stuffy traditions and foolish foibles of mankind provoke his comments. Amusedly, mockingly, and even wickedly, he debunks them and the way he does it definitely allies us on his side. In a potent language of complex symbolism he gives us mental stimulation as well as aesthetic satisfaction. Sometimes his handling will be mystic, delicate—again it will be harsh with emotional intensity. In every case it compels attention and in every case there is demonstrated the worth of craftsmanship.

Zerbe is alone in his use of encaustic—a medium of melted wax and pigment that was known to the old masters and rediscovered by Zerbe. Zerbe is enthusiastic about encaustic. Not only will it weather the years but with it he can capture the evasive charms of light and atmosphere.

Zerbe was born in Berlin, Germany, in 1903. He attended art schools in Munich and in Italy. When he left Germany at the age of 31 he was already recognized as one of the most promising young artists of republican Germany.

Discontented with the politics of his native country, Zerbe came to America in 1934 and became a citizen. That same year he held his first American exhibition at the Germanic Museum of Harvard University where his work immediately aroused favorable comment. Subsequently he spent two years in Mexico and a later year in France. Finally, in 1938, he returned to make his permanent residence in Boston where he heads the Department of Painting at the Museum of Fine Arts School.

Zerbe seemed to take to the American environment without any awkward period of adjusting. America also took to Zerbe. Of his recognition by Boston, our oldest and most cultural city, someone reasoned that it was because "His strongest talents lie in fields where New England art is weakest."

In his 11 years in America he has won several important awards, has had several one-man shows and in addition to private collections is included in the permanent collections of Boston Museum of Fine Arts, Fogg Art Museum, Germanic Museum in Cambridge, Mass., City Art Museum in St. Louis, Rhode Island Museum, Virginia Museum of Fine Arts, Phillips Memorial Gallery and many others.

● *"Troupers" was painted in the summer of 1943. In it I attempted to picture the dramatis personae of our human comedy—the Clown, the Fool, the Crook and the Tramp. Had I been a writer I might have written a 600-page novel, but I honestly believe it is better to have painted the picture. "Troupers" is painted in encaustic, an old technique in which beeswax is used as binding medium for the pigment.*

Karl Zerbe

TROUPERS
by Karl Zerbe
painted in 1943
Encaustic, 31 x 36 inches

126

TABLE OF CONTENTS

CREDITS AND ACKNOWLEDGMENTS

● The following list, page by page, shows the source from which each artist's photograph in this collection was gathered. The page numbers shown refer to the catalogue numbers on the page opposite that on which each photograph appears.

(1) Perls Galleries

(2, 4, 12, 23, 27, 31, 38, 45, 56, 59, 64, 66, 67, 71, 74, 76, 98, 99, 122, 125) Peter A. Juley & Son

(3) Dorothy Hoffman

(5) Stowall Studios

(6, 8, 17, 21, 28, 35, 36, 42, 47, 62, 68, 72, 75, 86, 92, 100, 103, 104, 113, 119, 124) Associated American Artists Galleries

(7) *Life* Magazine, George Silk, Photographer

(9) Stephen Deutch

(10) Willett Art Studios

(11, 22, 43, 44, 48, 58) Colten Photos

(13, 50) Downtown Gallery

(14) Alexander Brook

(15, 95) Pach Bros.

(16) Copeland C. Burg

(18) George Platt Lynes

(19) John Carroll

(20) Art Institute of Chicago

(24) Ila Ladany

(25) Ralston Crawford

(26) Francis Criss

(29) Johan Hagemeyer

(30) T. Harmon Parkhurst

(32) *Life* Magazine, Eric Schaal, Photographer

(33) Stuart Davis

(34) Julio de Diego

(37, 81, 89) Alfred Stieglitz

(39, 52, 53, 96, 123) Alfredo Valente

(40) Mrs. Lulu Green

(41) Lyonel Feininger

(46) Dorothy Hoffman

(49) Ellen Ehrman

(51) Robert Gwathmey

(54) Milch Galleries

(55) Charlotte Brooks

(57) Florence McAllister

(60) Peter Hurd

(61) Joseph Breitenbach

(63) Libsohn-Ehrenburg

(65) Carl Klein, N.Y.

(69) Jane Rogers

(70) Edward Weston

(73) Julian Levi

(77) R. V. Anderson

(78) Henry Lee McFee

(79) Laura Gilpin

(80) Harold M. Waingold

(82) Wilfrid M. Zogbaum

(83, 90, 91) Midtown Galleries

(84) Adrian Siegel

(85) Walter J. Russell, N.Y.

(87) George L. K. Morris

(88) A. George Miller

(93) Robert Carlen Gallery and Downtown Gallery

(94) Butler Art Institute

(97) Victor Haveman

(101) Doris Heydn, courtesy Midtown Galleries

(102) Andrée Ruellan

(105) Helen Morrison

(106) Harvey Croze of Cranbrook

(107) Charles Sheeler

(108) George Hurrell

(109) Everett Shinn

(110) Merrill Chase

(111) Wyatt Davis

(112) Robert Lewin

(114) Eugene Speicher

(115) The Phillips Studio

(116) Jack Gage Stark

(117) Ansel Adams

(118) Albert Sterner

(120) William Thoeny

(121) Konrad Cramer

(126) Karl Zerbe

● Acknowledgment is hereby made of permission given by the copyright owners for quotations used in various biographies in this
catalogue. The numbers shown are the catalogue numbers appearing opposite the biographies in which the quotations are used.

(1) From *Art News*, March 15–31, 1943, reprinted by permission
of The Art Foundation

(2) From *Art Digest*, December 15, 1944, reprinted by permission
of The Art Digest

(4, 5, 38, 56, 67, 76, 114) From *The American Artist and His
Times*, by Homer Saint-Gaudens, reprinted by permission of
Dodd, Mead and Company, Inc.

(20) From *The Magazine of Art*, June 1941, reprinted by permission of The American Federation of Arts

(32) From *Life*, April 19, 1936, reprinted by permission of Life

(45, 111) From *Gist of Art*, by John Sloan, reprinted by permission of American Artists Group, Inc.

(50) From *The Magazine of Art*, May 1944, reprinted by permission of The American Federation of Arts

(64) From "Morris Kantor—Late American," by Harry Salpeter,
in *Esquire*, June 1940, reprinted by permission of Esquire, Inc.

(67) From *Current Biography, 1942*, reprinted by permission of
H. W. Wilson Company

(80) From *The Magazine of Art*, July 1935, reprinted by permission of The American Federation of Arts

(81) From *John Marin—the Man and His Work*, by E. M. Benson,
reprinted by permission of The American Federation of Arts

(91) From "Rabelais in a Smock," by Harry Salpeter, in *Esquire*,
July 1936, reprinted by permission of Esquire, Inc.

(108) From *Millard Sheets*, by Dr. Hartley Burr Alexander, reprinted by permission of Dalzell Hatfield

(124) From *Current Biography, 1940*, reprinted by permission of
H. W. Wilson Company

PRINTED IN THE UNITED STATES OF AMERICA BY THE LAKESIDE PRESS, R. R. DONNELLEY & SONS COMPANY, CHICAGO